PETER AUREOL ON PREDESTINATION

STUDIES IN THE HISTORY
OF
CHRISTIAN THOUGHT

EDITED BY

HEIKO A. OBERMAN, Tucson, Arizona

IN COOPERATION WITH

HENRY CHADWICK, Cambridge
JAROSLAV PELIKAN, New Haven, Connecticut
BRIAN TIERNEY, Ithaca, New York
ARJO VANDERJAGT, Groningen

VOLUME LXXXIII

JAMES L. HALVERSON

PETER AUREOL ON PREDESTINATION

PETER AUREOL
ON PREDESTINATION

A CHALLENGE TO LATE MEDIEVAL THOUGHT

BY

JAMES L. HALVERSON

BRILL
LEIDEN · BOSTON · KÖLN
1998

This book is printed on acid-free paper.

Library of Congress Cataloging-in-Publication Data

Halverson, James L.
    Peter Aureol on predestination : a challenge to late medieval
thought / by James L. Halverson.
        p.   cm. — (Studies in the history of Christian thought, ISSN
0081–8607 ; v. 83)
    Includes bibliographical references and index.
    ISBN 9004109455 (alk. paper)
    1. Predestination—History of doctrines—Middle Ages, 600–1500.
2. Aureolus, Petrus, ca. 1280–1322—Contributions in doctrine of
predestination.   I. Title.   II. Series.
BT809.H35   1998
234'.9'092—dc21   98–16147
                                                                    CIP

Die Deutsche Bibliothek - CIP-Einheitsaufnahme

Halverson, James L.:
Peter Aureol on predestination : a challenge to late medieval thought /
by James L. Halverson. – Leiden ; Boston ; Köln : Brill, 1998
    (Studies in the history of Christian thought ; Vol. 83)
    ISBN 90-04-10945-5

ISSN   0081-8607
ISBN   90 04 10945 5

PRINTED IN THE NETHERLANDS

CONTENTS

ACKNOWLEDGEMENTS

This book began as a doctoral dissertation that I wrote at the University of Iowa, so I must first thank those who guided and supported my doctoral research. I owe the greatest debt to my advisor, Katherine Tachau, who introduced me to the late Middle Ages and provided immeasurable academic and personal support. I am also grateful to Scott MacDonald, James McCue, Constance Berman, and T. Dwight Bozeman for their careful comments and suggestions. My socii, Russel Friedman and Christopher Schabel, have supported and aided this project from beginning to end. The University of Iowa's Teaching-Research Fellowship and the Seashore Dissertation Fellowship allowed me two precious years of reflection and writing. I thank the Graduate College and the History Department for that support. The University Library staff, especially Pam Kacena and Chris Africa, were of invaluable help.

Many debts were also incurred in bringing this project to its present state. Richard Muller, Hester Gelber, and Curtis Daugaard read all or part of this monograph and gave helpful comments. My colleagues at Coe College and Judson College have been most supportive of this project. Much dreary, but crucial, editorial work was done by three wonderful students: Elizabeth Aylward, Kristen Rostis, Jeff Harron, and Joy Ellen Brewer. Julian Deahl and Theo Joppe at Brill have been more than patient with this novice author. Most importantly, I am grateful to Heiko A. Oberman for letting this project see the light of day.

Finally, I thank my wife, Terri.

J.L.H.
Elgin, Illinois
August, 1997

INTRODUCTION

Western Christian thought has long been preoccupied by soteriology. Of particular interest has been the relationship between divine and human agency in the process of salvation. Accounts of this relationship have ranged across the spectrum from the ancient Pelagian assertion that salvation is based on the individual's use of free will and moral integrity to the 17th-century Reformed position that both predestination and reprobation are carried out according to God's active, eternal, and irresistible will without respect to human morality. Such widely differing understandings of the soteriological process have been the occasion for controversy and division in Western Christianity. Augustine and his followers attacked Pelagius and others who seemed to ascribe too large a role to human free will in salvation; in the 16th and 17th centuries, soteriological differences were partly responsible for the Protestant Reformation and the further disunity among Protestant denominations.

The source for these differing opinions lies in the unstable relationship between three sets of assumptions. First, insofar as Christianity is situated in mainstream Western monotheism, it argues that God is, in some sense, good, just, omnipotent, and omniscient. Second, insofar as it is uniquely Christian, it argues that this God has, through the Incarnation and Resurrection of Christ, set into motion a process whereby the broken relationship between God and humankind is restored. Finally, particularly in Western Christianity, a third set of assumptions is emphasized: not every individual participates in the salvific work of Christ (i.e., some are not saved) and, based on the Augustinian refutation of the Pelagian heresy,[1] God initiates the process of salvation in those who are to be saved without regard to individual merit. The central question then is why does an omnipotent, good, and just God save some individuals and not others? Neither of the two possible responses completely accounts for all of the assumptions listed above. If the damned are rejected on account of their sin, then it seems that God takes into ac-

---

[1] The doctrines of Pelagius and his followers, which held that the human free will could merit salvation through the performance of good deeds, were condemned in their various forms in a series of councils during the 5th and 6th centuries. For an introduction to the history of Pelagius, Pelagianism, and semi-Pelagianism, see Jaraslov Pelikan, *The Christian Tradition: A History of the Development of Doctrine*, vol. 1: *The Emergence of the Catholic Tradition (100-600)*, (Chicago, 1971), pp. 314-330.

count human merit in His decision to damn and save. On the other hand, if sin is not the cause of a particular individual's damnation, then God does not seem to be either just or good. Nor does Scripture definitively settle the problem. For instance, opposing arguments can be taken from the same New Testament author. In *Romans* 9 Paul lays out a lengthy argument which seems to prove that salvation and damnation depend solely on the will of God; in *I Timothy* 2:4, however, Paul claims that God "desires all men to be saved and come to the knowledge of the truth" (NKJV).

While soteriological controversies have been the focus of the most scholarly interest, such controversy has not been a continuous state of affairs in the history of Western Christianity. Even though no positive doctrine of predestination was affirmed in the councils which settled the Pelagian controversy,[2] Medieval Latin theologians had, by the 13th century, arrived at a consensus position regarding predestination. According to them, God's elective will pertains only to some particular persons; the remaining, the reprobate, are ignored by God's elective will and, bereft of sanctifying grace, die in a state of mortal sin and suffer damnation. Medieval theology attempted to offer a third answer which would cut the Gordian knot of determinism and legalism: God saves certain individuals without regard to their merit, but damns others on account of their sin.

But this consensus did not last. During the Reformation, first justification, and then predestination, occupied a central role in interdenominational debate. This shift from consensus to controversy, however, was not a result of the Reformation; rather, the roots of modern predestinarian pluralism in Western theology lie in the 14th century. During the first half of the 14th century several influential theologians broke with the traditional view, arguing that the causal processes of predestination and reprobation must be parallel. In the first decades of the 14th century, Franciscan theologian Peter Aureol rejected the consensus position, particularly as it was held by fellow Franciscan John Duns Scotus. Instead, Aureol argued that although, strictly speaking, God does not take human merit into account in predestination, He takes into account the human response to the initial divine offer of grace. Within the next generation of scholars at least three other prominent theologians had adopted this view: William Ockham, Robert Holcot, and Thomas of Strassbourg. In the 1340s, the Augustinian Hermit theologian Gregory of Rimini, perceiving a Pelagian tendency in this new view, argued that God

---

[2] See above, n. 1.

both saves without regard to merit and damns without regard to sin. By 1350 the Medieval consensus had been irrevocably shattered.

The Late Medieval Setting

Gregory of Rimini's 1342-1344 lectures on Peter Lombard's *Sentences* at the University of Paris mark a watershed in late Medieval thought.[3] In these lectures two of the most important intellectual developments of the 14th century converge. Only in the 1340s did the "new English theology" — a methodological revolution based on a new analytical logic and natural philosophy which began as early as 1315 and was represented by such diverse figures as William Ockham, Adam Wodeham, Robert Holcot, and Walter Chatton — receive its first full and positive reaction at the center of continental learning.[4] In the 150 years after this initial reaction, the "new English theology" would evolve into the *via moderna*, an academic alternative to the *via antiqua* of Albertus Magnus, Thomas Aquinas, Bonaventure, Giles of Rome and John Duns Scotus, and which spread alongside the *via antiqua* as new universities were established across Europe. Not only were the Parisians of the 1340s the first continental theologians successful in incorporating the new theology, but one of them, Gregory of Rimini, became a representative of the movement in his own right. Within the 15th-century *via moderna* there was, in the judgment of some historians, a "via Gregorii" as well as a "via Ockhamistae".[5]

---

[3] Only Gregory's lectures on the first two books of the *Sentences* survive. They have been edited in *Gregorii Ariminensis OESA Lectura super Primum et Secundum Sententiarum*, 7 vols., eds. Damasus Trapp, Venicio Marcolino, et al., (Berlin, 1979).

[4] The best general description of this development is found in William J. Courtenay, *Schools and Scholars in Fourteenth-Century England*, (Princeton, 1987), pp. 250-306. Courtenay stresses the fact that the "new English theology" (*theologiae anglicana*) was distinct for its methodological approach and did not require any particular substantive positions. The complex reception of the epistemological aspects of the "new English theology" at Paris is thoroughly documented in Katherine H. Tachau, *Vision and Certitude in the Age of Ockham: Optics, Epistemology and the Foundations of Semantics, 1250-1345*, (Leiden, 1988). Although Oxford influences on Parisian theology are evidenced by the late 1330s, the initial institutional response was negative. See William J. Courtenay and Katherine H. Tachau, "Ockham, Ockhamists and the English-German Nation at Paris, 1339-1341", *History of Universities* 2 (1982), 53-96.

[5] An introduction to the problem of tracing the "via Gregorii" is found in Manfred Schulze, "'Via Gregorii' in Forschung und Quellen", *Gregor von Rimini: Werk und Wirkung bis zur Reformation*, ed. Heiko A. Oberman, (Berlin, 1981), pp. 1-126. The focus of research on the "via Gregorii" has been an effort to tie the theology of Rimini to the "Reformation breakthrough" in Luther's early writings. Heiko Oberman claims that Luther was influenced by Rimini through Staupitz and the Erfurt Augustinian monastery; Heiko A. Oberman, "Headwaters of the

Rimini also embodied another equally new and important trend: a renewed emphasis on and critical approach towards the writings of Augustine, especially the anti-Pelagian treatises.[6] His particular interpretation of the Augustinian doctrines of grace and merit made him

---

Reformation: Initia Lutheri — Initia Reformationis", *The Dawn of the Reformation: Essays in Late Medieval and Reformation Thought*, ed. idem, (Edinburg, 1986). Evidence suggests, however, that the Erfurt Augustinian *studium* was influenced by the theology of Biel rather than Rimini; see Wolfgang Urban, "Die 'Via moderna' an der Universitaet Erfurt am Vorabend der Reformation", *Werk und Wirkung*, ed. Heiko A. Oberman, pp. 311-330. Based on this, Alister McGrath argues that Luther did not encounter the theology of Rimini until the Leipzig debate of 1519; see Alister E. McGrath, *Intellectual Origins of the Reformation*, (Oxford, 1987), pp. 108-115. For more on Luther's encounter with Rimini's thought during the debate with Eck at Leipzig see Leif Grane, "Gregor von Rimini und Luthers Leipziger Disputation", *Studia Theologia* 22 (1968), 29-49.

[6] Damasus Trapp, "Augustinian Theology of the 14th Century: Notes on Editions, Marginalia, Opinions and Book-Lore', *Augustiniana* 6 (1956), 146-241; Courtenay, *Schools and Scholars*, pp. 307-326. Heiko A. Oberman, "'Tuus sum, salvum me fac'. Augustinreveil zwischen Renaissance und Reformation", *Scientia Augustiniana*, ed. Cornelius P. Mayer and Willigis Eckermann, (Wuerzburg, 1975), pp. 349-395.

For generations historians of Medieval thought assumed that the "new English theology" and the "Augustinian revival" were mutually exclusive, even antagonistic, trends. Oberman discusses this scholarly tradition in *The Harvest of Medieval Theology: Gabriel Biel and Late Medieval Nominalism*, (Cambridge, MA, 1963; repr. 1983), pp. 425-428. Much of the confusion is due to the use of the term "nominalism" to describe the "new English theology" and the later *via moderna*. Although "nominalism" properly refers to metaphysical and epistemological positions concerning the existence and knowledge of universals, this term was used to describe the philosophical and theological assumptions of the movement in general. It was formerly assumed that the (supposedly Pelagian) theological views of the "nominalists" were a function of their philosophy. Such an assumption forced the best scholars, such as Damasus Trapp and Heiko A. Oberman, to fit a square peg into a round hole by posing the question as an either/or proposition. Trapp argues that Rimini cannot be considered a nominalist, since he condemned the views of the more radical theology of his Parisian colleague, John of Mirecourt. See Trapp, "Augustinianism", pp. 182ff. William J. Courtenay, in "John of Mirecourt and Gregory of Rimini on Whether God Can Undo the Past" *Recherches de Theologie ancienne et medieval*, 39 (1972), 224-253 & 40 (1973), 147-174, calls into question Trapp's conclusion that Rimini led the condemnation of Mirecourt. In his early work Heiko Oberman was forced to label Rimini a "right-wing nominalist" even though he does not hold any of the positions that Oberman attributes to theological nominalism. See Oberman, *Harvest*, pp. 196-206, 423-428.

More recent scholarship has refuted this view. The claim that "nominalist" theology is derived from "nominalist" philosophy assumes, among other things, the existence of a generic "nominalist" philosophical school. But the "new English theology" was not a philosophical monolith. Even at its earliest stages the movement cannot be reduced to "Ockhamism". Katherine H. Tachau (*Vision*, pp. 335-384) shows that Oxford theologians such as Adam Wodeham, Walter Chatton, and Robert Holcot were critical of Ockham. Moreover, Rimini and the other early Parisian *moderni* encountered this movement in its complexity and added to it. Trapp ("Augustinianism", pp. 182-190) documents the critical attitude that Rimini had with respect to certain positions held by Ockham. Moreover, the current opinion among Ockham scholars is that even he himself was not a "nominalist". See

the central figure of this new trend as it manifested itself on the continent. Common scholarly opinion has it that Gregory of Rimini at Paris and Thomas Bradwardine at Oxford attacked the semi-Pelagian doctrines held by some theologians in the first half of the 14th century.[7] The list of "Pelagians" usually includes the Oxford theologians William Ockham, Adam Wodeham, and Robert Holcot, with some disagreement over the role of such Parisians as Peter Aureol and Durand of Saint-Pourcain. The controversy is presented by historians as a renewal of the battle first fought between Augustine and Pelagius over the role of human free will in salvation. In response to what Bradwardine and Rimini perceived as a revival of Pelagianism and based on a new source-critical approach to the writings of Augustine's anti-Pelagian treatises, these two authors developed soteriological doctrines which deny any human role in salvation.[8]

Marilyn McCord Adams, *William Ockham*, 2 vols., (Notre Dame, 1987); Courtenay, *Schools and Scholars*, pp. 198-200. There is also significant disagreement over which authors were "nominalist" and over which positions admit to a judgment concerning their "nominalism". The most important work detailing this problem is William J. Courtenay, "Nominalism and Late Medieval Religion", *the Pursuit of Holiness*, ed. C. Trinkaus and Heiko A. Oberman, (Leiden, 1974), pp. 26-59. The "new English theology" is typified by its particular application of logic, physics and mathematics to theology, not by any common metaphysical or epistemological standpoint. Courtenay, *Schools and Scholars*, pp. 250-263. Furthermore, this methodological shift does not necessarily entail adherence to certain theological positions, even though it does mean a different approach to the theological project. See McGrath, *Origins*, pp. 75-85; see also, idem, "'Augustinianism'? A Critical Assessment of the So-Called 'Medieval Augustinian Tradition' on Justification", *Augustiniana* 31 (1981) pp. 247-267, esp. p. 249.

[7] For Thomas Bradwardine see, Heiko A. Oberman, *Archbishop Thomas Bradwardine: A Fourteenth-Century Augustinian, A Study of His Theology in Its Historical Context*, (Utrecht, 1958); and Gordon Leff, *Bradwardine and the Pelagians: A Study of his 'De Causa Dei' and Its Opponents*, (Cambridge, 1957). For the anti-Pelagian motif in Gregory of Rimini's doctrines of grace and predestination, see Martin Schüler, *Prädestination, Sünde und Freiheit bei Gregor von Rimini*, (Stuttgart, 1934), pp, 39-69; Paul Vignaux, *Justification et Predestination au XIVe siecle. Duns Scot, Pierre d'Aureole, Guillaume d'Occam, Grégoire de Rimini*, (Paris, 1934); Gordon Leff, *Gregory of Rimini: Tradition and Innovation in Fourteenth-Century Thought*, (New York, 1961), pp. 185-204; Christoph Peter Burger, "Der Augustinschüler gegen die Modernen Pelagianer: Das 'auxilium speciale dei' in der Gnadenlehre Gregors von Rimini", *Werk und Wirkung*, ed. Heiko A. Oberman, pp. 195-240; see also, chapter 6 below.

[8] Trapp, "Augustinianism", details the development of an "historico-critical" approach to theology in general and the writings of Augustine in particular within the Augustinian order on the continent. Beryl Smalley, *English Friars and Antiquity in the Early Fourteenth Century*, (Oxford, 1960), documents a similar shift occurring at Oxford which was not confined to Augustinian Hermits, but centered around Bradwardine and raises the possibility that the development of a source-critical approach to texts may have been connected to the rise of classicist learning in Southern Europe. Oberman, "Tuus sum", pp. 349-357, argues that the continental Augustinianism of Rimini and the similar English Augustinianism of Bradwardine developed independently. McGrath challenges the view that Bradwardine was

Since Bradwardine and Rimini became highly influential theologians, their development of a strong anti-Pelagian attitude is significant whether or not their assessment of their opponents was correct.[9] While the reaction to Bradwardine's theology was negative as often as it was positive, his *De causa Dei* provoked passionate responses from all sides and focused scholarly attention at both Oxford and Paris on the issues of grace, justification, and predestination.[10] According to the most recent scholarship Rimini's anti-Pelagian soteriology is the basis of an entire theological school which seems to have had far-ranging influence. In spite of disagreeing over its influence on the early Luther, both Heiko A. Oberman and Alister E. McGrath concur that there was a discrete *schola Augustiniana moderna* in the later Middle Ages whose source was Gregory of Rimini.[11] Recent scholarship agrees that positions held by Rimini and his followers influenced both John Calvin and Peter Martyr Vermigli, arguably the two most important sources of Reformed soteriology.[12]

Realizing the importance of Rimini's soteriology, Medieval intellectual historians have paid a great deal of attention to his doctrines

---

Augustinian on the basis of Bradwardine's reliance on Aristotelian metaphysics and his lack of emphasis on the Fall. See McGrath, "Augustinianism", p. 255. But according to McGrath's definition of Augustinianism, which includes adherence to the vocabulary and assumptions of Augustine, there would be no Augustinians besides Augustine himself. Bradwardine's understanding of himself as defending the grace of God against the "modern Pelagians" reveals a conscious identification with Augustine and Augustine's theology of grace.

[9] Oberman, *Harvest* and idem, "Duns Scotus, Nominalism and the Council of Trent", Oberman, *Dawn*, pp. 204-233, maintains that Bradwardine's and Rimini's assessment is correct, while Alister E. McGrath, "The Anti-Pelagian Structure of 'Nominalist' Doctrines of Justification", *Ephemerides Theologicae Lovanensis* 57 (1981), 107-119, argues the opposite. In this study I will use the terms "Pelagian" and "anti-Pelagian", but in a restricted sense. "Pelagian" or "Pelagianism", when used to describe a Medieval or Early Modern author or doctrine, refers only to the fact that this author or doctrine elicited an anti-Pelagian response, regardless of whether the author or doctrine merited such a response. "Anti-Pelagian" or "Anti-Pelagianism" refers to an author who develops his soteriological doctrines in response to what he perceives as a revival of the ancient heresy of Pelagius or those doctrines themselves, regardless of whether the author's judgment is correct.

[10] Courtenay, *Schools and Scholars*, pp. 294-303 and 307-324.

[11] See above, n. 9.

[12] See McGrath, *Origins*, pp. 93-107; and Frank E. James III, "A Late Medieval Parallel in Reformation Thought: Gemina Praedestinatio in Gregory of Rimini and Peter Martyr Vermigli", *Via Augustini: Augustine in the Later Middle Ages, Renaissance, and Reformation*, ed. Heiko A. Oberman and Frank E. James III, (Leiden, 1991), pp. 157-188. James corrects the view of John Patrick Donnelly, *Calvinism and Scholasticism in Vermigli's Doctrine of Man and Grace*, (Leiden, 1976), who stressed the fact that Vermigli's training was at "Thomist" universities in Italy. According to James, Rimini's writings were well known and widely referred to in Italy in the 16th century, and there is ample evidence that Martyr had first-hand knowledge and a deep understanding of Rimini's thought.

of grace, justification, and predestination.[13] They consider the anti-Pelagianism of Bradwardine and of Rimini as essentially the same, since both supposedly responded to the same "Pelagian" challenge presented by the *pactum* theology of such Oxford theologians as Ockham, Wodeham, and Holcot.[14] This is not to say that modern scholarship views Bradwardine and Rimini as interchangeable. Bradwardine used the methodology of the "old" theology of the 13th century, while Rimini adopted the methods of the "new" theology gaining popularity in the 14th century.[15] Rimini placed a much stronger emphasis on the effects of the Fall than did Bradwardine.[16] Even so, it is generally assumed that Bradwardine and Rimini were fighting the same battle and thus defended many of the same soteriological positions. For the most part this is true; both stressed the incapacity of human beings to effect their salvation in any way; both stressed the sovereignty and gratuity of divine grace. But they differ on one very significant point.

Among the opinions for which both authors are said to have argued is the so-called "doctrine of double (or absolute) predestination". Indeed, modern scholarship assumes that a doctrine of double predestination was a feature common among and unique to late Medieval anti-Pelagian authors.[17] But if "double predestination" is taken in a weak sense to mean simply that God's decision to save particular people is intrinsic to God and precedes foreknowledge of merit, then "double predestination" is not unique to 14th- and 15th-century anti-Pelagianism, but it is rather the dominant opinion in Scholastic theology. But if it is taken in a strong sense to mean that,

---

[13] See above, n.5. See also, Courtenay, *Schools and Scholars*, pp. 307-326.

[14] *Pactum* or covenantal soteriology is based on the common Scholastic distinction between the unlimited set of possibilities which an omnipotent God could have actualized in eternity (*Dei potentia absoluta*) and the limited set of possibilities which God chooses to actualize in time (*Dei potentia ordinata*). Insofar as His omnipotence is considered simply, God is not obligated to save or damn anyone, but insofar as He has entered into a covenant (*pactum*) with humans, God saves those who do their best (*facere quod in se est*). For Holcot's doctrine, see Heiko A. Oberman, "'Facientibus Quod in se est Deus non denegat gratiam': Robertus Holcot O.F.M. and the beginnings of Luther's Theology", *Dawn*, pp. 85-103. Oberman traces the development of this doctrine from Ockham to Biel in *Harvest*, pp. 185-247. The best recent works on the history of this distinction in Scholastic thought are, William J. Courtenay, *Capacity and Volition: A History of the Distinction of Absolute and Ordained Power*, (Bergamo, 1990); and the collection of his earlier essays on the topic: *Covenant and Causality in Medieval Thought: Studies in Philosophy, Theology, and Economic Practice*, [coll. essays], (London, 1984).

[15] Oberman, *Bradwardine*, p. 222.

[16] McGrath, "Augustinianism", p. 255.

[17] McGrath, *Origins*, p. 104; Courtenay, *Schools and Scholars*, p. 309; Adolar Zumkeller, "Konrad Treger's Disputation Theses of 1521", *Via Augustini*, eds., Oberman and James, pp. 130-156, esp. 135-137; Schulze, "Via Gregorii", pp. 25-63.

in addition to actively deciding to save particular people, God possesses an eternal, intrinsic and *active* will to damn particular people before foreseen sins, then it is not held by even most anti-Pelagian writers.

The source of this misinterpretation of late Medieval anti-Pelagian doctrines of predestination lies in the ambiguity of the term "predestination", so we can make the distinction if we use more appropriate terms. This is especially important, since the predestinarian controversy in which Rimini took part was also fueled by the ambiguity of the terms "*praedestinatio*" and "*reprobatio*". In Medieval Scholastic discussions, predestination and reprobation may refer either to God's intrinsic salvific purpose or to the divine volitions and actions which carry out that purpose (i.e. the granting of grace and eternal life). In order to avoid these confusions, I will refer to God's intrinsic purpose by using the term "election", which is not similarly ambiguous.

There were at least three different concepts of election represented in late Medieval theology. The common Scholastic opinion was "single-particular election" (SPE). According to this doctrine both predestination and reprobation principally refer to God's election. Predestination refers to God's elective purpose to save some individuals; reprobation refers to the lack of elective purpose to save others which is synonymous with "double predestination" taken in the weak sense. "Double predestination" taken in the strong sense is best described as "double-particular election" (DPE). As in single-particular election, predestination and reprobation refer to God's elective purpose, but double-particular election claims that God has a positive elective purpose to damn certain individuals. The third position is called "general election"(GE). This position separates election from predestination and reprobation. According to a doctrine of general election, God's elective purpose does not refer to individuals, but rather kinds of individuals concerning whom certain conditions obtain. "Predestination" and "reprobation" refer only to the two possible sets of divine volitions and operations (granting of grace and glory or obduration and damnation) which apply to the different kinds of individuals.

Gregory of Rimini is one of the only known theologians of the later Middle Ages who maintains double-particular election.[18] In the

---

[18] Only two other late Medieval theologians that I know of, Pierre d'Ailly and Marsilius of Inghen, endorse DPE. None of the authors commonly cited as late Medieval anti-Pelagians and members of the *schola Augustiniana moderna*, besides Rimini, hold it. See below, chapter 7.

face of historians' assumptions that anti-Pelagian soteriology entails a doctrine of double predestination (presumably taken in the strong sense), this claim may be surprising. But the surprising aspect of 14th-century anti-Pelagianism is rather Rimini's concept of DPE, since the orthodoxy of DPE was questionable at the time.[19] Moreover, the earliest controversies over Pelagianism at Oxford had little to do with predestination. John Lutterell's charge that Ockham held Pelagian views specifically addressed Ockham's use of the distinction between God's power taken absolutely and how God has limited the scope of His own power through ordaining a certain state of affairs to argue that the presence of infused grace was not necessary for the divine acceptation of the sinner. Robert Halifax attacked Wodeham's (and by implication Ockham's and Holcot's) doctrine of fruition which claimed that a person could love God above all else without sanctifying grace.[20] The 1618 edition of Bradwardine's *De causa Dei contra Pelagium* is almost 900 pages long, but discussions of predestination are scattered, ambiguous and undeveloped.[21]

When the Oxford controversies were introduced at Paris the focus remained the same. Rimini devoted a long treatise contained in Book II, distinctions 26-28, of his commentary on the *Sentences* to attacking the doctrine of fruition defended by Ockham and Wodeham.[22] But in his treatise on predestination, where he combatted "modern" views that he considered Pelagian, he did not address the Oxford controversy. Rimini's doctrine of double-particular election was addressed to a wholly distinct "Pelagian" challenge. In Book I, distinctions 40-41, where he develops DPE, he does not explicitly name any opponents. Thanks, however, to the editors of Rimini's commentary, we know that his doctrine is implicitly direct-

---

[19] Double-particular election, arguably present in Augustine's later anti-Pelagian treatises and defended by his more intense followers, was condemned by the Council of Orange in the 6th century, see Pelikan, *The Christian Tradition*, vol. 1, p. 329. The decrees of this council were lost, however, until the 16th century. In the 9th century Gottschalk's version of double-particular election was condemned by the synod of Quiercy in 853, but upheld by the Synod of Langres in 855. See Pelikan, *The Christian Tradition*, vol. 3, pp. 93-94. None of these doctrinal statements seem to have carried any more than temporary and regional weight until the decrees of the Council of Orange were incorporated into the decrees of the Council of Trent.

[20] Courtenay, *Schools and Scholars*, pp. 296-297.

[21] *Thomae Bradwardini De Causa Dei contra Pelagium*, (London, 1618). The most influential recent scholar to examine Bradwardine, Heiko A. Oberman, expresses surprise that Bradwardine did not devote more effort to a fully developed doctrine of predestination. Oberman, *Bradwardine*, pp. 95-122.

[22] Rimini also includes Scotus in his attack. See Gregory, *Lectura*, vol. 6, pp. 17-114. See also, Burger, "Augustinerschüler".

ed against a doctrine of general election first taught by Peter Aureol and then modified by Thomas of Strassbourg.[23] Rimini's development of a doctrine of predestination well outside of the mainstream of Latin theology was occasioned by the Parisian development of a doctrine of predestination which itself had no precedent in Latin theology.

Even though DPE and GE had little immediate impact, the predestinarian conflict which developed at Paris between 1317 and 1344 is, nevertheless, significant for an understanding of late Medieval theology. First, by isolating it from the controversies over Pelagianism originating at Oxford and spreading throughout late Medieval universities, we can see that these controversies had very little effect on the consensus view of single-particular election. The Parisian developments may also be significant for an understanding of Reformation and post-Reformation thought, since DPE appeared again in the 16th century.[24] Moreover, predestination became a controversial topic in post-Reformation theology. As in the debate between Aureol and Rimini, the issue again focused on GE versus DPE. The two most prominent examples of post-Tridentine predestinarian controversy are, among Roman Catholics, that between the Jesuit followers of Molina and the Dominican followers of Bañez, and in Reformed theology the dispute between the Remonstrants ("Arminians") and Counter-Remonstrants ("Calvinists") which led to the Synod of Dort.[25] Given the post-Reformation re-emphasis on scholastic sources, the parallels are intriguing.

---

[23] Rimini, *Lectura*, vol. 3, pp. 325-326. Aureol's fullest development of the doctrine is contained in his massive commentary on the first book of the *Sentences* called the *Scriptum*, presented to John XXII in 1317. The only complete edition of the *Scriptum* is contained in *Commentariorum in Librum Primum Sententiarum auctore Petro Aureolo*, (Rome, 1596). The first 8 distinctions of the Scriptum have been edited by Eligius Buyteart in *Peter Aureoli Scriptum super Primum Sententiarum*, 2 vols. (St. Bonaventure, N.Y., 1952). The introduction to this edition also outlines Aureol's life and the dating of his major works. There is at least one other surviving redaction of his commentary of the first book of the *Sentences*. *Vatican Borghese 123* contains a copy of his lectures on the first book delivered at Paris in 1317, contemporaneously with his preparation of the *Scriptum*. This version contains an essentially similar, though greatly abbreviated, account of the doctrine of predestination to the account in the *Scriptum* (*Borghese 123*, ff. 172va-179va).

[24] Zumkeller, "Treger", pp. 132-137. Frank James (James, "Rimini and Vermigli", pp. 174-185) has pointed out the similarities between Peter Martyr Vermigli and Rimini on predestination and this includes double-particular election.

[25] In his recent study of Arminius, Richard Muller argues that the Remonstrant doctrine of general election initiated by Arminius was influenced by Molina and Jesuit theology. See Richard Muller, *God, Creation and Providence in the Thought of Jacob Arminius*, (Grand Rapids, 1990), passim.

PART ONE

PETER AUREOL ON THE DIVINE WILL
AND PREDESTINATION

CHAPTER ONE

THE SEMANTICS OF SIMPLICITY

Predestination is a divine act which involves some combination of the divine will, power, and intellect. Therefore, the doctrine of predestination depends on a doctrine of the divine attributes, especially those attributes (i.e. will, power, intellect) which account for divine activity. The dependence of the doctrine of predestination upon the doctrine of the attributes is particularly important for Aureol, since one of his main themes is the causal priority of the divine will over the divine intellect in predestination. So, before discussing Aureol's doctrine of predestination, a discussion of his doctrine of the attributes is in order. In the Scholastic context two issues must be addressed in a doctrine of the divine attributes: (a) the relationship between the attributes within a simple divine essence and (b) the relationship of God as willer, doer, and knower with the objects of His will, power, and knowledge. In this chapter I discuss the first of these issues.

The doctrine of divine simplicity in Scholastic theology has its origins in the Trinitarian doctrines of Latin Fathers such as Hilary of Poitiers and Augustine.[1] Primarily defending the compatibility of attributing three distinct persons, but one essence to God, they briefly developed the corollary that all divine attributes are unified in a single divine essence. In the 12th century this doctrine began to have a life of its own. It received its classic formulation in Latin theology with Anselm, who proposed a doctrine of divine simplicity independent from purely Trinitarian concerns. For Anselm the fact that God is perfect entails that He is simple:

> If the highest nature is so many good things, will it be composed by many good things, or rather are there not many good things, but rather one good signified by many names? For every composite thing requires those things from which it is composed, so that it may exist; and it owes its existence to those things, because whatever it is, it is through those things <which compose it>, and they are not what they are through that <composite> thing, and therefore, it is not the greatest thing...

[1] Hilary of Poitiers, *De Trinitate, Patrilogia Latina*, (Paris, 1878-1890), b. VII, p. 223; Augustine, *De Trinitate, Corpus Christianorum. Series Latina*, (Turnhout, Belgium, 1953-), b. VI, chs. 6-8, pp. 236-238.

> Since, therefore, this <highest> nature is in no way composite, yet
> in every way so many good things, it is necessary that all these many
> things be the same. Therefore, any one of them is the same as all,
> whether taken together or individually, so that when "justice" or
> "essence" is said, it signifies the same thing as the others, whether to-
> gether or individually. Therefore, just as whatever one is said essen-
> tially of the highest substance, the substance is whatever it is essential-
> ly, in one way and one consideration.[2]

Peter Lombard's inclusion in his *Sentences* of a separate distinction on
divine simplicity assured that every theology student at a Medieval
university would confront this doctrine and its Patristic sources.[3] In
the 13th century student commentaries on the *Sentences* carefully
dealt with all the issues that Lombard presented and many theologians composed systematic *Summae* which normally included a discussion of divine simplicity; yet no significant controversy arose during this time. While such authors as Thomas Aquinas, Bonaventure,
Henry of Ghent, and Godfrey of Fontaines disagreed about the precise nature of the relations between the persons of the Trinity, all
described the distinction between the attributes and the essence, and
among the attributes themselves, as being in some way due to the
created intellect.[4] Consequently, many authors seem unconcerned
with drawing a strict distinction between the various divine attributes as they pertain to predestination. Bonaventure argues that predestination is an act of the divine will, but says that one could equally
argue that it is an act of the divine essence. Thomas Aquinas and
Richard of Middleton argue that predestination is an act of the divine intellect, but for them the divine intellect possesses efficacious as
well as cognitive characteristics.[5]

Near the end of the century the picture changed with the development of the formal distinction. This distinction argues for an
extra-mental difference obtaining in the subject (*ex natura rei*), but
claims to avoid any real composition in the subject (i.e. God). John
Duns Scotus, often credited with its development and unarguably
the most influential theologian to defend it, based the formal distinction on a strong realist metaphysics.[6] Because his metaphysics al-

---

[2] Anselm, *Monologion, Anselmi Opera Omnia*, vol. 1, ed. Franciscus Salesius Schmitt, (Edinburg, 1946), c. 17, pp. 31-32.

[3] *Magistri Petri Lombardi Sententiae in IV libris distinctae*, 3 vols., (Rome 1971), b. I, d. 8, cc. 23-28, (vol. 1, pp. 98-103).

[4] Hester Goodenough Gelber, "Logic and the Trinity", (Ph.D. Dissertation, University of Wisconsin, 1974), pp. 1-59. This type of distinction is frequently called a rational distinction or a conceptual distinction. I prefer to use the term "conceptual distinction" because the meaning of the term "*ratio*" differs according to author.

[5] See chapter 3 for a detailed discussion of this issue.

[6] For the purposes of this study a realist position is any position which holds that

lowed for various levels of extra-mental ontological status, Scotus could argue for a distinction which was greater than a merely conceptual distinction, but not quite a real distinction. Scotus and the other authors who supported a formal distinction emphasized more a distinction between the attributes and less a doctrine of absolute simplicity.[7] One of the consequences of this shift was the development of a doctrine of divine voluntarism which emphasized the primary role of the will in divine causation, including predestination.[8]

Aureol entered the debate at this stage, addressing the problem in distinctions 8, 35, and 45 of his *Scriptum*. As is to be expected from positions he takes elsewhere, Aureol criticizes Scotus's stance and emphatically denies the applicability of the formal distinction to the doctrine of the divine attributes.[9] Aureol also faults the appeal to the notion of a merely conceptual distinction between the attributes as a way of preserving divine simplicity. His rejection of the formal distinction, or indeed any distinction *ex natura rei*, is not surprising considering the fact that Aureol consistently maintains a strong anti-realist position.[10] Aureol considers any distinction *ex natura rei* between

---

abstract terms like "essence", "justice", and "will" refer to things which possess ontological status independent of any particular, created intellect.

[7] The most recent account of the development of the formal distinction and its application to Trinitarian doctrine is in Gelber, "Logic", pp. 60-103. Another analysis of Scotus's version of the formal distinction is in Marilyn McCord Adams, "Ockham on Identity and Distinction", *Franciscan Studies*, 36 (1976), 25-44. Scotus applies various versions of the formal distinction to the problem of the divine attributes in his *Lectura*, in *Joannis Duns Scoti opera omnia*, ed. Luke Wadding, (1639; repr. 1891-1895) vol. 17, I, d. 8, p. 1, q. 4, n. 173; and the *Ordinatio*, in *Joannis Duns Scoti opera omnia*, ed. Charles Balic, (Vatican City, 1950-), vol. 5, I, d. 8, p. 1, q. 4, n. 191, pp. 260-1.

[8] Discussing the importance of the formal distinction in Scotus's doctrine of predestination, Wolfhart Pannenberg claims that "voluntarist" doctrines of predestination were largely undeveloped in the 13th century because of the lack of a sufficient distinction between the divine will and the divine intellect. In a theology where the attributes are only conceptually distinct, foreknowledge, providence, and predestination are not significantly different. See Wolfhart Pannenberg, *Die Prädestinationslehre des Duns Skotus*, (Göttingen, 1953), pp. 33-44.

[9] Aureol's criticism of Scotus's teachings is well documented. See Michael Schmaus, *Der "Liber propugnatorius" des Thomas Anglicus und die Lehrunterschiede zwischen Thomas von Aquin und Duns Scotus*, part 2; *Die Trintarischen Lehrdifferenzen*, (Münster, 1930); B. Lindner, *Die Erkenntnislehre des Thomas von Strassbourg, Beiträge zur Geschichte der Philosophie des Mittelalters*, 27/4-5, (Münster, 1930); Vignaux, *Justification*, pp. 43-96; Tachau, *Vision*, p. 105; Mark Henninger, *Relations*, (Oxford, 1989), pp. 151-158; A.E. McGrath, *Iustitia Dei*, vol. 1, (Cambridge, 1986), pp. 149-150.

[10] Perhaps the most fundamental difference between the two theologians is that between their respective doctrines of universals. Aureol claims that abstract terms refer only to concepts, and thus abstractions like "justice" and "humanity" exist only as intra-mental constructs. For a dated and unsympathetic study of Aureol's metaphysics, see Raymundus Dreiling OFM, *Der Konzeptualismus in der Universalienlehre des Franziskanerzbischof Petrus Aureoli, Beiträge zur Geschichte der Philosophie des Mittelalters*, 11/6 (Münster, 1913). See Gelber, "Logic", pp. 130-143, for Aureol's criticism of the formal distinction as Scotus applies it to Trinitarian questions.

the attributes and the essence, or among the attributes, to be tantamount to a distinction between separate realities or essences, which
would be contrary to divine simplicity. His rejection of the conceptual distinction is puzzling, however, for the very same reasons.
Nevertheless, Aureol finds the conceptual distinction inadequate for
expressing the relation holding among the essential attributes in
God, since it does not significantly distinguish among them.

Aureol assumes a third position. For Aureol, the distinction that
obtains between the essence and the attributes, and between the attributes themselves, is neither merely conceptual, nor formal, but
rather semantic or "connotative". The amount of space that Aureol
devotes to his doctrine of the attributes reveals the important place it
occupies in his theology. Moreover, the details of his stance are not
only important for the history of the doctrine of divine simplicity,
but also for the history of the doctrine of predestination. It is no coincidence that Aureol's doctrines of divine simplicity and predestination are both innovative. In Aureol's theology, predestination is primarily an effect of the divine will with the divine intellect playing a
secondary role; thus he needs to make a significant distinction between the attributes. But he is not willing to give up God's absolute
simplicity. According to Aureol, a "connotative" distinction solves
the problem. Like the formal distinction, it provides a sufficient distinction between the attributes, while at the same time maintaining
God's absolute simplicity.[11]

Aureol's Critique of the Conceptual Distinction

In describing the conceptual distinction between the divine attributes, Aureol singles out three different opinions. Although each
of these proposed a conceptual distinction, each argued for a different basis for the distinction. It is here that Aureol perceives the internal flaw of the conceptual distinction: none of the bases given for
the distinction is adequate to preserve divine perfection and simplicity.

The first opinion, which Aureol attributes to Thomas Aquinas,
teaches that the basis of the conceptual distinction lies in the inabili-
ty of the limited human intellect to conceive of God's entire perfec-

---

[11] Since Aureol's doctrine of the attributes is largely reactionary, I will outline his
rejection of previous doctrines, concentrating mostly on Aureol's account of them.
Thus, I do not propose to give a history of the doctrine of the attributes, but to gain
a better understanding of Aureol's own attitude towards his immediate tradition.

tion in a single conception.[12] Because of this, Aquinas had argued that the intellect is forced to conceive of divine perfection according to an aggregate of discrete, limited concepts. Aureol attacks this position on two grounds. First, since each attribute is itself infinite, then, according to Aquinas's account, the created intellect would not be able to conceive of a divine attribute in a single concept:

> ...any attribute is formally infinite, for according to the Prophet, "the wisdom of God is without limit"; nor is there any limit to the mercy of God. And so it is concerning the other attributes. Therefore, if divine infiniteness and human limitation cause many concepts to be formed that are attributable to divine perfection, on account of this many conceptions will be formed concerning divine wisdom and the other attributes.[13]

Or, if Aquinas were correct, it would then follow that the more limited the intellect, the greater the number of conceptions it would form, so that an illiterate person would conceive of more of the divine attributes than would a theologian or an angel.[14]

Aureol also attacked Aquinas's account of how the intellect conceives of God. Aquinas had claimed that a multitude of conceptions due to the limitation of the intellect occurs only when all are of the same nature, but for Aureol the concepts of the attributes are not of the same objective nature. By this he means that insofar as the attributes exist as concepts or objects of a created intellect, they are numerically distinct; thus they do not have the same nature. Hence, a created intellect conceives of the attributes according to different

---

[12] Aureol describes this position in two places: *Scriptum*, d. 8, s. 23, art. 1, n. 49, (Buyteart, vol. 3, p. 980): "Circa primum considerandum quod aliqui dicere voluerunt perfectiones divinas vere esse in Deo, non tamen fore distinctas; propter quod non repugnant divinae simplicitati. Earum enim distinctio oritur ex duobus: ex imperfectione siquidem nostri intellectus et ex plenitudine perfectionis divinae. Noster enim intellectus, cum limitatus, non potest unica conceptione attingere totam perfectionem divinam. Propter quod, format partitos et limitatos conceptus". He attributes this position to Thomas Aquinas, but in art. 2, nn. 6-9, pp. 986-988 the opinion is anonymous. While Aureol treats the two opinions as the same, the one in art. 2, nn. 6-9, pp. 986-988 includes language that is more like Bonaventure than Aquinas: "Et videtur quod repugnet divinae simplicitati, ponendo comparationem secundum *modum intelligendi*, pro eo quod differunt ex imperfectione intellectus nostri, necesse est de illa re haberi diversas conceptiones. Sed perfectio divina excedit nostram intellectionem. Habet enim in se unitissime omnem perfectionem communicatam omnibus creaturis. Omnem autem perfectionem intellectus noster concipere non potest unica conceptione. Ergo necesse est quod propter sui imperfectionem et excessum plenae perfectionis existentis in Deo formet diversas conceptiones." Gelber ("Logic", pp. 12-15) claims that *modus intelligendi* was a term distinctive to Bonaventure's doctrine.

[13] *Scriptum*, d. 8, s. 23. art. 4, n. 74, (Buyteart, vol. 3, pp. 994-995).

[14] *Ibid.*, n. 75, p. 995.

natures.[15] This does not mean that Aureol accepts the conceptual distinction. He never denies that attributes are distinct in the created intellect; he denies only that the distinction depends on the intellect, that the distinction is *merely* conceptual. Moreover, even though the intellect conceives of divine perfection through multiple, diverse conceptions, these do not divide divine perfection as Aquinas says, but each one comprehends divine perfection in its entirety.[16]

Within a generation after Aquinas, variations on the conceptual distinction had become popular. These new variations were based on the assumption that a conceptual distinction must be based on some extra-mental distinction. None of the authors holding these views denied that the limitation of the created intellect played a role in the conceptual distinction. Rather, they assumed that there must be some extra-mental basis in accordance with which the limited intellect conceptualizes the distinctions in God's perfection. The two views of this sort that Aureol deemed worthy of mention arose from a debate between Henry of Ghent and Godfrey of Fontaines.[17]

According to Aureol, Henry of Ghent had taught that the distinction between the persons of the Trinity and distinct conceptions of the attributes in the divine mind combine to account for the distinction between the attributes and essence and among the attributes.[18]

---

[15] *Ibid.*, n. 76, p. 995: "...quandocumque est conceptuum multitudo propter limitationem concipientis, omnes illi conceptus eiusdem sunt rationis, ut patet de videntibus albedinem clarius et minus clare: visiones enim eorum sunt eiusdem rationis... Sed conceptus attributales sunt alterius rationis obiectivae. Ergo eorum distinctio non oritur ex limitatione intellectus." Aureol's notion of "objective being" and the numerical distinction among the objects of the intellect are important features of his epistemology, on which see Tachau, *Vision*, pp. 89-104.

[16] *Ibid.*, n. 77, p. 995: "...intellectus potest quidem formare diversos conceptus de eadem re, et similiter diversos conceptus de eadem perfectione; non tamen illam rem dividendo aut illam perfectionem, quasi aliquid assumat, aliquid relinquat; immo per quamlibet conceptionem claudit totam perfectionem et totam rem."

[17] For details of this debate, see Gelber, "Logic", p. 35; John F. Wippel, *The Metaphysical Thought of Godfrey of Fontaines: A Study in Late Thirteenth-Century Philosophy*, (Washington, D.C., 1981).

[18] Henry of Ghent, *Quodlibeta*, (Paris, 1518), v. 1, Quod., 5, q. 1, ff. 223ff. Aureol reports Henry's view as follows in *Scriptum*, d. 8, s. 23. n. 52 (Buyteart, vol. 3, p. 972): "Fuerint ergo alii, concedentes quidem quod attributorum distinctio sumi habet per comparationem ad aliqua re distincta, sed distincta re non sunt creaturae, sed aliquid intra Deum, videlicet personae. Dicunt enim isti quod essentia divina accipi potest in se et absolute, in quantum res quaedam est, et sic est fundamentum omnium attributorum; est tamen unum quid simplicissimum, carens omni distinctione rei vel rationis. Alio modo prout simplici intelligentia concipitur a divino intellectu, et sic adhuc concipitur ut quid simplicissimum, carens omni pluralitate; est tamen in potentia ad pluralitatem. Tertio quoque accipi potest, in quantum intellectus quasi post primam apprehensionem negotiantur circa ipsam, reducendo omnia attributa de potentia in actum secundum duplicem coordinationem. Primam

On this view, the divine essence can be conceived of in three ways. Taken in itself, the essence is utterly simple, but still the basis for all the attributes. Second, the divine intellect conceives of the essence as intelligence, and while it lacks all plurality, the divine intellect can (in Aristotelian terms) reduce the essence's potential plurality of attributes into act, that is, into actual plurality. Finally, the essence can be conceived of *as if* the divine intellect were carrying out its ability to distinguish between the attributes by reducing each of them into act.

The essence as the divine intellect does this by assuming two sets of coordinating modes. The first set of coordinating modes reduces divine intellect into act. First, the essence assumes a declarative mode. In this mode the essence has the character of truth, and because of this character, it assumes the mode of that to which a declaration is posed, namely the understanding or intellect. Now the essence has assumed the modes of both the intellect and its object, i.e. truth. At this point the essence assumes yet a third mode: that by which an object acquires potentiality. In this mode, the essence has the character of an actual operation of the intellect—presumably that operation by which the divine intellect attains the truth. The second set of coordinating modes reduces the attribute of divine will into actuality. The essence assumes an appetitive mode, and thereby the very character of good itself. On account of this character, then, the essence takes on the mode of an appetitive object and, hence, assumes the character of the will's appetite for it. Since the divine essence is now both appetite and appetitive object, it assumes a third mode to mediate between the two: actual volition by which the will operates.[19]

With these two sets of coordinating modes, according to Aureol, Henry can now account for the basis of the conceptual distinction.

---

quidem ex parte intellectus considerando quod essentia divina induit modum declarativi, et habet per consequens rationem veri et induit modum illius, cui fit declaratio et sic est intellectus; et induit modum illius, quo potentia attingit obiectum, et sic habet rationem actualis intellectionis. Secundam vero ex parte voluntatis secundum quam induit modum allectivi, et ita rationem boni; et modum eius quod allicitur, et ita rationem voluntatis et appetitus et modum mediantis inter utrumque, et sic actionem actualis volitionis. Omnia autem attributa reducuntur ad duas personas Filii et Spiritus Sancti, realiter distinctas."

[19] Although this is a rather bizarre explanation, Henry's account is merely a version of a generally accepted understanding of how the divine intellect and will function. God's intellect knows things through God's essence as the essence is the cause and exemplar of all things; and God's will wills things through God's essence as the essence is the highest good. Aureol does not attack Henry for his view of how God knows and wills things, but rather how Henry describes the functioning of the divine attributes.

First, for Henry all other divine attributes (e.g., wisdom, justice, etc.) can be reduced to the coordinates true/intellect/intellection and good/will/volition. Second, the difference between these coordinates can be reduced to the distinction between the second and third persons of the Trinity. This is because the Word emanates through the mode of intellect and the Spirit emanates through the mode of will.[20]

Aureol finds fault with this position on three grounds. First, he does not believe that it adequately preserves the distinction among the attributes. He argues that divine understanding cannot account for the distinction between the attributes, because the divine intellect is one of the attributes so distinguished, and the act of distinguishing must precede the things distinguished insofar as they are distinct.[21] He goes on to argue that, even if the divine intellect could be the basis for the distinction between the attributes, this account is not adequate to explain how a conceptual distinction is formed in created intellects, since no one is privy to the divine mind.[22]

Furthermore, Aureol thinks, Henry's position impugns divine perfection by describing the divine intellect as functioning in a discursive or reflexive manner. Aureol realizes that Henry is only drawing an analogy, but contends that such an analogy is faulty. He maintains that we must not form multiple images of God's intellect: "in whatever moment God understands His essence, He comprehends His essence as perfect and reduces all its perfections into act in that very same moment".[23] Therefore, since God understands His essence through a simple understanding, and not any reflexive act, He also makes the attributes distinct through that same simple understanding. Aureol claims that, if this position is not maintained, it would then follow that God is blessed, or just, or perfect, only insofar as He assumes the characters of each particular attribute.[24]

---

[20] *Scriptum*, d. 8, sec. 23, n. 22, (Buyteart, vol. 3, p. 973).

[21] *Ibid.*, art. 3, n. 89, p. 999: "Distinguens enim praecedit distinctum, intelligere divinum non praecedit omne attributum, cum ipsum sit quoddam attributum. Ergo ipsum non distinguit omne attributum."

[22] *Ibid.*, n. 90, pp. 999-1000.

[23] *Ibid.*, n. 91, p. 1000: "In quandocumque enim signo Deus suam essentiam intelligit, in eodem ipsam perfectam comprehendit, et ducit in actum omnes perfectiones eius. Sed sine actu negotiante per simplicem intelligentiam suam essentiam cognoscit. Ergo per simplicem intelligentiam omnes divinas perfectiones distinguit, praesertim cum intellectus negotiativus aut reflexivus locum non habeant in divinis."

[24] *Ibid.*, n. 92, p. 1000: "Deus beatus non esset, nisi quatenus induit respectum rationis, nec perfectus nec iustus, et sic de aliis attributis..."

Finally, Aureol objects to the opinion on the grounds that Henry has incorrectly described the relation of the personal properties to the attributes. While Aureol claims that the distinction between the divine will and divine intellect can obtain in the personal properties of the Word and the Spirit, will and intellect are not the principles productive of the persons, but are only connoted by them. In Aureol's words:

> ...the distinction of some of the attributes in God, such as the will and the intellect, can be taken as applying to the person of the Word and <the person> of the Holy Spirit; although not as though <the Word and Spirit> were produced through the intellect and the will, but only insofar as they are connotated <by the intellect and the will>. For it is upon the intellect that the Word objectively shines <light>, <and it is> the will whom the Spirit leads to what it loves.[25]

Although Aureol, as we shall see, constructs his own doctrine of the attributes around a theory of connotation, he does not rely on the distinction between the divine persons as a sole or primary basis for the distinction between the attributes. Unlike Henry, he does not think it is possible to reduce all the attributes to the coordinates true/intellect/intellection/Word and good/will/volition/Spirit.[26]

Aureol was not the first one to attack Henry's doctrine of the attributes. While Henry was still formulating his own position, Godfrey of Fontaines, a younger contemporary of Henry and possibly his student, was developing an alternative approach. Like Henry, Godfrey denied that the created intellect can conceive of distinct divine attributes without any basis in an extra-mental distinction. He went further than Henry, however, in claiming that the basis for a conceptual distinction must be some real distinction.[27] For Godfrey the distinction between the persons of the Trinity was not real, since

---

[25] *Ibid.*, n. 208, p. 1032: "...quod distinctio perfectionum in Deo aliquarum quidem, puta intellectus et voluntas, sumi potest penes personam Verbi et Spiritus Sancti; non tamen quatenus sint producta per intellectum et voluntatem...sed quatenus sunt connotata. Est enim intellectus cui lucet Verbum obiective, voluntas quam defert Spiritus in amatum..."

[26] *Ibid.*, n. 208, p. 1032: "Nihilominus non omnes conceptus perfectionales habent Verbum et Spiritum pro connotato, sicut patet unitate quae sumitur ab indivisione, et potentia quae connotat creare aliquid circa creaturos; et sic de aliis multis."

[27] *Scriptum*, d. 8, s. 23, art. 1, n. 50, (Buyteart, vol. 3, pp. 980-981): "...nihilominus intellectus non posset huiusmodi conceptiones distinctas formare, nisi quia perfectiones in creaturis reperit realiter distinctas. Omnis enim distinctio rationis aliquorum ortum habet a reali distinctiones eorundem, alicubi reperta. Unde intellectus noster attributa distinguit per comparationem ad creaturas, ubi rationes attributales realiter distinguuntur."

it did not distinguish between discrete things.[28] On the other hand, there is a real distinction between attributes in creatures. So, instead of arguing that the basis for the conceptual distinction lay in the distinction between the divine persons, he claimed that the created intellect forms its conceptions of the divine attributes by making comparisons to the created order.

Aureol does not refute this position as it stands. About a decade after Godfrey had defended this opinion in his *Quodlibeta*, Hervaeus Natalis adopted a similar position, adding a few refinements.[29] Aureol found Hervaeus's modifications significant enough to include in the appraisal of Godfrey's opinion. Hervaeus's qualification of a conceptual distinction based on comparison to the created order reveals that he is concerned with the implications that such a theory might have for divine perfection. First, as he stresses, only the distinction between the attributes, not the attributes themselves, depends on the created order. God is absolutely just, wise, and good without reference to the created order.[30] Another implication of this position is that it seems to make the created order the cause of divine cognition of His attributes. Hervaeus denies this, and counters by saying that since created intellects are too limited to understand how the divine intellect conceives of attributes, we describe God's knowledge by comparison to the order in which a created intellect reaches understanding.[31] The created intellect supposes that, because such attributes in created beings really are distinct, the divine intellect (like the human) must form a conception of these separate attributes before arriving at any multiplicity of conceptions of the same perfections in the divine intellect.

---

[28] Gelber, "Logic", pp. 35ff.

[29] Hervaeus, a contemporary of Scotus, probably lectured on the *Sentences* in 1302-1303. For a more comprehensive account of his career at Paris, see Bruno Decker, *Die Gotteslehre des Jakob von Metz: Untersuchungen zur Dominikanertheologie zu Beginn des 14. Jahrhunderts, Beiträge zur Geschichte der Philosophie des Mittelalters*, 42/1, (Münster, 1967), pp. 73-77.

[30] *Scriptum*, d. 8, s. 23, art. 1, n. 51, (Buyteart, vol. 3, pp. 981-982): "...ipsa absolute Deo conveniant sine habitudine ad creaturam, vel comparatione ad extra. Est enim Deus absolute iustus et sapiens et bonus."

[31] *Ibid.*: "quod attributa distinguit per comparationem ad extra, non est intelligendum quod res extra causaret divinam cognitionem, cum non habeat causam nec intra nec extra; sed quod hic est ordo intelligendi in Deo secundum nostrum modum considerandi, ut sicut velle praesupponit intelligere et intelligere creaturarum intelligere suae essentiae, ita intelligere plura secundum rationem circa seipsam praesupponit pluralitatem realem earundem rationum intellectam circa creaturas. Unde secundum nostrum modum intelligendi, conceptio perfectionum attributalium, ut in creaturis realiter sunt distinctae, praecedit pluralitatem rationis earundem perfectionum in divino intellectu."

Aureol found three major difficulties in the position defended by Godfrey and Hervaeus. Most important, Aureol found unnecessary the whole idea of comparison to objects outside God. According to Aureol it is possible that one and the same thing can be understood in many ways, just as one and the same thing can be seen in many ways:

> For it remains that one thing can occasion many visions <in the sens-es of the observer>. It is clear that a color, from a distance moves <the sense> to a confused vision, but up close to a determinate vi-sion. Thus this color appears before this whiteness <does> and, like-wise, this animal <appears> before this man. Similarly the intellect potentially has many understandings of the same thing. Since, all else being equal, when an agent and a recipient are placed near to each other, an effect follows…; therefore, having posited a simple thing concerning which many conceptions can be formed and an intellect able to receive them, there appears no reason why such a thing can-not move the intellect to many concepts <distinguished> conceptual-ly, any comparison having been excluded.[32]

Nor is vision the only analogy which applies to this case. Aureol likens the intellect's passive capacity for many conceptions to the air's passive capacity for the sun's diverse effects. Just as air is in po-tency to light, heat, and greater thinning, so the intellect can be in potency to many concepts of the same thing.[33]

Second, while comparison to creatures plays some role in distin-guishing between the attributes, it is not the basis for a distinction. Aureol claims that we can conceive of the respective characteristics of each attribute without recourse to a comparison to creatures. We can do so, Aureol holds, by conceiving of a given attribute's defini-tion just as easily as we can by conceiving of that attribute as a qual-ity of a creature. By thinking of the definition of justice (i.e., that by which a person renders to someone what is his) and that of clemen-

---

[32] *Ibid.*, art. 3, n. 86, p. 998: "Constat enim quod una res potest habere plures vi-siones; ut patet quod color a longinquo movet ad visionem confusam, de propre autem ad visionem determinatam. Unde prius apparet hic color quam haec albedo, et similiter prius hoc animal quam hic homo; similiter etiam intellectus est in poten-tia ad plures intellectiones de eadem re. Sed, posito activo et passivo appropinquatis ad invicem, sequitur effectus, omni alio circumscripto. Ergo posita re simplici de qua possunt formari multae conceptiones et intellectu potenti recipere, non apparet cur talis res movere non possit intellectum ad plures conceptus secundum rationem, exclusa omni comparatione."

[33] *Ibid.*, n. 87, pp. 998-999:"…sicut patet de aere, qui est in potentia ad lucem et calorem et raritatem ampliorem; unde et sol omnia simul inducit in aere, activo et passiva eisdem existentibus. Ergo, cum intellectus sit in potentia ad plures conceptus de aliqua re…"

cy (i.e., that by which someone relieves another's suffering), two different concepts are formed.[34]

The obvious objection to this claim is that the created intellect must have something upon which to base its definitions. Aureol agrees that in the case of attributes like justice and clemency it is true that at some point the intellect must have had a basis for its definitions in creatures. Once the definition has been formed, however, the intellect need not repeatedly refer to the created order to distinguish between the attributes.[35]

Taken on its own this does not seem a successful reply, but when combined with Aureol's third objection, his point becomes clear. In this objection Aureol argues that there are some attributes that have no basis in the created order at all, particularly the divine will and intellect. For Aureol the divine will and intellect are distinct from one another by the fact that God knows evil things, but does not will them—a distinction that, unfortunately, does not obtain in the human will. Therefore, this distinction holds true even if the divine intellect and will are not compared to created intellects or wills:

> But <even> when the divine will is not compared to the created will, nor the <divine> intellect to the <created> intellect, still we find that contradictory statements <are made> concerning them as they are in God. For it is true that God knows evil things, but does not will them. Therefore, excluding all comparison to the distinction <between will and intellect> which those creatures possess, <will and intellect> are still distinct as they pertain to God.[36]

This explains the significance of the previous argument. Aureol is claiming that there is something about the attributes themselves that causes a distinction to be drawn between them. Aureol does not distinguish between different types or levels of attributes, so, if there is some extra-mental distinction between the intellect and the will,

---

[34] *Ibid.*, art. 3, n. 78, p. 996: "Non est enim de ratione iustitiae nisi quod sit id quo redditur unicuique quod suum est, nec de ratione clementia nisi quod sit id quo subvenitur alienae miseriae. Isti autem duo conceptus abstrahunt a clementia et iustitia, prout sunt qualitates creatae."

[35] *Ibid.*, art. 3, n. 79, p. 996: "Et si dicatur quod intellectus nesciret quid est reddere unicuique quod suum est, nisi ita conspexisset in iustitia creata; dicendum est quod est quod ita sit, nihilominus postmodum habet conceptum iustitiae indeterminatum; et similiter conceptum clementiae, absque hoc quod recurrat ad distinctionem quam habent iustitia et clementia in creatura."

[36] *Ibid.*, art. 3, n. 82, p. 997: "Sed non comparando voluntatem divinam ad voluntatem creatam nec intellectum ad intellectum, adhuc invenitur dici contradictoria de illis prout in Deo sunt. Verum est enim quod Deus intelligit mala, et non vult ea. Ergo, exclusa omni comparatione ad distinctionem, quam habent ista creatura, adhuc distinguentur prout reperiuntur in Deo."

then there is also one between justice and clemency. So, comparison to creatures, or to the persons of the Trinity for that matter, only reveals that prior extra-mental distinction.

But this does not mean that Aureol must accept that the distinction between the attributes is intrinsic to God. We must also keep in mind Aureol's first argument against Godfrey and Hervaeus: the intellect can have different conceptions of one and the same thing. Coupled with his reply to Aquinas, that a created intellect can comprehend divine perfection in one conception, Aureol presents a double-edged argument. On the one side, he denies that the created intellect in itself *must* form diverse conceptions of God. On the other side, although admitting that the intellect does form such diverse conceptions, he denies that there *must* be an intrinsic composition in the divine essence to account for the differing conceptions in the created intellect.

Aureol's Critique of the Formal Distinction

Aureol chose to solve the problem of holding that there is an extra-mental distinction which does not impugn divine simplicity, by arguing that there is a semantic distinction between the attributes. Yet this was not the most obvious option available to him. Within his own Franciscan order theologians, especially Duns Scotus, had argued that there was a formal distinction between God's attributes. Many of these authors claimed that there could be a distinction obtaining in the nature of the attributes themselves *(ex natura rei)* which, nevertheless, did not impugn divine simplicity.[37] Because of his anti-realist metaphysics, Aureol did not accept their argument; but to leave the debate at that would be an over-simplification.

Anti-realism is only the starting point of the later Franciscan critique of the formal distinction. True, both Aureol and William Ockham, two of the most influential Franciscan authors in the period after Scotus, rejected the formal distinction as philosophically untenable. Ockham, however, accepted the theological usefulness of the formal distinction as a way to explain a doctrine that is beyond philosophical inquiry.[38] Aureol, on the other hand, rejected the formal distinction altogether. Unlike Ockham, Aureol saw no need to

---

[37] For a detailed account of the development of this idea, see Gelber, "Logic", pp. 60-103.

[38] For an account of Ockham's philosophical critique and theological adoption of the formal distinction, see Adams, "Ockham on Identity".

resort to a philosophically absurd position in order to explain the
distinction between the divine attributes.[39]

Modern readers of Aureol have generally considered him a fair and
insightful reporter of the views of his opponents.[40] His critique of the
formal distinction is no exception. Aureol recognized, for instance,
that Scotus had developed his position through various stages. In his
earlier work, Scotus based his distinction on a multitude of "formalities" in God. In his *Reportata* and *Logica* he moved to a position called
"*secundum quid*" distinction or "formal non-identity".[41] Aureol responded to both of these positions in his critique of the formal distinction,
but he treated the later position as the more sophisticated and, therefore, more dangerous one. In addition to Scotus, Aureol cited William
of Ware and a certain Thomas of England as authors who had argued
for formal non-identity between the attributes.[42]

Aureol assumes that the move from a distinction between formalities to a distinction based on formal non-identity has been motivat-

---

[39] This does not mean that Aureol believed that the entirety of divine perfection
was understandable to the created intellect. In his Trinitarian theology, he argued
that there was a real distinction between the persons. While this did not accord with
his ontology, he held this position as a point of orthodoxy. It is interesting to note
that even when Aureol abandons his philosophical position, he does not defend a
formal distinction. For details of Aureol's Trinitarian doctrine see, Gelber, "Logic",
pp. 130-143. Gelber is mistaken in seeing Aureol's connotative distinction as a possible solution to the Trinitarian problem. The doctrine of the attributes and the
doctrine of the Trinity were separate issues for Aureol. The doctrine of the Trinity
was not philosophically definable. Aureol could have also taken this stance concerning the attributes, but instead he assumes that there is a philosophical explanation
to account for the doctrine that a simple divine being possesses various attributes.

[40] Henninger, *Relations*, p. 151; Stephen D. Dumont, "The Univocity of the
Concept of Being in the Fourteenth Century: John Duns Scotus and William of
Alnwick", *Medieval Studies*, 49 (1987), 1-74.

[41] The development of Scotus's formal distinction is discussed in Gelber,
"Logic", pp. 71-103; and Adams, "Ockham on Identity", pp. 25-43. Aureol does
not seem to impose any major distortions on Scotus's teaching. It is beyond the purposes of this study to judge to what extent Aureol correctly interpreted Scotus.
Consequently, I will concentrate on Aureol's exposition of the formal distinction
and not Scotus's own texts. This approach is also warranted by the fact that Aureol
attributes this position to other authors in addition to Scotus. Aureol's account of
the formal distinction is a composite drawing, and it is to this composite opinion
that Aureol responds. We do not know who his opponent(s) is(are) in distinction 45,
but Aureol is clearly responding to a tradition in which Scotus is only the most
prominent figure.

[42] He cites Scotus and Ware as his opponents in his attack in *Scriptum*, d. 8, sec.
23, art. 1, nn. 53-59 (Buyteart, vol. 3); he cites Thomas of England alone in distinction 45, *Vatican City, Biblioteca Apostolica, MS Borghese 329*, f. 496vb. The identity of
this Thomas of England is unknown, but circumstantial evidence points to Thomas
Wilton. Aureol made extensive use of Thomas Wilton's *Quodlibeta* in his *Scriptum*, see
Anneliese Maier, "Literarhistorische Notizen uber Petrus Aureoli, Durandus und
den 'Cancellarius'", *Gregorianum*, 29 (1948), pp. 213-251.

ed by a need to emphasize the simplicity of God. Instead of claiming that there is some sort of positive distinction between the attributes, formal non-identity entails only that there be a lack of adequate identity between the attributes. Because of this lack, the terms which signify the attributes are neither synonyms, nor convertible.[43] For example, essence must be predicated of intellect, but the converse is not true, because one can conceive of a non-intelligent being. This type of non-identity is described as a "non-identity *per se primo modo*", since convertibility is the "first mode" of identity.[44] Therefore, I will use the translation "in a certain respect" for *secundum quid*, because the relata differ with respect to their definitive natures: the definitive nature of one relatum is not included in the definitive nature of the other relatum.[45]

If this distinction was going to preserve divine simplicity, it had to show how relata of differing definitive natures did not entail compo-

---

[43] *Ibid.*, ff.497ra-b: "Tertius modus realis distinctionis, sicut primus. Tertius vero nullo modo denominat aliqua realiter esse distincta simpliciter et absolute, sed solum cum quibusdam modis negantibus identitatem, ut dicatur quod talia non sunt idem per se primo modo, aut convertibiliter, aut synonimice, aut inquantum. Et ratio huius est, quia quando aliquid dicitur de pluribus, de uno quidem simpliciter, de alio vero secundum quid, nullo modo attribuitur simpliciter et absolute et sine addito illi de quo secundum quid dicitur. Licet enim ens in potentia sit reale, prout res dividitur contra ens factum ab intellectu, nihilominus non potest absolute concedi quod res in potentia sit absolute res absque additamento alicuius quid faciat illud stare secundum quid. Unde bene conceditur quod Antichristus sit ens in potentia, non tamen conceditur simpliciter et absolute quod sit ens. Similiter non est concedendum quod essentia et voluntas distinguantur realiter, aut quod distinguantur ex parte rei, aut ex natura rei, aut quod sint distinctae formalitates, aut quod haec formalitas non sic illa, aut quod distinguantur formaliter, omnia enim ista sunt falsa, cum denotet distinctionem simpliciter et absolute esse inter illa.

"Et propter hoc oportet praemittere negationem identitatis istorum, aut positionem distinctionis aliquid pertinens ad secundum quid, ut dicatur quod aliquo modo non sunt idem realiter, vel aliquo modo distinguuntur ex parte rei, aut quod non sunt idem primo modo, aut inquantum. Et tunc, si inferatur quod realiter distinguantur, coincaretur duplex fallacia.

"Prima quidem secundum quid ad simpliciter arguendo a distinctione secundum quid ad distinctionem absolutam. Secunda vero fallacia consequentis arguendo a negatione inferioris ad negationem superioris, sicut si diceretur 'leo non est homo, ergo non est animal', constat enim quod esse idem convertibiliter, aut in primo modo per se, est quidem modus identitatis. Negare, ergo, omnem modum identitatis inter aliqua propter hoc quod non sunt idem convertibiliter, aut primo modo per se, est comittere fallaciam consequentis. Et eodem modo, si arguatur quod distinguatur realiter ex hoc quod distinguuntur ex parte rei, cum distinctio negationem identitatis importet, distingui enim ex parte rei idem est in proposito quod non esse idem convertibiliter et per se primo modo."

[44] *Scriptum*, d. 2, sec. 23, art. 3, n. 91, (Buyteart, vol. 2, pp. 597-598).

[45] *Ibid.*, d. 8, art. 1, n. 55, p. 985: "Est autem ista non unitas quidditativa, quia una non est de conceptu quidditativo alterius et formali ratione, ita quod, si definirentur, non ponerentur mutuo in definitionibus suis." It is worth noting that Aureol has framed the position in conceptualist terms.

sition. On this issue the position that Aureol attributes to Scotus and William of Ware differs from the one he attributes to Thomas of England. Aureol correctly describes Scotus's *secundum quid* distinction as obtaining in the attributes *(ex natura rei)*.[46] Thomas of England's position, however, holds that the distinction obtains in the attributes in only a limited sense.[47] Consequently these two positions stress different aspects of the *secundum quid* distinction.

Aureol sees the main defense of Ware's and Scotus's position to be a definitional argument, according to which a formal distinction can be understood in two ways. In the first way, the designation "formal" can refer to the relata and, thus, describe a distinction between two modes of existence. This sort of distinction applies between "Socrates in a house" and "Socrates in a theater", since to be in a house or to be in a theater is to be in a certain respect, even though Socrates is the same person in both cases.[48] But if being in a certain respect entails qualification, then there would be imperfection in God. The second way attempts to avoid that problem: in this understanding the qualifiers "formal", "formally", and "in a certain respect" refer to the distinction, not to the relata.[49] According to this position, two relata lack adequate identity, but are not distinct things, when they fail to fulfill the four requirements of a simple, real distinction: (a) each of the relata most be fully actual; (b) each of the relata must have formal, and not merely virtual, existence; (c) each of the relata has distinct, and not confused, existence; (d) the one relatum is non-identical with the other.[50] Formal non-identity fulfills

---

[46] *Ibid.*, pp. 983-985. In d. 33, q. 2, of the *Reportata* (*Opera omnia*, ed. Wadding, vol. 23, p. 403b) Scotus says: "Potest autem essentiae et relationis distinctio vocari distinctio ex natura rei."

[47] *Borghese 329*, f. 497ra: "Tertius vero nullo modo denominat aliqua realiter esse distincta simpliciter et absolute, sed solum cum quibusdam modis negantibus identitatem, ut dicatur quod talia non sunt idem per se primo modo."

[48] *Scriptum*, d. 8, sec. 23, art. 1, n. 54, (Buyteart, vol. 3, p. 983): "Primum quidem quod distinctio secundum quid, relato secundum quid accipi potest vel referendo secundum quid ad ipsa distincta, ut cum ea quae distinguuntur sunt entia secundum quid, —quomodo consuetum est dici quod 'Sortes in foro' et 'Sortes in domo' secundum quid distinguuntur et sunt idem simpliciter, pro eo quod esse in foro et in domo sunt esse secundum quid."

[49] *Ibid.*: "...vel sumi potest referendo secundum quid ad distinctionem, ita quod, licet quodlibet distinctorum habeat entitatem et realitatem simpliciter, tamen eorum distinctio secundum quid quasi sint eadem realiter et simpliciter, sed non eadem secundum quid. Et hoc modo attributa inter se et a divina essentia distinguuntur."

[50] *Ibid.*: "Prima siquidem, si illa sint tantummodo in potentia...Secunda quoque, si talia sint solummodo virtualiter et non formaliter...Tertia vero, quando illa permixta sunt quomodo dicimus quod miscibilia sunt in mixto...Quarta autem, quando sunt eadem simpliciter et transeunt in omnimodam unitatem simpliciter, sed relinquitur aliqua non identitas secundum quid." For more on the four levels of identity, see Adams, "Ockham on Identity", p. 38.

only the final requirement, that there be non-identity remaining in two relata sharing in the same simple unity. The relata are the same, although it is *as if* they were two different formal entities.

Thomas of England's version of formal non-identity also attempts to lessen the distinction between the attributes, but Thomas claims that the essence and the attributes cannot be called "simply distinct" (*ex natura rei*); rather they are "distinct in some way" (*aliquo modo ex parte rei*). This shift in terminology was meant to preserve divine simplicity, while arguing that the distinction still obtained, although in a qualified sense, in the attributes themselves. In this case "in some way" (*aliquo modo*) seems to function in the same way as the "as if" (*quasi*) functioned in the version attributed to Ware and Scotus. Thomas, however, does not make the distinction between relata and relation.

According to Aureol's account of Thomas's position, then, the best way to understand formal non-identity is to conceive of the attributes in terms of the transcendentals.[51] Indeed, the transcendentals "good", "true", and "being" are also divine attributes. Thomas claims that there are two ways to reveal the non-identity between the transcendentals. First, considering the opposites of good and being highlights the distinction. The opposite of good is evil, while the opposite of being is non-being. Second, the concept of goodness and the concept of being are not predicable of each other in the first way (*per se primo modo*), since "goodness is being" is not as true as "goodness is goodness", since there is some non-identity remaining between them.[52] But this does not mean that being and goodness are really distinct. The proposition "being is goodness" is not false; rather, it does not have the same level of truth as a tautology does.

---

[51] *Borghese 329*, ff. 496vb-497ra: "'Ens', enim, 'verum' et 'bonum' sic sunt illimitata per praedicationem, quod licet entitas, veritas, bonitas aliquo modo differant ex parte rei, ita quod entitas et formalis ratio movendi intellectum per se, absque hoc quod moveat ratio boni. Nihilominus de se invicem praedicantur, quia 'bonitas est enititas' et 'entitas est quaedam bonitas', similiter etiam in natura illimitata secundum perfectionem, qualis est natura divina, omnes proprietates et perfectiones attributales, licet ex natura rei distinguatur, nihilominus ratione illimitationis una de alia praedicatur in abstracto, nam bonitas est veritas et veritas iustitia, et econverso."

[52] The arguments presented here for distinguishing between the transcendentals were not universally accepted in Medieval philosophy. Without a more certain identification of this author and some knowledge of his metaphysics, we have no way of knowing the grounds upon which he makes these controversial claims. For an introduction to the problem of the theory of the transcendentals in Medieval philosophy, see Scott MacDonald, ed. *Being and Goodness: The Concept of the Good in Metaphysics and Theology*, (Ithaca, 1991), esp. his introduction and chapter 1.

Thomas is here referring to the four requirements mentioned above for identity and distinction: since being and goodness meet only one of the requirements of difference, they are not absolutely different. But they do meet the criterion that there be some non-identity remaining between them. Therefore, they are not mutually predicable in the first way.

Moreover, for Thomas, the transcendentals are the fundamental attributes to which the others can be reduced. The example most appropriate for our purposes is the one concerning the distinction between will and intellect.[53] Thomas distinguishes between will and intellect on the grounds that they are moved by different objects. The will is moved by an appetitive or attractive object, and an object is attractive insofar as it is good. Therefore, the characteristic of good is what moves the will. By contrast, the intellect is not moved by an object's goodness, but by its being—a thing is knowable only insofar as it is. Therefore, the characteristic of being is what moves the intellect.

Aureol may acknowledge that there were various different versions of the formal distinction, but he does so to demonstrate that the differences among them are irrelevant. At the most basic level, he rejects the position that formal non-identity is any improvement over a distinction between formalities. Second, he argues that every understanding of formal non-identity shares the same basic flaw. Both of these claims rest on Aureol's doctrine of universals: the formal distinction, in any guise, is tenable only in a realist metaphysics. For an anti-realist, such as Aureol or Ockham, any refinement or development in the doctrine of the formal distinction merely increases the complexity of the error.

In both distinctions 8 and 45, Aureol attacks the Ware/Scotus version of formal non-identity.[54] In order to show why formal non-identity was not another distinction between formalities or entities existing only in a certain respect, Scotus and Ware had claimed that such expressions as "in a certain respect" and "formal" referred to the distinction and not the entities distinguished. Aureol, to the contrary, claims that there cannot be a formal distinction unless it is a

---

[53] *Borghese 329*, f. 497rb: "Autem entis non est primo motiva ipsius, per hoc enim quod aliquid apprehenditur esse non habet allicere voluntatem ad prosecutionem, nec fugam."

[54] *Scriptum*, d. 1, sec. 23, art. 4, nn. 142-148, (Buyteart, vol. 3, pp. 1010-1013); and *Borghese 329*, ff. 497va-498va. For convenience I will refer only to the arguments in distinction 8 when they are not also in distinction 45. While Aureol does not present Scotus's version in distinction 45, he does restate his refutation of it.

distinction between formal entities. Aureol uses two arguments to prove this claim. In the first, he assumes Scotus's realist position that relation is an extra-mental reality, so that he can show the position's internal inconsistencies.[55] In the second, Aureol reverts to his own anti-realist position and argues that the semantic defense of the formal distinction amounts to so much grammatical nonsense.

Aureol's first argument is based on the assumption that, if relation or distinction has any independent existence, its kind of existence depends on the kind of existence possessed by the entities which serve as bases of the relation or distinction.[56] Furthermore, existing in a certain respect (*secundum quid*) is qualified or diminished existence. Instead of there being a diminished- or quasi-distinction between the attributes, there would be a distinction between attributes which possess only qualified existence. But such a distinction does not occur between the attributes, because they exist simply; thus, any distinction obtaining in the attributes (*ex natura rei*) must be a real distinction:

> For as is the distinction between them, so is the being of the principles distinguished, because the distinctive principles are primarily diverse and distinct in their entirety... Therefore, if they are entities only in a certain respect and are distinguished in their entirety, <then> the distinction will necessarily be in a certain respect; but if these beings exist simply and not merely in a certain respect, <then> the distinction which follows from them would exist simply and not merely in a certain respect. But in the perfections which are attributed to God simply, there is nothing which exists merely in a certain respect, but rather divine wisdom is a being simply and not diminished. Therefore, if they are distinguished between themselves, they are necessarily distinct simply, and not merely in a certain respect.[57]

In Aureol's second argument, he returns to his anti-realist attack on the formal distinction. For Aureol, a distinction or relation is not an independent thing. Relation is either merely a concept, and thus has no extra-mental reality, or it is the diverse connotations of certain

[55] Henninger, *Relations*, pp. 68-98.

[56] *Scriptum*, d. 8, sec. 23, art. 5, n. 142, (Buyteart, vol. 3, p. 1010): "Relatio namque non suscipit magis et minus, nec simpliciter nec secundum quid, nisi ratione fundamentorum, ut Philosophus dicit in *Praedicamentis*. Unde similitudo suscipit magis et minus, quia qualitas in qua fundatur hoc suscipit."

[57] *Borghese 329*, f. 497va: "Tanta enim est distinctio aliquorum, quanta est entitas principiorum distinctorum, principia namque distinctiva sunt primo diversa et distinguuntur se totis, ut patet 10 Metaphysicae. Si, ergo, sunt entitates secundum quid et distinguuntur se totis, necessario distinctio erit secundum quid. Sed in perfectionibus simpliciter quae Deo attribuuntur, nihil est quod sit secundum quid, immo non-diminutum, et sic de iustitia et bonitate et aliis attributis. Ergo, si seipsius distinguuntur necessitate, simpliciter distinguuntur et non secundum quid."

concepts, and thus exists only in particular things connoted by concepts.[58] Given this position, it is obvious why Aureol would not accept the argument that terms such as "formally" and "*secundum quid*" refer to the distinction and not the entities distinguished. The grammatical move to distinguish between a formal distinction and things formally distinct was itself a distinction without a difference, since there is no relation independent of the relata. Whether "formal" or "formally" is used, those terms must refer to the relata.[59]

By arguing in this fashion, Aureol has reduced formal non-identity to the earlier position that the attributes are distinct formalities. Consequently, he can argue that the formal distinction is a real distinction in disguise. Building on the previous argument he claims that a quidditative or *secundum quid* distinction is a distinction between quiddities. For Aureol the quiddity (literally, "whatness") of a thing is no different from its essence or reality. So, if a *secundum quid* distinction distinguishes between quiddities, then it distinguishes between realities and essences of things.

> If, therefore, these perfections are distinct quidditatively, then they are distinct through their quiddities... But it is manifest that total quiddities are none other than total realities, because the quiddity and the essence and the reality of a thing are the same... Therefore, it is necessary that perfections of this sort are distinct according to their total essences and realities. And thus they are totally and simply distinct.[60]

---

[58] For Aureol's doctrine of relation as a concept see, Henninger, *Relations*, pp. 150-174. For his doctrine of relation as connotative, see below, pp. 34ff.

[59] *Borghese 329*, f. 497vb: "Quaerundum est, ergo, si esse et voluntas distinguuntur in Deo ex natura rei, an distinguatur unum ab alio ex tota natura suae realitatis, aut ex parte naturae et per parte realitatis. Sed non potest dari secundum, esset enim tunc pars et pars in natura realitatis et in ipsa realitate, et per consequens realis compositio, quia non potest pars et pars alicubi reperiri sine compositione. Non potest, ergo, dici quod in Deitate et in eius perfectionibus, ubi summa simplicitas est et nulla compositio, aliqua distinguantur ex parte naturae suae realitatis. Ergo, necesse est quod distinguantur tota natura et tota sua realitate, et per consequens distinguentur naturaliter, totaliter, et non secundum quid; et distinguuntur totaliter, realiter et non solum aliquo modo, vero omni modo, nec solum diminute et secundum quid, immo simpliciter quod ex toto —quod absonum est in divinis."

[60] *Ibid.*, f. 498ra: "Praeterea, quaecumque distinguuntur quidditiva, distinguuntur per suas quidditates, secundum regulam prius assumpta. Ergo, si perfectiones istae distinguuntur quidditive, distinguentur per suas quidditates, aut, ergo, per totales quidditates, aut per partem. Non potest autem dici per partem ratione simplicitatis. Necesse est, ergo, quod per totale quidditates. Sed manifestum est quod totales quidditates non sunt aliud quam totales realitates, quia quidditas et essentia et realitas rei idem sunt, cum definitio quae explicat quidditatem explicet rei essentiam et entitatem, ut patet 7 Metaphysicae. Ergo, necesse est quod perfectiones huiusmodi distinguantur secundum suas totales essentias et realitas. Et ita totaliter et simpliciter distinguentur."

Aureol has no more patience for the version of the formal distinction which he attributes to Thomas of England. Aureol denies that terms can be more or less truly predicated of other terms. According to Aureol's theory of predication, if one of the attributes is not predicable *per se primo modo* of the other, then the former is not in any way predicable of the latter. Arguing that, if there is some reason intrinsic to the attributes which explains why they are not convertible, then they are simply distinct, Aureol takes as an example the proposition "justice is wisdom". Abstract terms or concepts such as "wisdom" and "justice", Aureol claims, signify the intrinsic character of those things which they represent when all extrinsic characteristics have been excluded. Thus, "wisdom" signifies precisely the intrinsic characteristic which makes a thing wise and not any of its other characteristics. Moreover, in a *secundum quid* distinction or in a case of formal non-identity, the lack of identity is due to the fact that the distinguished entities do not signify the same intrinsic characteristic. Therefore, the intrinsic character of wisdom is not precisely the same as the intrinsic character of justice. But if that is the case, then, according to Aureol, the proposition "wisdom is justice" is merely false, because the intrinsic character of one is not included in the other.

By rejecting the four levels of identity and sameness, Aureol has turned the tables on his opponents. Rather than being the basis for only a minimal distinction, formal non-identity entails an essential difference.[61]

---

[61] *Ibid.*, ff. 498rb-va: "Quod vero illimitatio non det quod talia de se invicem praedicari valeant in abstracto, si distinguantur quiddative et ex natura rei, immo quod multo minus praedicabuntur, quam si essent limitata, manifest apparet. Quaecumque enim se totis et totaliter distinguuntur, si fuerint infinita, non est dubium quod multo amplius distinguentur quam si fuerint finita, distinguentur enim per aliquid infinitum et modo infinito. Et propter hoc Deus in infinitum distare dicitur a qualibet creatura, creaturae vero distinguuntur et non distent ab invicem infinite. Sed manifestum est quod quae magis ab invicem distinguuntur, minus de se invicem praedicantur. Ergo, si 'sapientia' et 'iustitia' se totis distinguuntur ex natura rei, non dabit eis illimitatio quod de se invicem praedicentur, immo maxime aufert, quia erunt in infinitum distantia et distincta. Et si dicatur quod ratione illimitationis transeunt in identitatem realem propter quam de se invicem praedicantur realiter, licet non in primo modo, non valet utique, quia contradictio est quod distinguantur se totis et quod transeant in identitatem realem, nisi detur quod eorum totalitas accidat realitati et sit extra eam, omne autem quod est extra realitatem est extra ens, et per consequens realia erunt nihil. Praeterea, manente causa, manet effectus, sed tota causa, quare abstracta de se invicem praedicari non possunt, est illa quae tacta est, videlicet quia denotat rationem praedicati, quantumcumque praecisam et abstractam includi in ratione subiecti, quantumcumque praescindatur et abstrahatur, et propter hoc de humanitate non praedicatur, nisi illud quod includitur infra 'humanitatem'. Est enim 'humanitas' tantum et 'animalitas' quaedam et 'substantialitas', secundum Avicennam. Non est autem vera, nec multa, nec 'animalitas est rationalitas', propter hoc quod earum rationes ab invicem praescinditur. Ergo,

Aureol on the Attributes: the Connotative Distinction

By rejecting both major positions of his time concerning (a) the distinction between the divine essence and the attributes, and (b) between the attributes themselves, Aureol leaves himself in a very interesting position. He cannot accept the formal distinction on metaphysical grounds, but in order to claim that the divine will is significantly different from the intellect, he needs more than a merely conceptual distinction. To escape this dilemma Aureol argues for a third type of distinction between the attributes; he claims that the attributes differ through what they connote. For Aureol such a position entails redefining divine simplicity, the attributes, relation, and connotation.

Like those who had argued for a merely conceptual distinction, Aureol defines the attributes as concepts.[62] Because the attributes are merely concepts, he can claim that the divine will and the divine essence are both (a) one and the same thing, and (b) one and the same intrinsic characteristic (*idem secundum rem et rationem*).[63]

---

manente distinctione formali, sive in natura limitata, sive natura illimitata tolletur veritas talium propositionum, immo magis in natura illimitata, quanto magis distinctio illimitatorum distinctorum se totis potior sit et maior ratione illimitationis. Praeterea, facientes non causam, causam paralogizant seipsos. Sed constat quod illimitatio non potest esse causa quare praedicetur abstractum de abstracto, si tamen rationes obiectivae formaliter designatae ab invicem distinguantur. Iam enim illimitatio non excludit illud quod veritatem propostionis impediebat, quinimmo potius intendit cum abstracto et praecisio rationis unius ab alia, causa sit quare propsitio talis est falsa. Denotatur enim per huiusmodi propositiones quod abstracta ratio praedicati non praedicatur, nec abstrahitur a praecisa et abstracta ratione subiecti. Ergo, talia dicens paralogizat se ipsum. Nec valet si quis dixerit quod illimitatio ponit identitatem realem, quia realis identitas praedicati cum subiecto non denotatur per propositiones huiusmodi quae sunt in abstracto, sed potius designatur inclusio rationis formalis. Unde quia differentia est extra rationem generis, idcirco si praescindantur et abstrahantur rationes generis et differentiae, non possunt de se invicem praedicari."

[62] *Scriptum*, d. 8, sec. 23, art. 2, n. 68, (Buyteart, vol. 3, p. 991): "Ex praemissis potest concludi quid sit attributum definitive. Est enim conceptus indeterminatus principaliter et in recto secundum rem, includens in obliquo certum aliquod connotatum, pertinens ad perfectionem simpliciter, communis Deo et creaturae, in idem re et ratione coincidens cum illo in quod specificatur."

[63] For this claim as it applies specifically to the divine will, see *Borghese 329*, f. 494vb: "Quod voluntas sit in ipsum quod divina essentia et re et ratione intrinsece et quod solum penes extrinsece distinguuntur. Sed in oppositum videtur quod voluntas et ceterae perfectiones sint id ipsum quod ratio Deitatis, nullo penitus addito, sed tantum extrinseco connotato. Constat enim quod ratio Deitatis est perfectissima. Sed si non esset intriseca eadem ratio cum 'intelligere' et 'velle' et ceteris perfectionibus, non esset simpliciter perfestissima, immo inter omnes minus perfecta. Tum quia perficeretur per omnes. Tum quia non esset vivida, sicut rationes importatae per 'intelligere' et 'velle'. Tum quia non esset beatifica, nec haberet rationem finalis boni, sicut ipsum velle in quo consistit beatitudo principaliter et ultimate—

By using the term "*ratio*" in a highly technical sense in discussions of this sort, Aureol refers to the intrinsic character or characteristic of a concept.[64] So, for instance, he argues that the subject of theological enquiry is not the particular divine being, but rather that which is characteristic of the abstract concept "Deity" (*ratio Deitatis*).[65] Thus, if the attributes and the essence could not be reduced to the same *ratio*, then the attributes would not be part of the characteristic intrinsic to Deity. Or, if one maintained a strong realist stance, the divine essence would then contain multiple *rationes* which possessed their own ontological status. For a Latin Christian conceptualist, like Aureol, neither position can be acceptable.

The key to the originality of Aureol's doctrine lies in Aureol's definition of a concept.[66] A single concept can signify many different things;[67] moreover, concepts signify determinate things in more than

---

quae omnia sunt absurda. Ergo, necesse est dicere non solum catholice, immo etiam philosophice, quod ipsamet ratio Deitatis sit quoddam intelligere et quoddam velle. Et sic de aliis perfectionibus nullo intrinseco addito, solum adiuncto aliquo extrinseco connotato. Praeterea, non solum Deus perfectissimus est realiter, immo et ratio Deitatis est perfectissima ratio. Sed constat quod res Deitatis non esset perfectissima, nisi esset realiter quoddam intelligere et quoddam velle nulla realitate addita. Ergo, nec ratio Deitatis erit perfectissima ratio, nisi sit ratio intellectionis, volitionis et omnis alterius perfectionis simpliciter nulla penitus ratione intrinsecus adiuncta."

[64] This is not a common use of the terms "*secundum rem et rationem*". Aquinas, for example, in his doctrine of the transcendentals claims that they are the same *secundum rem*, but differ *secundum rationem*. One modern study of Aquinas's doctrine of the transcendentals interprets this as a distinction between sense and reference; on this interpretation, terms for transcendentals such as "being" and "goodness" refer to the same thing, but differ in sense. See Eleonore Stump and Norman Kretzmann, "Being and Goodness", *Being and Goodness*, ed. Scott MacDonald, pp. 98-128.

[65] *Scriptum*, Prooemium, sec. 5, art. 4, (Buyteart, vol. 2, pp. 312-313): "...ratio deitatis est formalis ratio subiectiva, respectu habitus theologici. Illa namque ratio, quae mediat inter Deum et omnia quae declarantur in hac scientia, et quae determinat sibi unum genus cognoscibilitatis et modum proprium istius habitus, illa quidem est ratio subiectiva. Sed Deitas est huiusmodi. Per rationem namque Deitatis, attribuntur Deo ea quae declarantur in hac scientia quasi partes, scilicet tres personae; de qualibet namque persona multae veritates in hoc declaritivo habitu inquiruntur; per eandem etiam rationem reducuntur in Deum perfectiones essentiales, quae sunt intelligere et velle, et similia; per eandem etiam reducuntur omnia quae cadunt sub omnipotentia, ut quod Deus potuit mundum creare, et unire Deum et hominem, et Virginem facere inviolatam parere, et similia; per eandem etiam reducuntur omnia contigentia quae subsunt divinae voluntati, ut quod Virgo peperit de facto, quod homo Deus fuit, et quod Abraham duos filius habuit, et universa quae de facto tenemus per fidem, et declarantur per theologiam."

[66] See Tachau, *Vision*, pp. 89-113.

[67] Aureol uses two terms to describe this property of indeterminate concepts. In *Scriptum*, d. 8, sec. 23, art. 2, n. 69, (Buyteart, vol. 3, p. 992), he uses the word "*significare*". In distinction 45, (*Borghese 329*, ff. 499ra-b) he uses the word "*importare*" which is commonly translated as "to convey". He seems to use these words as synonyms, so to simplify matters I will translate both as "to signify".

one way. This holds true for attributable concepts (i.e. concepts which describe things). The attributes immediately signify the concept "being"; for instance, the concept "justice" primarily signifies a being. Obliquely and secondarily, however, the attributes signify the actions—or the objects of the actions—of a being operating in a certain way.[68] "Justice" secondarily signifies a being rendering to someone what is his. Aureol thus assumes that before the intellect can conceive of an individual rendering to someone what is his, it must first conceive of that individual's existence.

This definition of attributes also applies to the divine attributes, with one difference: the concepts in this case signify a divine being as opposed to any being. The concept "divine will" primarily signifies the divine essence, or more precisely, the intrinsic characteristic of Deity.[69] It secondarily signifies willed objects.[70] The concept of "divine intellect", although also signifying the divine essence, connotes everything that God knows. Furthermore, Aureol claims, the set of things God knows and the set of things which He wills are not coextensive, because God knows both good and evil, but does not will cul-

---

[68] Aureol uses the terms *connotat* and *in obliquo* to describe this type of signification. I have chosen "secondary" as a translation for *in obliquo* instead of more obvious choices like "oblique" and "indirect", because these latter terms can imply some mediation between significant and significate. Aureol denies that connotation of this sort is mediated by any condition (*Borghese 329*, f. 496rb). I will treat "that which is connoted" and "secondary significate" as synonymous in this study. I use the term "secondary significate" at times instead of "that which is connoted" in order to accentuate the difference between connotation and primary signification.

[69] *Borghese 329*, ff. 501va-b: " Ad tertium dicendum quod utique verum est eandem esse rationem Deitatis quae sumi potest absolute absque omni extrinseco, et sic potest nomen sibi imponi, ut Deitas appellatur, potest etiam concipi cum aliquo connotato extrinsece, et sic idem Deitati nomen aliud imponetur significans quod idem quod nomen Deitatis intrinsece, et cum hoc demonstrans intrinsecum aliquid, et cum sint multa extrinseca talia poterunt nomina multa imponi vel potius in generali imposita applicari. Secundum hoc, ergo, 'scientia' et 'voluntas' et cetera nomina attributalia connotativa sunt, nomen vero essentiae non, nec propter hoc oportet ea aliam rationem intrinsecam designare, cum eadem ratio possit quidem sumi aliquando absolute, sine omni ex extrinseco et aliquando simul cum extrinseco aliquo."

[70] *Ibid.*, f. 496ra: "Sententiarum in distinctione praesenti, cum dicit quod 'intelligere' et 'velle' non aliud significant quam divinam essentiam, nisi quod non significant eam simpliciter et absolute, sed demonstrant aliqua sibi esse subiecta, ut 'intelligere' monstrat omne scibile Deitate fore subiectum, similiter 'velle' demonstrat omne quae Deus facit, Deitate libere esse subiecta. Constat autem quod demonstrare aliqua esse subiecta, non est aliud quam illa connotare. Si cui, ergo, connotationis vocabulum sit exosum utatur secure vocabulo Philosophi dicendo quod attributa differunt,sicut relativa secundum dici vel distinguuntur secundum dici ad aliquid extrinsecum aut utatur verbo Magistri quod non distinguuntur aliter, nisi quia demonstrant aliqua Deitati esse subiecta. Dum enim veritas teneatur, non est curandum de verbis more Aristotelis qui modicam sollicitudinem habebat de nominibus et multam de rebus, ut Commentator dicit in 1 Physicorum, capitulo primo."

pable evil (i.e. sin).[71] Therefore, the concepts "divine essence", "divine will", and "divine intellect" refer to the same intrinsic connotates, but differ according to what they connote extrinsically.

Aureol's argument rests on the claim that such concepts as the divine attributes have some connotative characteristic (*ratio connotativa*). To support this claim he turns to the Aristotelian doctrine of relations. Announcing that he follows Simplicius, Aureol believes that Aristotle had discussed two types of relation in the *Categories*. One, of course, is the category of relation. There also seemed to be a second type of relation discussed in Book 7, where Aristotle asks whether second substances and qualities are relative.[72] The problem, put in Aureol's terms, was that concepts like "hand" and "health" seemed to imply a relation. When one thinks of a hand, one thinks of it as belonging to a handed thing; similarly, the concept "health" implies relation to a standard against which health is measured. Aureol argues that these concepts are relative, but not in the same way as those things which belong to the category of relation. The latter are *essentially* relative (*relativum secundum esse*). A concept is relative *secundum esse* when its essence or intrinsic character is that it be relative to something else.[73] Concepts like "hand" and "health", however, are not essentially relative, since their intrinsic characteristic does not include a relation to something else; instead, they are relative only in a manner of speaking (*relativum secundum dici*):

---

[71] *Ibid.*, f. 501vb: "Ad octavum dicendum quod diversitas harum duarum propositionum, 'Deus cognoscit malum culpae', 'Deus vult malum culpae', ortum habet non ex modo significandi diverso, nec ex ipso significato intrinseco et in recto horum duorum verborum 'vult' et 'cognoscit', sed ex significato extrinseco, sive ex connotato, ut saepe dictum est."

[72] *Ibid.*, ff. 494vb-495ra: "Prima quidem quod ratio connotiva non est aliud quam relativum, sive ad aliquid secundum dici; nec distingui penes extrinseca est aliud, nisi sicut distingueretur unum et idem. Si diceretur ad aliquid sit relative ad plura, non quidem secundum esse, sed secundum dici. Ubi considerandum quod relativum secundum dici non est de praedicamento relationis, immo sationes aliorum praedicamentorum hoc modo relativae dicuntur, sicut patet de substantiis, quia 'caput' dicitur 'alicuius caput' (similiter et 'manus' et 'remus' et similia). Qualitates etiam hoc modo relative dicuntur, quia ratio virtutis et vitii dicuntur ad aliquid (ut 'pulchritudo' et 'sanitas' ut Philosophus 7 Physicarum dicit). Talia, ergo, relativa non possunt intelligi dici ad aliquid per modum fundamenti, nec per modum concreti ex fundamento et habitudo constituti, possumus enim intelligere quod hoc duplici modo possit aliquid dici relative."

[73] For more on Aureol's doctrine of relation *secundum esse*, see Henninger, *Relations*, pp. 150-173. Because he only looked at texts in which Aureol discusses the category of relation (*relativum secundum esse*), Henninger deals with only half of Aureol's doctrine of relation. Aureol held both a doctrine of relation as concept and a doctrine of relation as connotative.

> So, therefore, when we accept that something is called "relative" we
> are not able to say that a substance or something from the other cate-
> gories <except relation> is called relative according to its own intrin-
> sic character, for it would follow that the intrinsic character proper to
> substance or <the one proper> to quality would be an accident, as if
> something were constituted from a relation and its basis. Thus, some
> relation is not included in either the definitive characteristic of 'hand',
> or of "health", or of "beauty", for otherwise that character would be a
> composite and exist through an accident.[74]

Given this distinction between the two types of relation, Aureol must
still explain why we call certain second substances and qualities "relative", if it is not of their nature to be in relation to another. He answers that terms representing second substances like "hand" and
"flesh", immediately appropriate or "determine" to themselves other
extrinsic terms. Because of this immediate appropriation of terms,
whenever a person hears the word "flesh", that person always conceives of flesh as belonging to an animal; likewise, when a person
hears the word "hand", that person always conceives of a hand as
belonging to a being with a hand.[75] Moreover, this appropriation is
immediate, because the intellect need not conceive of the hand actually having the condition of belonging to a handed thing. Even if a
person has a concept of an amputated hand, the nature of a hand as
part of a handed thing occurs to the intellect. The same holds true
for certain qualities, and these types of qualities include the attributes. Besides claiming that one cannot conceive of an act of the will or

---

[74] *Ibid.*, f. 495ra: "Sic, ergo, accipiendo relative dici aliquid non possumus dicere
sit relativum secundum dici secundum suam propriam rationem, sequeretur enim
quod propria ratio substantiae aut qualitatis esset ens per accidens, quasi aliquid
constitutum relatione et suo fundamento. Unde in ratione quidditativa 'manus' non
includitur relatio aliqua, nec in ratione 'sanitatis' aut 'pulchritudinis', aliquin ratio
illa esset quid compositum et ens per accidens."

[75] *Ibid.*, ff. 495ra-b: "Est, ergo, considerandum ultimo quod rationes generum
aliorum, quae tamen sunt relativae secundum dici, possunt intelligi ultra illos duos
modos qui tacti sunt aliis duobus modis dici relative. Primo quidem immediate appropriando terminos; secundo vero immediate appropriando habitudines per quas
ad terminos referantur. Possumus enim intellegere vel quod ratio 'manus' immediate appropriet et determinet aliud tamquam extrinsecum terminum, sicut 'manuatum', ut secundum hoc sine respectu medio manus per rationem manus dicatur
'manuati', et 'caro' per rationem carnis determinet sibi 'animal', ita quod audito
nomine carnis semper concipiatur ut aliquid animalis ex sua propria ratione; vel
possumus intelligere quod non immediate 'manus' vel 'caro' determinent et approprient sibi quoddam extrinsecum per modum termini, sed potius quia prius sibi determinant et appropriant habitudinem quandam et mediante illa approprient sibi
terminum illum extrinsecum, ita quod audito nomine manus vel carnis statim coin-
telligatur relatio partis et ex hoc intelligatur terminus cuius pars dicitur 'caro' vel
'manus'. Secundum hoc enim non immediate 'caro' vel 'manus' per suas proprias
rationes determinant sibi extrinsecum terminum, sed mediante habitudine quam
sibi determinant per suas proprias rationes."

of the intellect without first conceiving a being who wills or knows, Aureol states further that no one can conceive of an act of the intellect or an act of the will without also conceiving of an object known or an object willed. This is because when someone wills or knows, that person wills something or knows something:

> Thus no one can conceive of an act of the intellect or an act of the will, but that <the act> is apprehended along with some extrinsic known or willed object, since whoever knows or wills, knows or wills something... Thus when "volition" is taken as an abstract <noun> like "whiteness" or "shape", even then <it is the case>, since the object to which "volition" refers belongs to the secondary understanding of <volition>.[76]

If we apply this to the divine will and intellect, we can see how the connotative distinction functions. Both "divine will" and "divine intellect" primarily signify the divine essence, the being who wills and knows. Within the divine essence the act of knowing and the act of willing are not distinct; it is only through the extrinsic *connotata* of the acts that any difference appears. The act of the divine intellect has all things, both good and evil as its object, but, because the divine will does *not*, God does not will sin.

One can describe the connotative distinction, then, as an extra-mental distinction the basis of which is not the divine essence. On Aureol's account, the conceptual distinction is forced on the intellect by the very nature of the concepts pertaining to the attributes. The intellect is not able to conceive of the divine will without conceiving of both its intrinsic identity to the divine essence and its extrinsic differentiation from that essence. But because of the intrinsic identity of the essence and the attributes, the basis of this distinction is not Deity itself. By formulating an extra-mental distinction between the attributes that does not entail a distinction intrinsic to them, Aureol has attempted to ease the tension between his anti-realism and his voluntarism. If he is going to maintain a doctrine of predestination which stresses the primary role of the divine will, he must (if he is consistent) have a doctrine of divine simplicity which will not render such a distinction meaningless. Aureol's connotative distinction is a conceptualist's version of the formal distinction. While it does not allow any distinction *ex natura rei*, it performs, as we shall see, the same theological functions as an *ex natura rei* distinction.

---

[76] *Ibid.*: "Non est autem ita de 'manu', statim enim ducit in 'manuatum', quantumcumque fuerit amputata et ratio huius est, quia 'manus' ex sua ultima ratione appropriat sibi aliquid aliud extrinsecum cuius sit."

CHAPTER TWO

THE SEMANTICS OF VOLUNTARISM

Aureol's doctrine of predestination involves the divine will at two different points. First, there is God's intrinsic will to save all human beings. Second, God wills to carry out the salvation of those who do not resist His grace. Accordingly for Aureol, the divine will can be understood in two ways. On the one hand, God's will can be understood as the universal divine love for all creation. On the other hand, the divine will can be understood as the particular acts of divine willing which direct God's particular actions in the world. Both in general and pertaining to predestination in particular, this two-fold understanding of the divine will seems initially incoherent: how can the will understood as a universal love for creation irrespective of the disposition of particular creatures be the basis for particular divine acts in time, or rather on what basis does God act in a certain way; apropos to predestination: on what basis does God, who desires the salvation of all humankind, carry out this will for some and not others? Aureol addresses this problem as it pertains to the divine will in general in the final two treatises on the divine will in his *Scriptum*.

A reader of Aureol's *Scriptum* may be surprised that in distinction 46 Aureol poses the problem: Whether there is in God, truly and in the proper sense of the term, a characteristic of will.[1] After all, has he not already gone to great lengths to explain how God's will is distinct from all the other attributes? The problem, however, is not whether God is a willing God, but how God wills and whether human language is able to describe correctly how God wills.[2] Aureol points out that often terms signifying a willing being convey imperfections, like unmet desires and movement, which in no way should be attributed to God. Even terms which directly signify (the) will as

---

[1] *Ibid.*, f. 502vb: "Quaestio 73: Utrum ratio voluntas vere et proprie sit in Deo?"
[2] Vignaux, *Justification*, pp. 61-80, gives a brief description of Aureol's doctrine of the divine will. Vignaux was trying to stress the conflict between Scotus and Aureol concerning such issues as the necessity of created habits of grace. Vignaux recognized the importance of Aureol's doctrine of the attributes, but given the scope of his study, was not able to develop his analysis in detail. For instance, while he was aware of the importance of such terms as *potestas* and *complacentia* in Aureol's doctrine of the will, he was not able fully to describe Aureol's crucial and idiosyncratic appropriation of these terms.

capacity (*voluntas*), as willing activity (*velle*), or as a particular act of will (*volitio*), carry meanings which are not suitable to a concept of divine will. On the other hand, Scripture uses many terms which convey imperfection, but nevertheless ought not be denied to God.[3]

As in his treatise on the attributes in general, Aureol adopts a semantic approach in his discussion of the divine will. The impact of this type of approach is clearly seen in the organization of his treat-

---

[3] *Borghese 329*, f. 502vb: "Quod ratio voluntatis non proprie in Deo. Et videtur quod non, quia ratio vera et propria voluntatis et potissime actualis volitionis videtur consistere in aliquo intrinseco et absoluto, sed in praecedentibus dictum est quod velle in Deo non ponit rationem aliquam intrinsecam absolutam, sed tantum aliquid extrinsecum et consignificatum. Ergo videtur quod propria et vera ratio voluntatis non sit in Deo. Praeterea, actus connotatus per misericordiam, videlicet alteri subvenire, competit Deo, similiter et actus connotatus per furorem et iram, videlicet expetere vindictam. Sed nullus dicat quod furor aut ira aut passio misericordiae vere et proprie sit in Deo, sed tantum figurative quia habet se ad modum irati vel furentis vel miserantis. Ergo nec voluntas vere et proprie erit in Deo, cum nihil ponat in Deo, nisi suum proprium connotatum. Praeterea, voluntas et appetitus et desiderium idem esse videntur. Sed ratio desiderii et appetitus in Deo non est, cum imperfectionem importet; non enim appetitur, nisi perfectio et bonum. Ergo ratio voluntatis vera et propria non habebit locum in Deo. Praeterea, voluntas movetur a fine et est movens motum, sicut patet in tertio De anima et 6 Ethicorum ubi dicitur quod mens practica movet sicut cuius gratia respectu voluntatis; et similiter Anselmus dicit in libro De similitudinibus quod voluntas est instrumentum seipsum movens. Sed manifestum est quod Deus non movetur a fine nec habet rationem moti cum sit primum movens immobile. Ergo ratio voluntatis, proprie accepta, non habet locum in Deo. Praeterea de ratione voluntatis, est quod sit libera et ad utrumlibet ad contingens, quia nihil est tantum in potestate nostra, quantum voluntas, secundum Augustinum. Sed contingentia omnino repugnant Deo nec actus aliquis intrinsecus Deo potest esse in alicuius potestate, cum sit ipsum quod Deus. Quicquid autem est Deus de necessitate est Deus. Ergo dici non potest quod ratio vera et propria voluntatis in Deo sit. Praeterea, voluntas esse non potest absque libero arbitrio quia quicquid habet voluntatem, habet etiam arbitrandi libertatem, sed liberum arbitrium Deo repugnat, cum consilium praesupponat et per consequens discursum. Ergo id quod prius.

"Quod ratio voluntatis proprie sit in Deo. Sed in oppositum videtur quod ait Apostolus ad Romanos duodecimo, 'Probetis quae sit voluntas Dei beneplacens et perfecta'; et ad Romanos nono, 'voluntati cius quis resistet'; et ad Ephesios capitulo primo ait quod praedestinavit nos secundum propositum voluntatis suae secundum [bene]placitum eius; et Propheta dicit, 'omnia quaecumque voluit Deus fecit in caelo et in terra' et ubique scriptura magnificat voluntatem divinam. Ergo in Deo est vere et proprie ratio voluntatis.

"Praeterea, omnis perfectio simpliciter secundum suam veram et propriam rationem ponenda est in Deo. Sed voluntas est perfectio simpliciter quia in unoquoque melius est quod sit volens quam si nullo modo sit volens. Ergo ratio propria voluntatis erit vere in Deo.

"Praeterea, si id quod minoris dignitatis est in Deo ponitur secundum suam propriam rationem, multo fortius ponendum est quod est maioris dignitatis. Sed ratio voluntatis nobilior est et dignior et altior quam ratio intellecus, quia voluntas tenet arcem in regno animae et est motrix aliarum virtutum, secundum Anselmum. Ergo cum ratio intellectus vere et proprie sit in Deo, ut supra est probatum, oportet multo fortius quod sit in eo ratio propria voluntatis."

ises on the divine will. The generations before Aureol were concerned with many of the traditional problems of a religious tradition which argues for an omnipotent, benevolent God.[4] Is God free to will whatever He wills? Is God's will always fulfilled? If so, does His will impose necessity on the created order? Does God will the evil that occurs in the world? In distinctions 45-47, Aureol divides his discussion into ten articles. Specific questions such as these are relegated to a single short article at the end of distinction 47. For Aureol these problems arise out of unclear and imprecise language about God. If a theologian can construct an appropriate language, which in turn allows for an appropriate concept of Deity and the divine attributes, these problems simply vanish.

In order to accomplish this task Aureol rigorously applies a rule— which I call "Aureol's Law of Attribution"—to determine whether any term or concept can be used to signify the divine will or any other attribute:

> No conceivable attributable characteristic which has not been stripped of all imperfection is or ought to be conceptualized as belonging to God... If therefore <this rule> is not able to be carried out, it is impossible that <the characteristic in question> be truly attributed to God.[5]

Using this method, Aureol proceeds to examine all the various ways that contemporary theology has described the divine will. Not surprisingly, Aureol argues that Latin theology suffers from the limitations imposed by a fundamentally flawed language for describing God. Directing his attacks principally against Thomas Aquinas,

---

[4] In this chapter I will reconstruct the development of the doctrine of the divine will only as it pertains to Aureol's own theology. There has been some research on Scotus's doctrine of the divine will. A solid, but cursory, account of Scotus's doctrine can be found in B.M. Bonansea, *Man and His Approach to God in John Duns Scotus*, (N.Y.: 1983). Since the author is himself a Scotist, however, his account is not accessible to someone not already familiar with Scotist presuppositions. Douglas C. Langston, *God's Willing Knowledge: The Influence of Scotus' Analysis of Omniscience*, (London: 1986) puts Scotus's doctrine in the context of contemporary philosophical debate. Although Langston is correct about the connection between Scotus's doctrine of divine foreknowledge and the divine will, he fails to recognize that Scotus's doctrine of the will, like the doctrines of other voluntarists, has its own implications for human free will apart from the question of future contingents. One of the significant aspects of voluntarism is that it occasions entirely new problems once the problems of divine omniscience have been "solved".

[5] *Borghese 329*, f. 504vb: "Constat enim quod nulla attributalis ratio conceptibilis est aut concipi debet in Deo, quae non possit praescindi ab omni imperfectione, sic quod formaliter remaneat, exclusa omni imperfectione—pro regula enim generali datur quod sequestranda est: omnis imperfectio a ratione quacumque reperta in creaturis—si debeat ad divina transferri. Si ergo sequestrari non possit, impossibile est quod vere attribuatur Deo."

Henry of Ghent, and John Duns Scotus, Aureol claims that their doctrines of the divine will violate God's perfection by compromising variously His simplicity, infinity, goodness, and omnipotence. Most of these problems stem from an indiscriminate use of terms signifying the concept of will which do not sufficiently distinguish between created and divine natures. In most cases, the terms used to signify the concept of created will are not able to be stripped of their imperfect connotations, and therefore inherently convey imperfection. Often even those terms which are able to be stripped of meanings conveying imperfection are used without first applying this law of attribution. Even though such terms *can* be stripped of imperfect connotations, until they are, they are no better than terms which inherently convey imperfection.

Aureol divides his critique of earlier views into two parts. The first, which occupies the whole of distinction 46, deals with the concept of divine will as an intrinsic characteristic of Deity. The second part, which occupies the first two articles of distinction 47, deals with the concept of the divine will as it is active in the created order, and directly addresses the problem of the efficacy of the divine will. This distinction between intrinsic characteristic and extrinsic act is defined in terms of a distinction between God's will as ultimate love/delight (*amor complacentiae* or *amor delectationis*) and God's will as executive power (*potestas executiva* or *potentia executiva*). Aureol was not the first to draw this distinction. Scotus had drawn a similar distinction in his *Reportata*, *Ordinatio*, and *Quodlibeta*.[6] But Aureol is not merely following Scotus on this point. Scotus deployed the distinction as a solution to the problem of evil; for Aureol, however, this distinction is fundamental for his entire doctrine of the divine will. He argues that, because of the specific meanings conveyed by the terms *"amor"* and *"potestas"*, these are the only words appropriate for immediately signifying the divine will.

---

[6] *Lectura*, I, d. 47, q. 2, (Vives, vol. 22, p. 510a): "In Deo est velle complacentiae simplicis respectu possibilis, et sequitur intellectionem simplicium; efficax vero non est in Deo, nisi respectu eorum, quae vult fieri." *Ordinatio*, I, d. 47, q. 1, (Balic, vol. 6, p. 381): "Et utrumque in nobis potest distingui, ut velle distinguatur in velle efficax et remissum: ut dicatur 'velle efficax' quo voluntati non tantum complaceat esse voliti, sed si potest statim ponere volitum in esse, statim ponit; ita etiam 'nolito efficax' dicitur qua non tantum nolens impedit aliquid, sed si possit, omnino illud destruit. 'Voluntas remissa' est qua ita placet volitum, quod tamen voluntas non ponit illud in esse, licet possit ponere illud in esse; 'nolitio remissa' est qua ita displicet nolitum quod non prohibeat illud esse, licet posset." *Quodlibeta*, quod. 16, (Vives, vol. 26, p. 190a): "Licet necessario voluntas divina habeat actum complacentiae respectu cuiuscumque intelligibilis, in quantum in illo ostenditur quaedam participatio bonitatis propriae, tamen non necessario vult quodcumque creatum volitione efficaci, sive determinativa illius ad existendum."

Only after Aureol has carefully constructed his new language does
he address other problems. At the end of the entire discussion of the
will, Aureol finally turns to issues of necessity, contingency, and evil.
He also deals with a problem not usually addressed in its own right in
the 13th century: the question of priority between the will and the intellect in divine causality. It is significant for our study of his doctrine
of predestination that Aureol argues for voluntarism in his doctrine of
the divine will. That is to say, divine actions are carried out primarily through the will, but also because of the will; everything God does
He does by His will, simply because He has willed to do it.

Complacentia: The Will of God as Divine Delight

Aureol divides the concepts of will which are attributed to God as an
intrinsic characteristic into two groups. First, there are those concepts that can immediately be attributed to the divine will, once
their corresponding terms have been stripped of all imperfection.
Second, there are those concepts that, although traditionally attributed to the divine will, have corresponding terms that are not able to
withstand his law of attribution. The latter are attributed to God
only by way of secondary signification or connotation.[7] Sensitive to
the complexity of such terms, Aureol often unpacks terms like "love"
or "command" so that he can apply his law of attribution to their
various differing significations. In this way "love", conceptualized in
a precise way, would immediately signify the divine will, but in any
other way could at most *connote* the divine will.

The identification of God's will with His love does not constitute a
solution for Aureol, but only the proper point of departure. Framing
his discussion around Aquinas's claim that the primary act of God's
will is an act of love,[8] Aureol criticizes Aquinas's concept of divine

---

[7] *Borghese 329*, f. 507ra: "Quod nulla alia ratio alicuius actus voluntatis locum
habet in Deo quantum ad immediatum consignificatum et connotatum, nisi complacentia sola et amor delectationis, possunt tamen rationes aliae aliquo modo sibi
competere propter secundaria connotata."

[8] *S. Thomae Aquinatis Doctoris Angelici. Opera omnia. Iussu impensaque Leonis XIII, P.M,
edita*, (Vatican City, 1882-), vol. 4, q. 20, art. 1, p. 252: "...quod necesse est ponere
amorem in Deo. Primus enim motus voluntatis, et cuiuslibet appetitivae virtutis, est
amor. Cum enim actus voluntatis, et cuislibet appetitivae virtutis, tendat in bonum
et malum, sicut in propria obiecta; bonum autem principalius et per se est obiectum
voluntatis et appetitus, malum autem secundario et per aliud, inquantum scilicet
opponitur bono; oportet naturaliter esse priores actus voluntatis et appetitus qui respiciunt bonum; his qui respiciunt malum; ut gaudium quam tristitia, et amor quam
odium. Semper enim quod est per se, prius, est eo quod est per aliud.
"Rursus, quod est communis, naturaliter est prius; unde et intellectus per prius
habet ordinem ad verum commune, quam ad particularia quaedem vera. Sunt

love at two points.[9] First, even though Aquinas had distinguished between love as desire (*desiderium, concupiscentia*) and love as pleasure or delight (*delectatio, gaudium, complacentia*),[10] he seems to have attributed both types of love to God. Aureol argues that for God to desire something, even if He desires it for another and not Himself, is contrary to God's intrinsic characteristic of ultimate delight. If there is

autem quidam actus voluntatis et appetitus, respiciens res bonum sub aliqua speciali conditione: sicut gaudium et delectatio est de bono praesenti et habito; desiderium autem et spes, de bono nondum adepto. Amor autem respicit bonum in communi, sive sit habitum, sive non habitum. Unde amor naturaliter est primus actus voluntatis et appetitus.

"Et propter hoc, omnes alii motus appetitivi praesupponit amorem, quasi primam radicem. Nullus enim desiderat aliquid, nisi bonum amatum: neque aliquis gaudet, nisi bono amato. Odium etiam non est nisi de eo quod contrariatur rei amatae. Et similiter tristitiam, et cetera huiusmodi, manifestum est in amorem referri, sicut in primum principium. Unde in quocumque est voluntas et appetitus, oportet esse amorem: remoto enim primo, removetur alia. Ostensum est autem in Deo esse voluntatem. Unde necesse est in eo ponere amorem."

[9] *Borghese 329*, ff. 505ra-b: "Opinio Thomae parte 1, q. 20. Circa secundum vero considerandum est quod aliqui dixerunt ex actibus voluntatis aliquos esse in Deo secundum propriam rationem, aliquod vero non. Et quidem ratio amoris proprie est in Deo secundum eos, ille namque voluntatis actus qui est naturaliter et simpliciter primus. Oportet quod ponatur secundum propriam rationem in omni habente voluntatem, sed amor est actus primus simpliciter et naturaliter in omnes actus voluntatis, quod patet quia praecedit omnes qui tendunt et respiciunt malum cuiusmodi sunt odium et tristitia, cum appetitus per prius tendat in bonum quam respiciat malum. Non enim respuit malum, nisi quia tendit in bonum et iterum prior est amor caeteris actibus qui respiciunt bonum pro eo quod illud est naturaliter prius quod est communius. Nunc autem omnes alii actus respiciunt bonum sub aliqua propria ratione, ut gaudium et delectatio sunt de bono praesenti et habito, desiderium autem et spes de bono nondum adepto, amor autem respicit bonum in communi,sive sit habitum sive non habitum. Unde amor est naturaliter primus actus voluntatis quem omnes alii praesupponunt tamquam primam radicem, ita ut nullus desideret nisi bonum amatum, nec gaudeat nisi de bono amato, nec etiam odiat nisi illud quod rei amatae contrariatur. Ergo propria ratio actus amoris est ponenda in Deo, cum voluntas proprie sit in eo. Cum hoc etiam odium est in Deo, quia, licet peccatores amet inquantum sunt et inquantum ab ipso sunt, inquantum tamen sunt peccatores proprie non sunt, sed ab esse deficiunt et hoc in eis a Deo non est. Unde secundum hoc odio habentur ab ipso, sicut scriptum est, 'odisti omnes qui operantur iniquitatem. Cum hoc etiam gaudium et delectatio, secundum quod sunt actus appetitus intellectivi, non autem secundum quod sunt passiones appetitus sensitivi locum habent in Deo secundum suas proprias rationes. Addunt autem isti quod Deus habet velle intrinsecum, sed quod vult uniquique creaturae secundum suam propriam bonitatem, hoc autem est amare et velle alicui bona et propter hoc dicitur proprie actu intrinseco Deus creaturas amare."

[10] Aureol distinguished these two kinds of love first in *Scriptum*, art. 1, n. 54, (Buyteart, vol. 2, p. 396): "Quod complacere et delectatio idem sint ex terminis apparet. Nam idem est dictum 'delector in te' et 'complacet mihi in te', 'placibilis es mihi' et 'delectibilis es mihi'. Sed omnis amor est desiderium vel complacentia, desiderium quidem sicut gluto diligit morsellum et caupo vinum, cuius dilectio nihil aliud est quam desiderium et concupiscentia; complacentia vero vel in re habita realiter, vel saltem habita in conceptu. Ergo evidenter apparet quod omnis amor vel est desiderium, vel delectatio."

some object which God desires, then His delight is not ultimate (i.e. fulfilled/*complacentia*), but unfulfilled and imperfect. Aureol explains:

> ...<this opinion> which claims that God loves creatures with some kind of desire, not because He desires them for Himself, but because He loves them and wills the good that they have, is deficient. For either it is understood that He wills the good to them by being pleased in their goodness from the fact that He is pleased in His own goodness, or He wills the good for them, not by being pleased <in their goodness>, but by desiring or wanting the good for them. But the second <reason> cannot be given, since to want or desire, even universally, some object as some future good is repugnant to God according to His own intrinsic characteristic. Thus, it cannot be said that God desires something, either for Himself, or for another... Therefore it is necessary that the first <reason> be given, namely that God does not love creatures <for any reason> other than because He is pleased in His own goodness and from the fact that He is said to be equally and eminently pleased in all beings.[11]

If God is pleased with all things, then God does not "hate" according to any normal sense of the term. This is the second criticism that Aureol levels against Aquinas: just as love is divided into pleasure and desire, hate is divided into displeasure and aversion. Since these are parallel distinctions, God can no more be averse to something than He can desire something. Nor can He be displeased with anything; His pleasure with His creatures is infinite, since He is pleased with creatures through His own goodness.[12] As for things insofar as they do not participate in His goodness, it is more appropriate to describe God as passively "un"pleased, rather than actively displeased.

Aside from the possible implications that such a doctrine has for divine omnipotence and the problem of evil, with which he deals at

---

[11] *Borghese 329*, f. 505ra: "Tertio vero deficit in eo quod ait Deum amare creaturas quodammodo amore concupiscentiae, non quia eas sibi concupiscat, sed quia eas amat et vult bonum quod habent. Aut enim intelligitur quod velit eis bonum complacendo in bonitate earum ex hoc ipso quo complacet in sua bonitate aut vult eis bonum non complacendo, sed appetendo et optando eis bonum. Sed non potest dari secundum quia tale appetere, desiderare, vel optare et universaliter motus aliquis respiciens bonum aliquod ut futurum repugnat Deo secundum propriam rationem. Unde dici non potest quod Deus appetat aliquid, vel sibi, vel alteri, ut magis inferius apparebit. Ergo necesse est quod detur primum, videlicet quod Deus non alter diligat creaturas, nisi quia complacet in bonitate sua. Et ex hoc complacuisse dicitur in omni entitate equipollenter et eminenter."

[12] *Ibid.*: "Secundo vero deficit in eo quod ponit rationem odii formaliter esse in Deo. Constat enim quod odium dividitur in displicentiam et fugam, sicut amor in desiderium et complacentiam; unde quod oditur, ideo dicitur odiri quia displicet vel quia odiens, fugit et respuit oditum. Sed manifestum est quod nulla displicentia cadit in Deo, immo complacentia infinita, similiter nec aliqua fuga appetitus Ergo nullo modo aliqua propria ratio odii est in Deo."

a later point, Aureol must first abide by his own method. Stripping the concept of desire from the concept of love is only the first step; love considered only as delight or pleasure must itself be analyzed as well. If such a concept of love conveys imperfection, then it, too, must be rejected as a concept attributable to God.

Aureol admits that taken in certain ways the concept of love as delight does convey imperfection if imputed to Deity.[13] "Divine delight" can signify either the unconditioned characteristics pertaining strictly to Deity or the actual acts of a divine will. Since each particular volition has its own limited, individuating characteristic, "delight" taken in this way would convey imperfection in Deity. Aureol argues, however, that "delight" only secondarily signifies individual acts of the will; what "delight" immediately signifies is a quality deposited in the soul by which the willer is content in the object of love. As applied to Deity, the concept must, of course, be abstracted from the substance-quality distinction inherent in the created will, so that there is no real distinction between essence and delight. Given that, this concept of divine delight in no way conveys imperfection in God. Aureol believes that he has stripped the term "delight" of all connotations of imperfection, so that it may now become part of a suitable theological language. Thus,

> by abstracting the concept of absolute perfection which 'delight' (*complacentia vel amor delectationis*) expresses, we can say that <delight> is "that by which someone is spiritually content in something". So, therefore, by accepting <this> characteristic of delight and, similarly, by abstracting the characteristics of all acts of will, it may be discovered that this characteristic alone lacks all imperfection—indeed it is perfection absolutely—and that all other <characteristics> include imperfection.[14]

---

[13] *Ibid.*, ff. 505va-b: "Sed istis non obstantibus dicendum est sicut prius ubi considerandum quod actus voluntatis, de quibus inquirimus, possunt considerari secundum suas realitates et rationes proprias absolutas. Et sic non est dubium quod non sunt perfectiones simpliciter, cum sint quaedam rationes specificae limitatae ad genus et differentiam arctatae et propter hoc nec sub aliqua ratione absoluta et determinata transferuntur ad divina. Vel possunt considerari secundum illud quod connotant immediate, quia delectatio est qualitas quaedam posita in voluntate, secundum quam volens dicitur quietari, non quia qualitas illa sit formaliter quies, cum quies solum sit privatio motus, sed quia posita illa qualitate cessat omnis appetitus et spiritualiter conquiescit in ipso delectabili, tamquam in fine."

[14] *Ibid.*, f. 505vb: "Et sic abstrahendo conceptum perfectionis simpliciter quem exprimit 'complacentia' vel 'amor delectationis', possumus dicere quod est 'illud quo quis spiritualiter in aliquo conquiescit'. Sic ergo accipiendo rationem complacentiae et conformiter abstrahendo rationes omnium actuum voluntatis, invenietur hoc sola ratione carere omni imperfectione, immo ipsam esse perfectionem simpliciter, et omnes alias includere imperfectionem."

Aureol explains this conclusion by enumerating the various ways that a human being can will.[15] For Aureol all human acts of the will fall under one of eleven kinds of will(ing). Most have to do with unmet desires or displeasure, which Aureol has already dealt with. But there remain two acts of the will which can be signified by "delight". One is the delight in something which one does not yet have. The other, which he calls "ultimate delight", is pleasure in an object possessed by the willer. And it is only "ultimate delight" that can be stripped of all imperfection and can signify a divine attribute. After all, delight in an object not already possessed by the willer by its very nature excites and compels the will to desire the absent object; but any such notion of desire must be stripped from the concept of divine love. The concept signified by "ultimate delight", however, does not inherently convey imperfection, so once it is abstracted from the concept of created will, it conveys no imperfection.

Once a concept has been stripped of all covert signification of imperfections, it is then, and only then, that the theologian can shift from semantics to theology proper and ask whether God actually possesses an attribute described by that concept. Besides briefly citing authoritative texts from Aristotle and Averroes, Aureol builds two arguments for attributing delight to God.[16] His first is based on the claim that any intelligent creature, i.e., one that possesses the ca-

---

[15] *Ibid.*: "Hoc autem potest simul et generaliter declarari considerando quod actus iste et ratio eius sic abstracta, habet modum actus finalis, omnes autem aliae habent modum actuum ordinatorum ad istum tanquam in finem. Et hoc quidem apparet discurrendo per omnes actus voluntatis, respicientes bonum vel malum, sive sint irascibilis et cum quadam assurrectione sive sit concupiscibilis, omnes quidem actus voluntatis reduci possunt ad XI numerando eos conformiter et proportionaliter ad passiones appetitus sensitivi. Possumus quidem dicere quod omnis volens aut nolens dicitur velle vel nolle, vel quia amat complacendo in eo quod nondum habet, vel quia illud desiderat, vel quia in illo iam habito delectatur et complacet ac voluptas amando ipsum amore complacentiae ultimato, vel dicitur nolle ex hoc quod odit et illud sibi displicet adhuc absens vel quia detestatur ipsum et fugit, vel quia in eo praesente iam displicet et tristatur, vel possumus dicere quod velit aliquod bonum futurum sperando, vel quia etiam velit tamen desperando, vel quia nolit aliquod malum futurum conando ipsum repellere et contra ipsum audendo, vel quia nolit audendo, sed potius cadendo sub ipso et timendo, vel quod nolit malum iam praesens contra ipsum insurgendo et irascendo. Et quicquid vult homo aut quicquid voluntatem hiis necessario vult, aut non vult aliquo istorum undecimum modorum. Nam eligere est quoddam desiderare, secundum quod Philosophus dicit tertio Ethicorum quod electio est desiderium praeconsiliati, frui autem est delectari, ut superius visum fuit. Uti vero est, vel desiderare id quod est ad finem propter finem, vel etiam delectari in eo quod est ad finem proter ipsum finem et generaliter verum est quod omnes actus voluntatis reducuntur ad istos sive quis velit aut nolit sibi sive velit vel nolit alteri."

[16] *Ibid.*, f. 506rb: "Secunda vero propositio est quod propria ratio complacentiae ultimatae et amoris voluptuosi ac delectationis in Deo est inter actus caeteros vo-

pacity both to apprehend and to understand, possesses the characteristic of delighting in or being saddened by the apprehended objects. "Understanding" does not itself imply any desire or aversion, even though in an intelligent creature's sensory apparatus there will be a concomitant appetite which apprehends the object as, for instance, either pleasing or displeasing to the senses. This claim of course—excluding the role of the senses—applies even more clearly to God, inasmuch as God is the highest intellect, maximally capable of apprehension and understanding. Therefore, it is necessary to attribute delight to God. However, because God is perfect and His delight is infinite, displeasure is not attributed to God as it is to all other intelligent creatures.

Aureol's second argument is based on the claim that since all absolute perfections ought to be attributed to God, and to delight in the good absolutely is an absolute perfection, God delights in the good. To support the minor premise of his argument, Aureol claims that it is better for anyone to experience the good than to not experience it. Surely, he proceeds, this is even more true for God who is the highest good; after all, God would be most imperfect if He did not experience His own goodness.

Aureol and Traditional Theological Language

Divine delight is, for Aureol, the only concept that either can or ought to be used immediately to signify divine love and the intrinsic divine will. But this does not mean that he completely rejects any other language. Latin theology had traditionally used many terms and concepts to describe the divine will, many of which had come from the Vulgate translation of the Bible. Hence, Aureol must make room in his theological vocabulary for these imperfect concepts and their corresponding terms. To do this, he once again turns to semantic solutions. Now that he has clearly marked out the theological problems inherent in terms and concepts which ascribe hate, sadness, and desire to God, Aureol can bring these concepts back into his theology in a mitigated way. Aquinas, and scholastic thought in

---

luntatis et hoc quidem patet, quia Philosophi Deo attribuunt huiusmodi actum, ait enim Philosophus 7 Ethicorum quod si aliqua natura sit simplex et semper eadem, actio eius delectabilissima erit propter quod Deus una semper et simplici delectatione gaudet; similiter idem dicit 12 Metaphysicae, dicit enim quod Deus vivus aeternus in fine voluptatis, quod exponit Commentator, commento 39, dicens quod voluptas Dei est per comprehensionem sui ipsius; et subdit quod ista voluptas semper est in eo et est multo magis nobilis quam in nobis et magis admirabilis. Constat autem quod hoc non disisset, nisi hoc quodammodo notum esset lumine naturali. Ergo vera et propria ratio huius actus ponenda est in Deo."

general for that matter, were certainly not wrong to speak about God's hate or desire; but for Aureol they were wrong in using these terms loosely, and thereby implicitly impugning God's simplicity and perfection.

In order to use these concepts and their corresponding terms in a precise theological language, Aureol argues that one must consider the various modes of signification each one has.[17] For instance, the terms "sadness" (*tristitia*) and "anger" (*ira*), when used to describe a creature possess a three-fold signification. They *signify* a quality in the appetite; they *connote* the restlessness of the creature existing under some present evil; and they *secondarily connote* the extrinsic operation of the will arising from that restlessness which seeks to change the situation.[18] When used to describe the divine will, however, such terms do not properly signify at all three levels. Obviously they are not able to signify a quality inherent in God for in God there is no distinction between substance and quality, such that God would be, for instance, essentially sad. Nor do they con-

---

[17] *Ibid.*, f. 507ra: "Licet attribuantur quodammodo ceterorum actuum rationes propter secundaria connotata. Est enim considerandum quod tristitia in creaturis significat qualitatem quandam positam in appetitu contristato et hoc quidem formaliter est aliquid absolutum, connotat tamen quandam inquietudinem sub malo praesent, ex qua oritur exterius aliqua operatio correspondens, sicut videmus quod tristes prae tristitia aliquid operantur. Similiter et ira immediate quidem connotare videtur assurrectionem in malum, extrinsecus autem expetitionem vindicte aut aliquid huiusmodi. Secundum hoc ergo possumus Deo attribuere alios actus appetitivos inquantum Deitas est principium omnium exteriorum actuum qui consequitur actus istos. Si poneretur intrinsece in Deo, nam et vindictam expetit, ac si esset iratus et quaerelatur in Scriptura, ac si esset dolens vel tristis et bona tribuit aliquibus, ac si optare et vellet intrinsece eis bona et unum profert alteri, ac si esset in eo intrinsece actus electionis: nullus autem istorum actuum potest in Deo cadere, quantum ad permansivum et per se connotatum, cuius ratio est quia nullus actus imperfectionem aut inquietudinem includens poni potest in Deo, secundum suam propriam rationem. Sed manifestum est quod omnes actus, excepta complacentia et amore delectationis, ultimate, inquietudinem quandam includunt in voluntate, nam qui optat alteri bonum, nondum est in quiete et qui eligit alteri bonum aut vult aut appetit est etiam inquietus ex ratione istius actus; similiter et qui tristatur et qui desiderat et qui sperat et sic de aliis. Et ergo nullo modo vere et proprie rationes istorum actuum sunt in Deo, quamvis denominari possit ab istis propter quasdam operationes extrinsecas quas conformiter elicit, ac si esset talibus actibus intrinsece affectatus."

[18] It seems that Aureol is here drawing a distinction between two different levels of connotation. He does not make use of this distinction when he explains his theory of connotation in distinctions 8 and 45. If he is distinguishing between two levels of connotation, then secondary connotation should not be confused with secondary signification. Rather, according to Aureol's scheme a term can perform three semantic functions: (a) primary signification; (b) secondary signification or connotation; and (c) secondary connotation. The example that Aureol uses implies that a connotation is secondary when it presupposes another connotation.

note any state of being in God besides ultimate delight. Strictly speaking, they refer only to what they connote secondarily: the extrinsic operations of the divine will through which divine love is expressed, in what to humans seems like anger or sadness.

Speaking of the divine will in terms of love and hate was only one of the traditional ways of describing the divine will. Even though Aureol finds the proper way to describe the divine will in the language of divine delight, he does not ignore or reject other approaches. On the contrary, he attempts to incorporate them in his new theological language. Aureol first addresses a relatively recent discussion carried out by two of his most important predecessors, Henry of Ghent and Duns Scotus.[19] Both were interested in developing an acceptable theory for describing God's justice and wisdom as moral virtues possessed by the divine will. Given the fact that this does not seem to be a traditional issue, but only a rather recent concern, coupled with the fact that Aureol rarely passes up the opportunity to inveigh against these two opponents, one would expect Aureol to dismiss this idea out of hand. Instead, Aureol attempts to save the idea from what he perceives to be the fuzzy thinking of Henry and the unwarranted and untenable metaphysical assumptions of Scotus.

Henry's doctrine, according to Aureol, rests on two assumptions.[20] First, God is a willing God, and His will is an active power (*potentia activa*). By granting that nothing other than the divine will itself really inclines this power to act, creatures can conceptualize God as possessing a habit which inclines the will to act; that is, since real habits mediate between potency (*potentia*) and act in creatures, we may describe divine causality using the concept of habits (*habitus secundum rationem*). Second, it is proper to attribute the habits of the moral virtues to God, because they are absolute perfections. Therefore, the moral virtues are the habits which ought to be thought of as inclining the will to act.

For Aureol the whole trouble with this doctrine revolves around

---

[19] *Borghese 329*, f. 503rb: "Opinio Henrici articulo 45 in Summa sua et 95 articulo 46. Circa primum ergo considerandum est quod aliqui dicere voluerunt rationem voluntatis potentiae et rationes habituum voluntariorum et virtutum moralium vere et proprie debere poni in Deo."

[20] Aureol's account of Henry's arguments is a brief interpretation of a lengthy discussion. Instead of his usually careful recapitulation of an opponent's view, Aureol concentrates on inferences drawn from Henry's arguments that Henry may or may not have meant to imply. Because of the length and complexity of Henry's argument, any quotation which would fit in a footnote would not do it justice. See Henry of Ghent, *Summa Quaestionum Ordinarium*, (Paris 1520; repr. Bonaventure, NY, 1953), aa. 45-47, ff. 16r-28v (esp. a. 46, q. 2, fols. 20v-23r).

the term that Henry uses for power: "*potentia*".[21] "*Potentia*" has both passive and active meanings; it can mean "power", but it can also mean "potentiality". Aureol accuses Henry of failing to distinguish sufficiently between these two senses, with the result that his entire argument rests on an equivocation.[22] The term "*potentia*", especially when it is used with a term like "*habitus*", inherently conveys the signification of perfectibility, which of course implies imperfection. In this case it gives the concept of divine will (*voluntas*) a passive meaning. On account of this, in order for the passive divine will (*voluntas*) to become an active divine willing (*velle*) the habits of moral virtue must provide the inclination to particular acts of will (*volitiones*).

Henry's claim that the use of terms like "*potentia*" and "*habitus*" does not describe divine reality, but is only a useful way of thinking about God, does not forestall Aureol's reaction to the theory. That God is really perfect entails that He must also be conceptualized as perfect, but to have an imperfect concept of God means that one conceptualizes God as imperfect:

> But this manner of speaking, which claims that the characteristic of potential will and, similarly, the characteristic of a habit mediating

---

[21] *Borghese 329*, f. 503rb: "Sed hic modus dicendi est impossibilis in eo quod ait rationem voluntatis potentiae posse vere concipi circa Deum, et similiter rationem habitus existentis mediam inter potentiam et actum. Sicut enim Deus est perfectissimus realiter, ita est perfectissimus ratione. Sed in eo quod realiter est perfectissimus concipi non potest aliqua res potentialis, quia ex hoc conciperetur non esse res perfectissima cum res potentialis sit imperfecta. Ergo, in Deo, cum sit perfectissimus ratione, concipi non poterit aliqua ratio potentialis, cuiusmodi est ratio habitus quae est medium inter actum et potentiam, et ratio voluntatis potentiae quae magis distat ab actu quam habitus. Et si dicatur quod quia voluntas et habitus non distant ab actu propter hoc non habent rationem imperfecti, non valet utique quia vel indistantia ab actu excludit totaliter potentiae rationem, et per consequens nulla ratio potentiae concipi vere poterit circa Deum, et ita nec ratio voluntatis nec ratio alicuius moralis habitus aut illa indistantia rationem potentiae reliquit, et sic habetur propositum. Nam imperfectio adeo est annexa rationi potentiae quod ab ipsa separari non potest, potentia quidem importat perfectibile, sicut actus perfectionem. Unde concedere quod ratio alicuius potentiae vere concipi possit circa Deum est necessario concedere quod circa ipsum vere concipi possit ratio quae ex se imperfecta est et indigens perfici per aliam rationem. Praeterea, ratio voluntatis potentiae non solum consistit in elicere actum, quinimmo in recipere et perfici per ipsum. Unde nec voluntas dicitur velle ex hoc quod elicit volitionem, sed ex hoc quod recipit eam, nam secundum Priscianum in fine Minoris, 'omnia verba ad animam pertinentia significant passionem', ut intelligere et velle, sed ratio receptiva et perfectibilis non potest vere concipi circa Deum, cum omnes rationes attributales conceptuales circa Deum sint perfectiones simpliciter et infinitae formaliter, et per consequens non sunt perfectibiles per extrinsecam rationem, sed habent intrinsece infinitam perfectionem. Ergo nullo modo ratio voluntatis potentiae aut habitus vere potest concipi circa Deum."

[22] Henry, in fact, does distinguish between the passive and active senses of "*potentia*". He attributes the active sense to will and the passive sense to intellect. This was presumably insufficient for Aureol. See *Summa*, a. 45, q. 2, f. 27r.

between potency and act can be truly conceptualized as belonging to God, is impossible. For just as God is really most perfect, He is in the same way conceptually perfect. But a potential thing cannot be conceptualized as belonging to that which is most perfect, since on that very account of this it would not be conceptualized as the most perfect thing, because what is <still> potential is imperfect. Therefore, since He is most perfect conceptually, any such potential characteristic, as that of a habit which mediates between act and potency, or a characteristic of potential will which is farther from the act than the habit is, cannot be conceptualized as belonging to God.[23]

Whereas Aureol refutes Henry's claims by appealing to language, Scotus had done so by appealing to metaphysics.[24] Scotus argues

---

[23] *Borghese 329*, f. 503rb: "Sed hic modus dicendi est impossibilis in eo quod ait rationem voluntatis potentiae posse vere concipi circa Deum, et similiter rationem habitus existentis mediam inter potentiam et actum. Sicut enim Deus est perfectissimus realiter, ita est perfectissimus ratione. Sed in eo quod realiter est perfectissimus concipi non potest aliqua res potentialis, quia ex hoc conciperetur non esse res perfectissima cum res potentialis sit imperfecta. Ergo, in Deo, cum sit perfectissimus ratione, concipi non poterit aliqua ratio potentialis, cuiusmodi est ratio habitus quae est medium inter actum et potentiam, et ratio voluntatis potentiae quae magis distat ab actu quam habitus."

[24] *Ibid.*, f. 503va: "Opinio Scoti in primo suo. Propterea dixerunt alii quod ratio voluntatis potentiae est in Deo, non autem quod sit ratio receptiva respectu actus. Quamvis enim ratio voluntatis et ipsum velle in Deo formaliter distinguantur et ex natura rei, sunt tamen idem realiter, et ideo maiorem identitatem habet velle cum voluntate quam si reciperetur in ea, ut perfectio eius, sicut esset in nobis, si velle esset idem cum voluntate realiter. Constat enim quod propter identitatem realem voluntas perfectius et intimius posset dicere velle, quam nunc denominetur velle propter receptionem ipsius. Et similiter voluntas in Deo, licet non sit ratio receptiva, respectu volitionis, nec perficiatur aut etiam informetur per eam, nihilominus dicitur voluntas perfectissime velle propter identitatem realem volitionis cum ea. Nec tamen sic potest dici quod intellectus velit, licet sit idem realiter cum volitione propter ordinem immediatiorem quem habet voluntas ad velle, qualem enim ordinem habent aliqua ut sunt distincta realiter, talem habent nisi distinguuntur formaliter et secundum rationem. Sed ubi velle et intelligere distinguuntur realiter ab intellectu et voluntate, voluntas habet ordinem per se et immediatum ad suum velle, mediatum autem et per accidens ad intelligere et similiter intellectus habet immediatum ordinem et per se ad intelligere, per accidens autem respicit velle. Ergo in Deo ubi formaliter distinguuntur, eundem ordinem habebunt, et ita Deus dicetur velle per suam voluntatem et non per intellectum et intelligere per intellectum, non autem per voluntatem; unde sicut quodam ordine pullulant istae perfectiones essentiales ab essentia ut primo pullulet intellectus quam voluntas et intelligere quam velle, ita ordine quodam sunt in ea et dicuntur de ipsa, ut vere dicatur velle per voluntatem et intelligere intellectu."

Aureol seems to be referring to a passage in distinction 45 of Scotus's *Reportata*. There is a discrepancy, however, between Aureol's account of this passage and the version that appears in the Vives edition. Aureol claims that Scotus argued for both a conceptual and a formal distinction between the divine *voluntas* and divine *velle*. The version contained in the Vives edition argues for only a conceptual distinction, which is not significantly different from Henry's position and is open to the same critique. There are at least two possible reasons for this discrepancy. One is that Aureol simply got it wrong. This would be easy to assume since this passage is em-

that God's perfection can be preserved, if one clearly distinguishes
the ontological status of the created will from the ontological status
of the divine will. In a creature there is a real distinction between
the passive characteristic of will, the activity of willing, and the particular acts of the will. In God they are really identical, being only
formally distinct. Because of this real identity it is mistaken to say
that the will is perfectible only by receiving inclinations to particular
acts of will through habits. The divine will is perfect in itself, since it
is at once attribute, activity in general, and particular act.

Aureol bases his critique of this argument on his refutation of the
formal distinction: the distinction must pertain to the relata and not
the relation, so that those things which are formally distinct exist
only formally. Aureol assumes that the formal distinction between
voluntas and *velle* amounts to this: that the quiddity or definitive nature of *voluntas* includes imperfection, while the quiddity of *velle* does
not. Therefore, according to Aureol's critique of the formal distinction, the quiddity of *voluntas* not only includes imperfection of the
will, but the quiddity of *voluntas* *is* imperfection of the will. The formal distinction can be reduced to a real distinction, and thus Scotus's position is no better than Henry's. In fact, for Aureol it is
worse; at least Henry had kept the discussion at the conceptual level.
On account of this conceptual rather than ontological basis, Aureol's
own position is a reconstruction of Henry's after extensive use of his

---

bedded in one of Scotus's longest and most intricate discussions of the formal distinction, which Aureol was almost obsessed with refuting. On the other hand,
Aureol may have been using a manuscript of the *Reportata* which reported Scotus
arguing for a formal distinction between *voluntas* and *velle*. This is also plausible.
Aureol rarely makes such blatant alterations to his opponents' positions. Moreover,
the *Reportata*, as the name implies, are only student notes of Scotus's Parisian lectures on the *Sentences*, and were never edited by Scotus. It is possible that a manuscript containing Aureol's version existed. I will assume in my analysis that Aureol is
addressing a position that really existed outside of his mind and was attributed to
Scotus. Scotus's version is presented here for purposes of comparison.
    Reportata, I, d. 45, q. 2, (Vives, vol. 22, p. 507): "...dicendum quod quia in volun-
tate creata actus volendi non est idem cum voluntate, ideo oportet quod recipiatur
in voluntate ad hoc quod dicatur velle per voluntatem, quia non potest actus voluntatis habere maiorem identitatem cum voluntate creata, quam recipi in ea, ut perfectio eius. Sed si posset actus voluntatis esse idem realiter voluntat creatae, verius
diceretur creatura rationalis velle voluntate quam modo, et ideo Deus, in quo idem
sunt realiter voluntas et velle verius dicitur velle voluntate, quam reciperetur in ea,
ut quid distinctum realiter. Dices forte, si propter identitatem realem actus volendi
in Deo ad suam voluntatem, diceretur Deus velle voluntate, cum actus volendi in
Deo sit idem realiter cum intellectu, diceretur tunc Deus per intellectum velle.
Respondeo, qualem ordinem habent aliqua, ubi sunt distincta realiter, talem ordinem habent, ubi sunt distincta secundum rationem; et ideo voluntas respectu
actus volendi in Deo, est immediate in suo ordine, sicut si distingueretur; et sicut
aliqua exeunt ab essentia, ita redeunt; et ideo non dicitur velle per intellectum, licet
sint eadem realiter."

law of attribution. Aureol carefully explains what attribution of the moral virtues in general to God may not imply.[25] The will of God is, both really and conceptually (*etiam secundum rationem*), unelicited and subsistent. This is the case because of the absolute identity of *voluntas*, *velle*, and *volitio* in the divine essence and the will's absolute identity with the divine essence. Neither God's willing nor the particular acts of His will are externally elicited or produced, because each is the divine essence itself:

> For since the reality of volition (*res volitionis*) and the reality of the essence (*res essentiae*) are the same, if the reality of volition is produced, it is necessary that even the reality of the essence be elicited and produced, too, which is altogether ridiculous. Therefore, it is necessary that the characteristic of volition not be produced, even conceptually, but that it be understood as existing from itself, and not from some elicitating principle. Thus, it is clear how what they <Henry> meant, namely that the will elicits in God an act of volition according to our mode of understanding, is false, because the opposite ought to be understood, namely that Deity is the kind of active willing (*velle*) which is altogether from itself, not brought forth from some passive will (*voluntate*), since <Deity> is pure volition.[26]

---

[25] *Ibid.*, f. 503vb: "Restat ergo nunc dicere quod videtur sub triplici propositione. Prima quidem quod omnis intellectus concipiens circa Deum rationem voluntatis potentiae aut rationem habitus inclinantis voluntatem ad actum, concipit quod circa Deum apprehendi non potest sine errore et falsitate, et ideo decipitur, ac si conciperet in eo rationem materiae, vel lapidis aut alicuius alterius imperfectionem importantis."

[26] *Ibid.*, ff. 504ra-b: "Quod in Deo non est velle elicitum, etiam secundum rationem, sed omnino inelicitum et subsistens, quo non obstante adhuc est liberum immo liberrimum. Secunda vero propositio est quod velle in Deo non est elicitum, etiam secundum rationem, sed quid omnino inelicitum et subsistens et nihilominus liberrimum, isto non obstante. Et primum quidem patet quia omnis perfectio simpliciter multo intimius competit Deitati quam alicui formae creatae, sed aliqua forma creata reperibilis est quae sic est velle intrinsece, quod si poneretur inelicita et subsistens, velle suum esset omnino inelicitum et subsistens. Sicut patet de qualitate, quae est volitio formaliter in voluntate creata, illa quidem si poneretur realiter inelicita et subsistens, necessario volitionis ratio esset in ipsa inelicita et subsistens. Ergo et Deitas sic erit suum velle quod nisi ipsa nec eius velle elicietur. Constat autem quod essentia non est elicita nec producta realiter aut secundum rationem, non ergo velle divinum concipi debet, ut elicitum aliquo modo secundum rationem ab aliqua voluntate. Praeterea, quandocumque aliqua idem sunt et re et ratione, impossibile est quod unum sit secundum rationem elicitum vel productum, quin reliquum sit productum. Sed probatum est supra velle divinum non esse aliud realiter aut secundum rationem intrinsece, nisi ipsammet Deitatem et rationem Deitatis. Et constat quod ratio Deitatis nullo modo producta est, neque elicita ab aliqua potentia, ergo nec velle divinum concipi debet, ut elicitum ab aliqua potentia sed ut a se existens absque principio elicitivo. Praeterea, non est magis inconveniens, nec minus conceptibile quod ratio volitionis actualis concipiatur esse a se et a nullo alio elicitive secundum rationem quam quod realitas ipsius concipiatur esse a se et non elicita secundum rem, sed manifestissime est cuilibet fideli quod secundum dari oportet. Cum enim res volitionis et res essentiae idem sint, si produceretur res

Aureol's position on the simplicity of the divine will mirrors his position on the divine essence: once again, he has rejected both the
merely conceptual distinction and the formal distinction as adequate
to account for the complexity of reference imparted by a simple concept. In Deity *"voluntas"*, *"velle"*, and *"volitio"* are distinguished only
according to their connotates; both really and conceptually they intrinsically signify the divine will itself, but each differs according to
what they connote extrinsically.[27] Some of the extrinsic connotates
of the divine will are the moral virtues, provided that our concept of
them is stripped of all imperfection.[28] This is done by conceiving of
virtues, like justice, as virtuous acts and not as habits. In this way the
virtues do not convey a concept of potency in the divine will which

---

volitionis, necessario et res essentiae esset elicita et producta, quod omnino absonum est. Ergo nec ratio volitionis oportet quod sit producta, etiam secundum rationem, sed intelligetur, ut existens a se et non ab aliquo principio elicitivo. Unde
patet quomodo falsum est quod aliqui sunt dicere voliti, videlicet quod voluntas in
Deo eliciat actum volitionis secundum nostrum modum intelligendi. Debet enim
per oppositum apprehendi, scilicet quod Deitas est quoddam velle omnino a se, non
egrediens ab aliqua voluntate, cum sit volitio pura."

[27] *Ibid.*, 504rb: "Secundum etiam patet, videlicet quod sit subsistens, illud enim
quod concipi non potest ut inhaerens alicui nec secundum rem nec secundum rationem, necessario habet concipi subsistens. Sed velle divinum non potest concipi ut
inhaerens realiter alicui voluntati, ut statim patet. Nec etiam ut inhaerens secundum rationem, cum non sit in Deo ratio voluntatis potentiae, sed omnino ratio puri
actus, sicut si qualitas illa, quae est in voluntate creata poneretur per se existere separate, ergo Deitas debet concipi per modum cuiusdam velle subsistentis. Unde
sicut supra dicebatur de intelligere, sic oportet tenere de velle et potest imaginatio
manuduci quia si quis conciperet volitionem rosae existentem in voluntate alicuius
separatim subsistere sine omni voluntatem, et similiter volitionem floris, et volitionem lapidis, et sic de omnibus rebus, et cum hoc apprehenderet quod omnes
istae volitiones essent una volitio. Sic intelligi debet Deus, ut quoddam velle subsistens omnium rerum, et ita propriissime vult, non quod habeat voluntatem quae per
velle perficiatur, sed quia est ipsummet velle, quo vult et realiter et secundum rationem intrinsece, licet ipsum velle addat extrinsece aliquod consignificatum."

[28] *Ibid.*, f. 504va: "Tertia quoque propositio est quod licet ratio habitus nullatenus
sit in Deo, recipit tamen denominationem moralium virtutum, ut dicatur pius, iustus, longanimis. Ubi considerandum quod virtutes morales possunt accipi vel pro
habitibus vel pro ipsis actibus virtuosis. Habitus autem haben rationem mediantis
inter potentiam et actus et inclinantis ac determinantis voluntatem ad virtuosos
actus. Non est ergo ratio virtutum moralium in Deo, sic intelligendo virtutes, quia
non indiget aliquo inclinante nec est in eo ratio voluntatis potentiae, ut declaratum
est supra. Actus autem virtuosi accipi possunt tripliciter. Primo quidem exteriores,
sicut actus iustitiae est reddere unicuique quod suum est. Secundo vero interiores
qui sunt principia actuum exteriorum, ut velle reddere unicuique quod suum est.
Tertio vero actus interiores praevenientes vel consequentes et istud est delectari de
operibus virtuosis vel complacere in eis. Sic ergo morales virtutes attribuuntur Deo
quantum ad actus, non autem quantum ad habitus, nam et reddit unicuique quod
suum est et Deitas ipsa est principium reddendi multo perfectius quam qualitas illa
creata quae ponitur in anima iusti, et similiter complacet in iustitia, complacendo in
essentia sua. Et ita Deitas nulla ratione formali addita intrinsece est vere iustitia
actus, non autem habitus, et sic intelligendum de aliis denominationibus virtuosis."

must be reduced to act by intermediates. If taken as acts, however, they are connoted by the divine will, since the latter is the basis for all virtuous acts and is pleased in all virtuous acts. There are, however, different levels of connotation. Justice is attributed to God through simple connotation, while chastity is attributed through more indirect connotation.[29] But God loves and delights in chastity, and therefore wills chastity in creatures.[30]

Not only has Aureol thus saved the language of moral virtue in theology, but by applying his law of attribution he believes that he has shown that the concepts of the moral virtues are more properly attributed to God than they are to creatures. Since the most perfect concept of virtue does not include a quality or habit, it follows that moral virtue can only be attributed to creatures in an imperfect sense. Hence moral virtues, strictly speaking, are more applicable to God than to creatures, "since all those virtuous descriptions more properly correspond to Deity than to some created quality...".[31] Aureol argues, therefore, that he makes an even stronger case than

---

[29] It is not clear whether this distinction between direct connotation and indirect connotation is the same as the one between secondary signification and secondary connotation.

[30] *Borghese 329*, f. 504vb: "Est autem ulterius attendendum quod virtutum quaedam sunt quae principaliter consistunt in moderamine passionum aut actuum intrinsecorum, sicut temperantia, castitas et sobrietas et actus talium proprie non denominant Deitatem. Non enim dicitur Deus castus vel sobrius, quamvis habeat actum complacentiae inquantum dicitur amator castitatis aut complacens in sobrietate. Quaedam vero sunt quae consistunt in actionibus ad extra principalius et directe, ut iustitua in reddendo unicuique quod suum est et liberalitas in essendendo et magnificentia in conferendo ampla donaria et talia propriissime denominant Deitatem, quia magis proprie et multo excellentius Deitas est id quo Deus largitur dona magnifica quam quaecunque magnificentia creata. Et propter hoc dicit Propheta quod magnificentia eius et virtus eius in nubibus, et idem intelligendum de iusititia et libertate. Unde dicitur dator largifluus et per magnificus. Quaedam vero sunt quae consistunt et in moderatione passionum quibus moderatis, moderantur actus exteriores, sicut mansuetudo in moderatione irae et exterioris vindictae, et sicut patientia in moderatione tristitiae interioris et toleratione exteriorum. Et secundum hoc virtutes istae denominant Deitatem, non quo ad actus interiores sed prout est principium actuum exterorum. Unde dicitur Deus longanimus et patiens et mansuetus inquantem per rationem Deitatis, vindictas moderat, exercendas in peccatores et differt in longum tempus; pius autem misericors inquantum totaliter aliquando relaxat. Et ita patet quod non oportet propter hoc addere rationem aliquam intrinsecam Deitati, cum omnes istae virtuosae denominationes magis proprie competant Deitati quam alicui qualitati creatae quantumcumque iustitia vel patientia vel longanimitas dicatur. Unde magis est ista intime Deitas quam creata qualitas, ut ex superioribus patet."

[31] *Ibid*: "...et magnificentia in conferendo ampla donaria et talia propriissime denominant Deitatem, quia magis proprie et multo excellentius Deitas est id quo Deus largitur dona magnifica quam quaecunque magnificentia creata."

Henry's for attributing the moral virtues to God. Henry had to settle for only a conceptual attribution, while Aureol can claim that God is really just. For Aureol, Henry's ambiguous language was doubly inadequate: on the one hand, it did not attribute to the divine essence all perfections; on the other hand, it did attribute to the essence the imperfect concepts of potency and quality.

While the problem of appropriating the language of the moral virtues for divine attribution was a relatively recent development, the distinction between the divine will and its five signs had long been a commonplace in Scholastic theology. Peter Lombard had argued in his *Sentences* that according to the figurative language used in Scripture to describe the divine will such terms as "command", "prohibition", "counsel", "permission", and "operation" are applicable to the divine will in so far as they refer to particular signs of the divine will (*beneplacitum*).[32] Because of its inclusion in the *Sentences*, this position had become generally accepted. By the late 13th and early 14th centuries, the discussions focused on two topics: how to distinguish among the signs, and the traditional problem of whether God either commands or permits evil.[33]

Before addressing these points, Aureol re-examines how such terms are applied to the divine will. The Scholastic tradition had been content to fall back on the common notion that Scripture and theologians speak metaphorically about God, as, for example, when speaking of divine "operation", "permission", etc. Lombard had called these descriptions "tropes" or "figures". In Aureol's generation, Durand of Saint-Pourcain, following Aquinas in this case, argues that the signs of the divine will are attributed to the will of God itself metaphorically, on account of their similitude and "proportion" to the created will.[34] Aureol agrees that the signs are used metaphorically to refer to the di-

---

[32] Lombard, *Sententiae*, I, q. 45, (vol. 1, pp. 310-312).

[33] The examples of such discussions are too numerous to mention here. All the Scholastics cited here discussed these issues in their lectures on the *Sentences*.

[34] Durand of Saint-Pourcain, *In libros Sententiarum. Redactio tertia*, (Venice, 1571), I, d. 45, q. 3, f., 118b; "...sed voluntas signi dicitur metaphorice voluntas Dei, eo modo quo signum nominatur metaphorice nomine rei cuius est signum, ut imago Herculis vocatur Hercules. Et hoc potest esse dupliciter, uno modo ratione similitudinis inter signum et signatum, ut in exemplo iam posito. Alio modo ratione proportionis, quasi arguendo quod sicut se habent signum et signatum in uno, sic se habent in alio. Et sic est in nostro proposito. Quia enim in nobis ille qui praecipit vel consulit aliquid fieri, videtur illud velle. Similiter qui prohibet aliquid fieri, videtur velle illud non fieri. Qui autem aliquid facit, vult illud fieri. Qui vero permittit aliquid fieri cum possit impedire, videtur illud velle. Ideo in Deo idem ponitur, scilicet quod praeceptum, consilium, prohibitio, operatio, et permissio sunt vel dicitur voluntas divina, propter dictam similitudinem, vel magis proportionem."

vine will, but they can only be used after being stripped of all that points to imperfection.

In order to do this, Aureol distinguishes between two kinds of signs: those signs that are likenesses or similitudes of their significate, and those signs that are not similitudes, but rather signify something as an effect signifies a cause.[35] This first kind of signification, which Aquinas and Durand attribute to signs, conveys imperfection. Commands, prohibitions, permission, counsel, and operations imply desire; therefore, if there were similitude between the nature of these signs and the thing signified, then the presence or occurrence of these acts would imply desire on the part of the willer. In God, however, the acts of the will are signs of the characteristic of simple Deity that in no way includes motion or desire.

By moving from similitude to cause and effect Aureol seems to have left the realm of metaphor. The signs need not be mere metaphors if they are effects of God's will that in no way impugn His perfection. But Aureol does not reject the metaphorical language of Lombard.[36] For Aureol there are two ways to understand the signs of the divine

---

[35] *Borghese 329*, f. 507vb: "Signorum enim quaedam significant per hoc quod similitudinem gerunt significati et hoc modo prosecutio hominis et operatio eius signum est interioris desiderii et suae volitionis quae non est aliud quam quaedam interior prosecutio. Quaedam vero sunt quae ita significant aut repraesentant, ut nullam similitudinem gerant, sed tantummodo arguant sicut effectus causam et per hunc modum divina operatio, cum aliquid producit vel agit, significat ipsius voluntatem, non quidem aliquem actum conformem isti prosecutioni exteriori. Non enim est in Deo ratio desiderii secundum quem aliquid prosequatur aut etiam fieri velit vel appetat, nihilominus aeque profluit huiusmodi operatio ab ipsa Deitate."

[36] *Ibid.*: "Ulterius vero considerandum quod voluntas signi dupliciter potest intelligi. Primo quidem intransitive ut intelligatur voluntas quae est signum, ita quod signa ipsa dicantur voluntates, sicut consuetutum est dici quod hoc est praeceptum et regia voluntas, et sic metaphorice dicitur voluntas divina eius operatio vel consilium vel praeceptum, ut Magister dicit in littera. Secundo vero potest intelligi transitive quodammodo signum divinae voluntatis, ut praeceptum vel operatio non dicatur voluntas, sed signum voluntatis, et hoc modo non dicitur voluntas transumptive, sed aliquo modo proprie secundum aliquem intellectum. Si enim quis intelligat quod in Deo sint rationes actuum voluntariorum quibus correspondeant ista signa, sic non est verum quod in eo sit appetitus vel desiderium quo oportet fieri illud quod praecipit vel consulit vel per se ipsum producit. Si vero quis intelligat quod Deus per rationem simplicem Deitatis, non interveniente aliqua alia ratione, sit principium exterioris operationis aut promulgationis consilii vel praecepti et Deitatem, ut sic voluntatem appellet, vel potius quoddam velle, sic utique verum est quod operatio et consilium signa sunt voluntatis vel potius effectus. Actus namque voluntarii in appetitu creato habent duo et unum est perfectionis reliquum imperfectionis, imperfectionis quidem est quod sint quidam motus spirituales et quaedam inquietudines appetitus correspondentes proportionaliter exterioribus motibus. Perfectionis vero est quod sit principium exteriorum motiunum et in primo consistit ratio istorum actuum intrinseca et formalis et maxime propria; in secundo vero non adeo proprie consistit, sed tantum aliqualiter proprie, quia nulla creatura potest esse principium talium, nisi mediante actu intrinseco voluntatis."

will. Lombard points out one way used in Scriptural passages where the distinction between sign and significate is metaphorically collapsed so that, for instance, "divine counsel" stands for divine will. But this metaphorical collapsing of sign and significate must be understood as a conflation of cause with effect, not of a significate with its representative similitude.

Aureol himself realizes major problems with this position: if the effect is not a similitude of the significate, how can it function as a sign? Moreover, he admits,

> <something> is not called a sign which does not have a significate. But it has been declared that there are no acts of the will in God designated through these signs, because the divine good pleasure (*beneplacitum*) by which God delights in His essence and in every being is not revealed by <its> "operation" <or production>, for God delights equally in creatures which have not been produced as in those which have been produced. Therefore it does not seem that signs of this sort may be rightly assigned <to the divine will>.[37]

Indeed this reveals the main difficulty with Aureol's entire conception of the divine will as divine delight. If God's intrinsic will is merely to delight in all things as they exist and participate in His goodness, two questions arise: (1) how is the divine will the basis for any particular volition; and (2) why does God will the particular things He wills?

Aureol replies to his own objection by arguing that the well-pleased divine will (*divinum beneplacitum*) can be understood in two ways. First, it can be construed as delight in the way that Aureol has so laboriously articulated, but then, these signs do not signify divine delight. The divine will can also be understood "as the guiding principle for all acts and operations and beings which effectively depend on Him".[38] The signs at issue signify this guiding principle, and be-

---

[37] *Ibid.*: "Praeterea, signum non dicitur quod non habet signatum, sed declaratum est quod in Deo non sunt actus voluntatis designati per huiusmodi signa, quia nec divinum beneplacitum quo Deus complacet in sua essentia et in omni entitate non declaratur per operationem. Aeque enim complacet Deus in creaturi non productis, sicut et in productis, non ergo videtur quod bene assignentur huiusmodi signa."

[38] *Ibid.*, f. 508ra: "Quando sunt actu quam complacuit ab aeterno. Secundo vero accipi potest divinum beneplacitum pro dominativo principio omnium actuum et omnium operationum et entitatum ab ipso dependentium effective. Illud enim quod executivae potentiae dominatur consuevit beneplacitum appellari, movet enim appetitus executivam potentiam in creaturis. Et sic Deitas ipsa, nulla ratione intrinseca addita, dicitur beneplacitum prout est denominativum principium operationis, promulgationis, consilii et praecepti ac prohibitionis et hoc modo correspondent sibi quinque signa praedicta."

cause both "delight" and "ruling power" refer to Deity itself, the signs do signify the divine will.

But this distinction seems on the face of it to do more harm than good for Aureol. The notion of divine delight may not convey imperfection, but neither does it account for God willing outside Himself. In order to arrive at a complete explication of the divine will, Aureol must form a conception of an efficacious divine will which at the same time is both compatible with the concept of divine delight and accounts for God's actions *ad extra*.

Potestas: The Will of God as Power

One of the major problems with any theory of God's will as it is active in the created order is how to reconcile God's goodness and omnipotence with the presence of evil in the world. If God does not will evil, then it seems from evil's presence that God's will is not always fulfilled. To avoid this conclusion, Scholastics often distinguished between efficacious and non-efficacious types of divine will. By Aureol's time there were two different ways to draw this distinction. He rejects both of them.

The more common was the distinction between God's antecedent and consequent will. Introduced to Scholastic discourse by John the Damascene's *De fide orthodoxa*, it explained how, for instance, God wills that no one commit murder, yet murder is committed.[39] The antecedent will is a conditional will by which God wills something based on the actions of creatures. The consequent will is the will which is actually carried out based on the antecedent will and the actions of creatures. Aureol, however, rejects this position as it was defended by Aquinas.[40] Aquinas had held that the consequent will

---

[39] John of Damascus, *De fide orthodoxa*, ed. Eligius Buyteart, (Bonaventure, NY, 1955), II, c. 43, nn. 10-12, p. 160.

[40] *Borghese 329*, f. 511ra-b: "Opinio Thomae in Scripto. Propterea dixerunt alii quod voluntas Dei efficax et inefficax differunt, quia una est antecedens et alia consequens. Voluntas quidem consequens est secundum quam Deus vult simpliciter et perfecte; voluntas autem antecedens secundum quam vult aliquid secundum quid et imperfecte, nec ista imperfectio est ex parte voluntatis, sed ex parte voliti. Est enim econtrario de voluntate et cognitione speculativa: cognitio quidem speculativa perficitur in abstractione a singularibus, sed voluntas, et quicquid aliud est ordinatum ad opus, perficitur in particulari circa quod est operatio. Illud ergo est simpliciter et perfecte volitum quod subiacet voluntati, secundum omnes conditiones sigulares circumstantes ipsum particulare et hoc pertinet ad voluntatem consequentem quae respicit opera, et dispositiones quibus aliquid sufficienter ordinatur ad hoc quod sit sibi conveniens illud quod Deus dicitur illi velle, ut salus vel aliquid huiusmodi. Et talis voluntas, cum sit perfecta et simpliciter, dicitur efficax et impediri non potest. Illud autem quod est rectum et bonum secundum aliquam conditionem rei, in uni-

differed from the antecedent will, because the former was perfected through the completion of a particular operation, given that all the conditions of the antecedent will had been met. But Aureol argues that Aquinas was mistaken in saying that the consequent will was intrinsic to God. If the consequent will was intrinsic to God, then particular divine operations *ad extra* would be identical with the divine essence, and thus come about from absolute necessity.

A more recently developed option was Scotus's distinction between God's complacent will and His efficacious will.[41] The flaw in this account according to Aureol was Scotus's further distinction be-

versale consideratam, non habet rationem voliti simpliciter, sed secundum quid tantum, sicut istum hominem, inquantum homo est non est nisi bonum salvari, eo quod natura sua ad hoc est ordinata et hoc dicitur Deus velle, voluntate antecedente, et non simpliciter, sed secundum quid, et talis voluntas dici potest inefficax, nec semper impletur."

Aureol cites Aquinas's version of the distinction found in his *Sentences* commentary, *Sancti Thomae Aquinatis opera omnia*, ed. Robertus Busa, (Stuttgart-Badd, 1980), I, d. 47, art. 1, vol. I, pp. 119a-119b: "Respondeo dicendum, quod quidquid vult deus voluntate consequente, totum fit; non autem quidquid vult voluntate antecedente; quia hoc non simpliciter vult et perfecte, sed secundum quid tantum, nec ista imperfectio est ex parte voluntatis, sed ex conditione voliti. Est enim e contrario de voluntate et cognitione speculative: cognitio enim speculative perficitur in abstractione a singularibus; sed voluntas, quidquid aliud est ordinatum ad opus, perficitur in particulari, circa quod est operatio, illud ergo est simpliciter et perfecte volitum quod subjacet voluntati secundum omnes particulares conditiones circumstantes ipsum particulare; et hoc pertinet ad voluntatem consequentem, quae respicit opera et dispositiones, quibus aliquis sufficienter ordinatur ad hoc quod est sibi conveniens et debitum: et hoc est quod dicitur deus velle simpliciter, ut salutem vel aliquid huiusmodi: et ideo talis voluntas non potest impedire, sicut nec praescientia, cui subiicitur res secundum illas conditiones quibus in actu consistit. Illud autem quod est rectum et bonum secundum aliquam conditionem rei universalem consideratum, non habet rationem voliti simpliciter, sed secundum quid tantum; sicut istum hominem, inquantum est homo, non est bonum salvari, eo quod natura sua ad hoc est ordinata, et hoc deus vult voluntate antecedente, secundum quam non dicitur aliquid velle simpliciter; et ideo talis voluntas potest non impleri."

[41] In the *Lectura* and the *Ordinatio* Scotus presents two different versions of this distinction. In the *Reportata*, the version that Aureol addresses, he makes a further distinction between an intensified efficacious will and a diminished efficacious will. *Reportata*, I, d. 47, q. 1, (Vives, vol. 26, p. 510a): "Velle autem uno modo accipitur pro actu simplici voluntatis, quo quis aliquid simplici complacentia, non tamen movet ad consequendum illud, sicut aliquis desperans de sanitate, vult quidem sanitatem, et habet simplicem complacentiam respectu sanitatis; quia tamen desperat de ea non laborat ad consequendum eam. Aliud est velle efficax, quo quis non solum vult aliquid, sed movet ad obtenendum volitum; et illud velle est duplex, quoddam intensum, ut cum aliquis perfecte vult aliquid, movet perfecte ad illud consequendum. Aliud est velle remissum, ut cum aliquis vult aliquid, non tamen operatur, quantum potest ad illud consequendum, sicut si vellem aliquid portare, quod bene possem, non tamen volo portare, nisi alio mecum concurrente ad portandum; et sicut distinctum est de velle, ita potest distingui de nolle, quod quoddam est intensum, et quoddam remissum."

Scotus seems to be drawing the distinction between "intense" and "diminished" willing from developments in Medieval physical thought. For a discussion of this de-tween two types of efficacious will which ought not to be attributed to God. God's intensely efficacious will (*velle intensum*) is always fulfilled; but often God wills things in some diminished way, such that He allows its fulfillment to be impeded (*velle remissum*). The evangelical counsels should be considered examples of this diminished will. Aureol responds that *any* divine volition is infinite; therefore one can not attribute a limited (*remissum*) will to God without attributing imperfection to God.

Although Aureol rejects the aforementioned distinctions, he does not deny that he must distinguish God's efficaciousness from divine delight. Not only is the incompatibility of delight and efficaciousness implied in distinction 46, but in distinction 47, Aureol explicitly enumerates reasons why this is the case.[42] This is because Aureol's def-

---

velopment, including Scotus's role in it, see Edith Sylla, "Medieval Quantification of Qualities", *Archive for History of the Exact Sciences*, 8 (1971), 9-39; see also: John E. Murdoch, "*Mathesis in philosophiam scholasticam introducta*: the Rise and Development of the Application of Mathematics in Fourteenth-Century Philosophy and Theology, in *Arts liberaux et philosophie au moyen age*, (Montreal, 1969), pp. 215-254.

[42] *Borghese 329*, ff. 511rb-va: "Quid dicendum secundum veritatem, et primo quod velle complacentiae non habet in Deo activitatis seu efficaciae rationem. Restat ergo nunc dicere quod videtur sub triplici propositione. Prima quidem quod velle complacentiae non habet rationem activitatis aut efficaciae, sic quod voluntas Dei efficax dici possit amor ille quo complacet in sua bonitate et in omni participante eam. Constat enim quod voluntas Dei efficax non habet necessitatem simpliciter et absolutam, alioquin quae facit Deus circa creaturas, ageret necessitate absoluta. Sed manifestum est quod amor complacentiae infinitae qua Deus complacet in se et ex hoc complacuisse dicitur in omni bono, est amor necessarius simpliciter et absolute, ea quidem ecessitate, qua Deus est complacens in omni bono et in omni entitate, iuxta illud sapientis Sapientiae 11: 'Diligis omnia quae sunt, nec enim odiens aliquid constituisi', ergo huiusmodi velle non est efficax nec activum, nec principium productivam eorum quae fiunt ad extra. Praeterea, nullum velle quod habet rationem quietis et finis dicitur activum aut motivum ad extra, desiderium quidem alicuius rei movet ad prosecutionem illius delectatio. Vero aut complacentia non movet immediate, nisi pro quanto excitat desiderium et huius ratio est quia complacentia habet rationem spiritualis quietis et non alicuius motionis. Et propter hoc non sequitur exterior motio immediate nisi quatenus ex complacentia quadam spirituali et intrinseca motio in appetitu consurgit, sed velle efficax est illud quod est activum et motivum ad extra. Ergo velle complacentiae divinae, licet sit infinitum, non tamen habet efficaciae rationem. Praeterea, ex hiis quae experimur in nobis assurgimus ad divina, sed experimur quod velle complacentiae in nobis non movet nec est efficax ad agendum, nisi ex complacentia desiderium excitetur. Volumus enim omnes bona et complacemus in eis, eligimus autem nequaquam, ut Philosophus dicit 8 Ethicorum, et experimur quod quantumcumque adsit complacentia immediate, respectu alicuius rei, si fuerit sine disiderio et appetitu sive electione prosequendi et acquirendi illam rem, nullus ex illa complacentia movetur, quantumcumque intensa. Ergo nec Deus producit ex suo velle complacentiae quod producit, et propter hoc ratio efficaciae non potest attribui illi velle. Praeterea, illud quod indifferenter se habet ad aliqua nec plus determinatur ad unum quam reliquum, non est causa immediate quod altissimum determinate fiat, sed velle divinae complacentiae indifferenter se habet, sive res sint sive non sint. Aeque enim com-

inition of divine delight as "that by which God is pleased in His goodness and in all beings participating in it"[43] is unable to be a definition of the efficacious will of God. First of all, God loves, of necessity, His goodness and beings which participate in His goodness. If divine delight were also the divine will *ad extra*, then all things would come about of necessity. Second, the definition of divine delight must be stripped of all meanings except those conveying the characteristic of spiritual contentment. Efficacious will, however, is an active and motive force in the created order. Thus, the characteristics of spiritual contentment and efficaciousness are incompatible.

This is not to say that God's activity in the world is somehow incompatible with His nature. Aureol merely wants to make clear that God does not act in the world on account of His delight in His creatures. While He is pleased by the things He produces, and is even pleased in His act of production, His pleasure in no way determines Him to any particular act. This is because He is pleased whether certain things are brought about or not.[44] Aureol's position requires some explanation, for it leaves very little room for the divine will to operate in the created order. This is by design. The distinction that

---

placuit Deo ab aeterno in seipso et omni quidditate creabili et in omni bono, sicut complacet hodie rebus creatis. Ergo ex illo velle complacentiae non determinavit se Deus magis ad producendum quam ad non producendum. Ex his ergo apparet quod licet Deus producat complacenter quicquid producit, non tamen ex complacentia determinatur ad producendum et propter hoc sapiens dixit alloquens Deum, nihil odiens constituisti, immo diligens et complacens omnia fecit et similiter complacens cuncta possit adnihilare. Patet etiam quod velle efficax et inefficax non differunt in nobis, sicut velle complacentiae intensum et remissum, sed velle efficax est desiderium prosequendi determinate in tali instanti, est enim electio quia quod eligimus, efficaciter volumus, electio autem est desiderium ut Philosophus dicit 3 Ethicorum."

[43] *Ibid.*, f. 511rb: "Prima quidem quod velle complacentiae non habet rationem activitatis aut efficaciae, sic quod voluntas Dei efficax dici possit amor ille quo complacet in sua bonitate et in omni participante eam."

[44] *Ibid.*, f. 511va: "Praeterea, illud quod indifferenter se habet ad aliqua nec plus determinatur ad unum quam reliquum, non est causa immediate quod altissimum determinate fiat, sed velle divinae complacentiae indifferenter se habet, sive res sint sive non sint. Aeque enim complacuit Deo ab aeterno in seipso et omni quidditate creabili et in omni bono, sicut complacet hodie rebus creatis. Ergo ex illo velle complacentiae non determinavit se Deus magis ad producendum quam ad non producendum. Ex his ergo apparet quod licet Deus producat complacenter quicquid producit, non tamen ex complacentia determinatur ad producendum et propter hoc sapiens dixit alloquens Deum, nihil odiens constituisti, immo diligens et complacens omnia fecit et similiter complacens cuncta possit adnihilare. Patet etiam quod velle efficax et inefficax non differunt in nobis, sicut velle complacentiae intensum et remissum, sed velle efficax est desiderium prosequendi determinate in tali instanti, est enim electio quia quod eligimus, efficaciter volumus, electio autem est desiderium ut Philosophus dicit 3 Ethicorum."

Aureol seeks to draw is not one between two aspects of the will as divine attribute, but instead one between what is *intrinsic* to the divine will and what is *extrinsic* to it:

> If one holds that through some intrinsic will, proper to the formal characteristic of volition, He determines Himself to produce, it would be inevitable that God would produce from absolute necessity whatever He produces. For that which necessarily follows from something simply and absolutely necessary is certainly simply and absolutely necessary. But it is manifest that when God of necessity wills the production of the world (or something else) <to occur> at some instant, the production follows in that instant, otherwise, with <His> will remaining <the same>, the production could not follow, which is altogether repugnant to God. It remains, however, that if some such intrinsic will is attributed to God, that <will> is simply and absolutely necessary, since it would be God Himself. Whatever God is, however, He is from absolute necessity. Therefore the production of the world has followed, with absolute necessity, from something absolutely and simply necessary, and consequently this <production> is necessary. And whatever God produces immediately, He produces of necessity.[45]

This was certainly not a common opinion. Most Scholastics— Aquinas and Scotus being only the most prominent examples—did not hold that a doctrine of an active will intrinsic to God entailed fatalism. Traditional Latin theology attempted rather to explain how a necessary cause could produce contingent effects. The most common method was to distinguish between two types of necessity: absolute necessity and conditional (*ex suppositione*) necessity.[46] Since God's goodness is His own end, He wills Himself from absolute necessity. Secondary objects, however, which are not needed for God to attain His end, are not willed from absolute necessity. Since creatures do not add any perfection to God, it is not the case that God wills them necessarily; indeed, God could have chosen to *not will* (*nolle*) the existence of creatures. The only type of necessity which applies to creatures, therefore, is some sort of conditional necessity. Although God could have willed otherwise, once He has willed the existence of creatures, the existence of creatures is necessary.

---

[45] *Ibid.*, f. 509va: "Producit, si ponatur quod se determinet ad producendum per aliquod velle intrinsecum, participans formalem rationem volitionis. Illud enim quod necessario sequitur ex aliquo necessario simpliciter et absolute, illud quidem tale est necessarium simpliciter et absolute. Sed manifestum est quod Deo volente productionem mundi aut aliquid aliud pro aliquo instanti de necessitate, productio sequitur in ipso instanti, alioquin stante voluntate, posset non sequi productio, et per consequens non esset efficax voluntas et posset frustrari, quod omnino deo repugnat."

[46] See for Aquinas, *Summa*, q. 19, a. 3, (Leonine, vol. 4, p. 235); for Scotus, *Reportata*, d. 46, (Vives, vol. 26, pp. 473-476).

Aureol argues that this is a false distinction.[47] First of all, the disposition (*habitudo*) that the divine will has towards secondary objects of the will is necessary and not contingent. This is because this disposition is not a relation between the will and the objects of the will

---

[47] *Borghese 329*, ff. 509ra-b: "Prima quidem quod impossibile est habitudinem illam quam habet velle divinum ad obiecta secundaria esse contingentem et non necessarium absolute, si ipsum velle fuerit in se necessarium absolute. Illa namque habitudo quam habet velle divinum ad s cundaria obiecta, cum dictis quod Deus vult creaturas, vel est id ipsum realiter et ratione quod ipsumet velle divinum, vel est realis relatio addita ipsi velle, vel relatio rationis. Sed non potest dari quod sit relatio rationis, quia illa non habet esse in intellectu obiective, et sic nullo intellectu apprehendente istam habitudinem non est huiusmodi habitudo, et per consequens Deus volet, obiecta secundaria quod erroneum est. Nec potest dici quod sit relatio realis, quia Dei ad creaturam nulla realis relatio est et iterum nihil potest esse reale in Deo quod Deus non sit, secundum regulam Augustini 11 de Civititate Dei, capitulo 10, qui dicit quod quicquid habet Deus, Deus est, et per consequens talis habitudo relatio realis poni non potest. Relinquitur ergo quod sit ipsummet velle divinum. Et per consequens, si habitudo illa contingens est, et velle contingens erit. Positum est autem quod velle divinum inse et absolute sit necessarium. Ergo necesse est quod sit necessaria absolute illa habitudo quae transit super quodcumquae obiectum. Praeterea, ideo voluntas, stante habitudine necessaria respectu finis, habet habitudinem contingentem ad ea quae sunt ad finem, quia actus ille quo vult finem praecise est alius ab actu illo quo vult illu, quod est ad finem propter finem. Alio namque actu vult quis sanitatem absolute, et alio potionem propter sanitatem, quod apparet, quia in primo actu finis est volitus praecise, in secundo vero non est volitus sed intentus, et est circumstantia actus, et ideo possibile est quod actus qui transit super finem sit forsitan necessarius, et cum hoc quod actus transiens super illud quod est ad finem propter finem remaneat contingens. Sed in Deo non est nisi unicus actus quo vult Deus bonitatem suam et omnem creaturam, ergo si habitudo quam habet illud velle est necessaria et habitudo illa necessaria erit quam habet ad bonitates creatas, unde eadem necessitate complacet in omni bonitate praticipata qua placet in sua bonitate, impossibile quidem est quod Deus non diligat omnem entitatem participantem suam bonitatem. Et confirmatur quia secus est de eo quod diligitur propter finem quasi inductivum finis ipsius et de eo quod non inducit finem, sed est quaedam derivatio et participatio eius, non diligit enim Deus creaturas, ut mediantibus ipsis acquirat perfectionem, sed quia sunt participationes suae perfectionis, unde ea necessitate qua complacet in se ipso, complacet in omni quidditate creabili vel creata et ita non habet ad bona creata habitudinem contingentem. Praeterea, illa habitudo est necessaria quam impossibile est non esse et fuit impossibile ab aeterno, sed si divinum velle intrinsecum habet habitudinem ad creationem mundi, ita quod Deus voluerit pro illo instanti quod mundus fieret, habitudinem illam impossibile fuit non esse etiam ab aeterno, quia detur oppositum quod fuit possibilis non esse, sequitur quod habitudo opposita potuit inesse, videlicet quod Deus potuit ab aeterno nolle mundum creare pro illo instanti quo creavit. Si autem potuit nolle, sequitur quod illud nolle potuit esse Deus, quia Deus cst suum velle et suum nolle et quicquid est in seipso. Constat autem quod quicquid potuit esse Deus, de necessitate est Deus et hodie est Deus, quare si aliquo velle intrinseco potuit Deus ab aeterno nolle mundum umquam creare et hodie oportet quod habeat illud nolle. Cum ergo non habeat, cum iam creaverit, sequitur quod habere non potuerit tale nolle et ita habuit voluntatem creandi de necessitate, sic quod impossibile fuit aliter se habere. Sed hoc est totaliter absonum et erroneum. Ergo dici non potest quod velle divinum habeat habitudinem contingentem immo nec aliquam habitudinem secundum quam sit verum dicere quod voluerit Deus aut noluerit mundum creare."

independent of either, but it is the will itself. If, therefore, the disposition of the will towards its objects is contingent, then the divine will itself is contingent. Second, Aureol argues, one should not distinguish between primary and secondary objects of the divine will, inasmuch as God wills His goodness and all creatures in a single act. Thus, the same necessity applies to God's willing of creatures as to His willing His own goodness. Finally, Aureol stresses, there is no distinction between what God could have intrinsically willed and what He did will. What God wills, He wills from eternity. So, if He had an intrinsic will to not create the world, it is necessary that that will presently be in God. However, since He has created the world, He must never have had such an intrinsic will.

The only way for Aureol to avoid fatalism, given his understanding of the divine will, is to hold that "God's intrinsic will" does not refer to any action in particular. Since the divine will is delight, Aureol argues that the will is indifferent to either side of a contradiction (A or not-A). Far from limiting divine freedom, Aureol believes he has strengthened the case for it: the divine will is not necessitated, since it can simultaneously and equally delight in and bring about either part of a contradiction. "But", Aureol concludes,

> not only can the power <of God> be brought to bear upon either part of a contradiction successively, rather it also can be brought to bear more upon the one at T1, more upon the other at T2. Therefore, the divine will is able not only to be brought to bear simultaneously upon either, but upon both more or less equally..."[48]

Although this position does avoid fatalism, it also seems to deny that God's will is in any way efficacious, since divine delight is indifferent to particular divine actions. But by distinguishing between the intrinsic will and the extrinsic will, Aureol believes that he has revealed the nature of divine freedom. On this distinction, freedom is attributed to the intrinsic will of God, and willing action is attributed only to the power that God has over the created world:

> Nevertheless God is said to produce freely and willingly what he produces. Freely because He produces with delight, for He is pleased in all created beings and all possible beings, whether they exist or not, and thus whatever comes about is pleasing to Him. Thus by delighting in His goodness He could annihilate the world just as He created it. And He is always pleased, whether He annihilates or creates. But

---

[48] *Ibid.*, f. 509va: "Praeterea, tanti ambitus est actus, sicut potentia sicut assumunt ista ponentes, sed non solum potentia ferri potest super utramque partem contradictionis successive, immo etiam magis referri potest nunc super unam, nunc super aliam. Ergo velle divinum non solum super utramque simul feretur, immo super utramque magis vel saltem aequaliter, si ratio eorum procedit."

He is said to act voluntarily because there is a characteristic of will
which has authority over exterior acts and has them in its power.[49]

Aureol realizes that such a distinction is not sufficient as it stands to
account for actions in the world. Although the will may have authority over the created order, Aureol's doctrine of the will restricts
its capacity to implement that authority. It is only when the characteristic of authority is joined to God's omnipotence that the will becomes efficacious.[50] The divine will in and of itself is not efficacious;
rather, its efficaciousness depends on divine omnipotence. This view
must be understood in the context of Aureol's doctrine of divine
simplicity. Divine will and divine power are really the same, since
they are both intrinsically the divine essence itself.[51] However, the
terms naming them connote different things, and it is through these
different connotates that the attributes can be thought of as mediating for one another. So, for instance, for something to be an object-
being-willed presupposes that it is also known.[52] In the same way an
object that is produced must also be a willed object.

This distinction between an object as willed and as produced
makes sense given Aureol's doctrine of the will. Acts of the divine

---

[49] *Ibid.*, f. 510rb: "Nihilominus tamen Deus dicitur libere et voluntarie producere
quae producit. Libere quidem quia complacenter producit, complacet enim in entitate creaturae et in entitate quam importat productio, sive sit sive non sit. Et ideo
quicquid fiat totum est sibi complacens, unde Deus complacendo in sua bonitate
posset mundum adnihilare, sicut creavit, et semper uniformiter complacet, sive ad-
nihilet sive creet. Voluntarie vero dicitur agere quia de ratione voluntatis est quod
sit respectu exteriorum actuum domina et habens illos in sua potestate."

[50] *Ibid.*, f. 511vb: "Tertia quoque propositio est quod efficacia divinae voluntatis
non debet referri ad aliquem actum intrinsecum, ut dictum est, sed potius ad
Deitatem prout induit rationem voluntatis, ex hoc quod habet plenum dominium et
liberam facultatem super utramque partem contradictionis, unde prout adiungitur
omnipotentia tali dominio, consurgit ratio efficacis voluntatis. Et hoc expresse innu-
it Augustinus Enchiridion, capitulo 111, ait enim quod quantum ad angelos et
homines malos attinet quod Deus noluit, fecerunt, quantum vero ad omnipotentiam
Dei attinet, hoc ipso quod contra eius voluntatem fecerunt, de ipsis facta est voluntas eius. Et subdit, capitulo 114, quod omnipotentis Dei voluntas semper vindicta
est, nec nisi volens quicquam faciat et omnia quaecunque vult, facit. Hoc siquidem
Augustinus vocat divinam voluntatem, non aliquod desiderium aut aliquem motum
intrinsecum quo Deus inclinetur ad aliquid faciendum vel non faciendum, sed vocat
plenitudinem dominii super utramque partem contradictionis et facultatem ac libi-
tum sic agendi vel non agendi voluntatem Dei quae semper impletur."

[51] Aureol discusses divine simplicity and omnipotence in *Scriptum*, d. 42, q. 1, a. 2,
(Rome, p. 968): "...omnipotentia ipsam Deitatem, addito certo connotato, videlicet
productione omnis possibilis".

[52] *Ibid.*: "Omnia attributa coincidunt immediate in rationem Deitatis, addito
certo connatato, ut superius dictum fuit, nec unum attributum mediat inter essentiam et aliud attributum, nisi quantum connotatum unius mediat inter connotatum
alterius, ut quia connotatum volitionis supponit connotatum ipsius intellectionis per
modum cuiusdam praevii, quia non est volitum, nisi quod prae-est intellectum per
modum preavii."

will are identical with the divine essence and are thus eternal. Moreover, the objects of the divine will (i.e., those things in which God delights), since they are willed in one act with divine goodness, are also eternal. The same does not hold true for divine power; while there is an identity between *velle* and *volitio* in God, there is no such identity between *potestas* and *operatio*—and this is the basis for the connotative distinction between divine will and divine power:

> Therefore, it must be maintained...that an act of the executive power is some real action flowing from Deity itself; and <it must be maintained> that it is not really the essence of God, but rather that it is in creatures insofar as they are its subjects, just as any other action is transferred to the recipient; and <it must be maintained> that it is not the intrinsic divine will, and that omnipotence is not the same attribute as will, but <omnipotence> is a certain executive power coinciding formally and intrinsically in the characteristic of Deity, although extrinsically a determinate connotate is added <to authoritative power>.[53]

For Aureol efficaciousness is not attributed strictly to either divine will or divine power; neither one is efficacious in and of itself. "Efficacious will" refers, rather, to the common extrinsic connotates of both the divine will and power, that is, the set of things both willed in eternity and actualized in time. "The efficacy of the divine will", according to Aureol,

> ought not to refer to some intrinsic act, as has been said, but rather to Deity as it assumes the characteristic of will in which it has full authority and free power over either part of a contradiction. Whence, as omnipotence is joined to such authority, the characteristic of efficacious will arises.[54]

Having already attacked Henry of Ghent's use of "*potentia*" on account of its passive connotations, Aureol is not about to reintroduce the term without addressing this problem. Although Latin theologians customarily used the term "power" (*potentia*) to describe God, Aureol prefers using terms, such as "authority" (*potestas*) and

---

[53] *Ibid.*: "Sic ergo tenendum...quod actus executivae potentiae est quaedam realis actio profluens ab ipsa Deitate, et quod ipsa non est realiter Dei essentia, immo est subjective in creatura, sicut et omnis alia actio transiens est in passo; et quod non est velle divinum intrinsecum; et quod non est omnipotentia idem attributum cum voluntate, sed est quaedam executiva potentia coincidens formaliter et intrinsece in rationem Deitatis, licet addat extrinsece determinatum connotatum, eo modo quo dictum est."

[54] *Borghese 329*, f. 511vb: "Tertia quoque propositio est quod efficacia divinae voluntatis non debet referri ad aliquem actum intrinsecum, ut dictum est, sed potius ad Deitatem prout induit rationem voluntatis, ex hoc quod habet plenum dominium et liberam facultatem super utramque partem contradictionis, unde prout adiungitur omnipotentia tali dominio, consurgit ratio efficacis voluntatis."

"strength" (*virtus*), which convey no sense of passivity or potentiality.[55] It is clear here and elsewhere that, in Aureol's theological vocabulary, the term "*potentia*" must be read as "*potestas*" or "*virtus*" when he is talking about God.

Divine Voluntarism

With Aureol's distinction between intrinsic and extrinsic will in mind, we can now turn to Aureol's description of how the attributes relate in divine causality. Unlike the positions of 13th-century theologians, Aureol's position on the relative efficacy of the divine will and intellect need not be pieced together from various treatises. Aureol specifically addresses the issue as raised by Durand of Saint-Pourcain.[56] Durand had argued that the will was more immediately related to divine action *ad extra* than was the intellect. He explained divine causality as following a logical order: God knows, God wills, God acts. Using the analogy of purchasing an automobile, we can

---

[55] *Scriptum*, d. 42, q. 1, a. 2, (Rome, p. 971a): "...oportet attributere Deo, unde magis coinceditur, quod est eo potestas activa vel virtus activa, quam quod sit potentia, quia ratio potentia videtur includere illam primam rationem potentialitatis et possibilitatis, quae nullo modo est in activa potentia Dei, licet in potentia creaturae."

[56] *Durand*, d. 45, q. 2, 117va-118ra: "Alius modus dicendi quem credo veriorem quod in omni agente a proposito creato vel increato, voluntas magis de prope se habet ad productionem rei, quam intellectus, vel secundum rem, ubi intellectus et voluntas realiter differunt, vel secundum rationem, ubi differunt solum secundum rationem, ut in Deo. Quod patet primo quia in habentibus ordinem plus distant extrema ab invicem, quam distet medium ab extremis, sed in agente a proposito sive libere haec se habet per ordinem: scire, velle, et operari, ita quod scire et operari sunt extrema inter quae medium est velle. Ergo magis de prope se habet velle ad operari quam scire. Maior de se patet. Probatio minoris, quod enim operari sit ultimum supponens scire et velle, patet quia aliter non esset opus a nostro proposito. Item constat quod velle supponit scire, ergo vellet est medium inter scire et operari.

"Secundo patet idem sic: qualem ordinem realem habent actus voluntatis et intellectum in illis, in quibus differunt solum secundum rationem; sed in nobis, in quibus differunt realiter habent talem ordinem realem quod actus voluntatis immediatius se habet <ad> operationem artis quam actus intellectus etiam secundum istos. Ergo in Deo, in quo actus intellectus et voluntatis solum differunt secundum rationem, talis est ordo rationis: quod actus voluntatis immediatius se habet ad productionem rerum creatarum quae producuntur per artem divinam quam actus intellectus."

Borghese 329, f. 510rb: "Opinio Durandi. Propterea dixerunt alii quod immediatius voluntas se habet ad productionem rei quam intellectus in omni agente a proposito creato vel increato in habentibus quidem ordinem plus distant extrema ab invicem quam medium ab extremis, sed in omni agente a proposito per ordinem se habent scire, velle et operari, ita quod scire et operari sunt extrema, medium autem velle. Operari namque praesupponit scire et velle, alias non erit agens a proposito, velle autem praesupponit scire, ergo immediatius se habet velle ad operari quam scire."

visualize how Durand believes the causal process works: John sees a red convertible in the showroom window; based on this he wishes to buy it; based on his wish to buy the automobile, he actually enters the showroom and purchases the automobile. The will thus functions as a medium between intellect and action. While the will is a more immediate cause of things, it functions as an instrumental cause, directed by the intellect. By so subordinating the will to the intellect, Durand proposes what we think of as an "intellectualist" appreciation of divine causality.

Aureol claims that Durand has asked the wrong question. To inquire about which divine attribute is more immediate to the object of divine causality leads to an incorrect conception of that causality, for each attribute is the divine essence itself, and hence all are equally immediate to divine acts. He argues that "the intellect's apprehension, the will's determination and the executive power's activity concur in one perfect causality".[57] The question, Aureol insists, should not be which is more immediate to the object, but which is logically prior in the causal sequence.[58] If Durand is concerned chiefly with *how* things come about, Aureol is concerned with *why* they come about. Although God's intellect directs and specifies particular acts, it is the will that chooses which acts will be carried out. Neither will nor intellect is causal in itself, but within the context of that single causal act, it is the will which has priority. By approaching the issue with a "why" question, Aureol positions himself diametrically opposite Durand: in the created order the will, for Aureol, is the primary causal agent, followed by the executive power, and then the direction of the intellect. But since it is a question of divine actions *ad extra*, the determinative and executive capacities of the will are the same in all respects, while still differing from the intellect connotatively.[59]

---

[57] *Borghese 329*, f. 510vb: "Sic apprehensio intellectus, determinatio voluntatis et activitas potentiae executivae concurrunt ad unam perfectam causalitatem."

[58] *Ibid.*, f. 510rb: "Inquirendum quidem fuit quae causalitas est potior, dirigere videlicet vel imperare, non autem quae immediatior, nam quaelibet est intimissima et penitus immediata."

[59] *Ibid.*, f. 513rb: "Est autem considerandum quod in divinus ista tria reducuntur ad duo, non enim executiva potentia est indeterminata, ut expectet determinationem intrinseci imperii voluntatis, alioquin sequeretur quod vis executiva in Deo esset in potentia et indigeret extrahente ipsam in actum, sicut in nobis indiget praesentia voluntatis et assistentia imperii, ut consurgat una causalitas perfecta. Unde qui imaginantur Deum indigere interiori motione voluntatis ad hoc quod aliquid producat exterius, imaginantur in ipso non esse semper et in actu et de necessitate causalitatem ultimatam, et per consequens imaginantur ipsum in potentia, ut supra deductum est dum ageretur de potestate Dei. Sic ergo in naturalibus virtus activa unita, simplex existens habet haec tria. Est enim vis determinata ad agere et specificata ad tale agere in creaturis vero voluntariis et appetitivus dividuntur haec tria et vis eliciens attribuitur executivae potentiae, determinatio vero volitioni, specificatio autem et directio appre-

Returning to John and his red convertible, we can recast the analogy to explain Aureol's claim. John decides that he wants to buy a red convertible. So, he goes to the dealer and looks over the entire lot for a red convertible to buy. After looking at all the automobiles he picks out and buys a red convertible. Although, in God, the choice and the direction are one act, His decision to act, just as is in the case of John buying a car, is more basic to the act than the direction of the act. The connotative distinction between determination/execution and direction is also apparent. Determination and execution refer to a particular thing (i.e. the red convertible); directive knowledge refers to all things in general (i.e. all the cars in the lot). Whereas Durand allowed the will only an instrumental role in causality, Aureol reverses the process and makes the intellect an instrument of the will.

Such a voluntaristic scheme prompts another "why" question for both Aureol and the reader: why does God will what He wills? Clearly the will does not *depend* on the intellect for its decision. But given that the object of the will is divine goodness, the question can be restated: does God will something because that something is good, or is it good because God wills it? If the divine will is taken as delight, God does not will something on account of its goodness in the sense of willing directed toward an end, because movement towards something implies incompleteness.[60] His goodness does not in-

---

hensioni. In divinis vero dividuntur in duo, nam executiva potentia est determinatissima nec expectat imperium voluntatis, non tamen est specificata ex se, immo indiget directione intellectus secundum varietatem producibilium creaturarum. Quare autem determinatio executivae potentiae divinae tribuatur, et non specificatio, statim apparet consideranti quod determinatio in ea ponit perfectionem, nam expectaret aliunde determinari, nec posset ex se prodire in actum, nisi aliunde determinata non indigeret assistentia extrahentis ipsam de potentia in actum. Specificatio vero poneret imperfectionem in ea, esset enim tunc arctata ad unum effectum specificum et unum modum, sicut vis ignitiva specificatur ad calefaciendum, nec propter hoc quod vis executiva caret specificatione, indiget extrahente ipsam de potentia in actum. Non enim specificatio extrahit ad agere, sed ipsa determinatio unde non se habet directio intellectus, ut extrahens, sed tantum ut specificans, nam extractio ad agere est proprie determinare.

Ex his itaque patet quid importat efficacia voluntatis in Deo, non enim significat determinationem volitionis interioris, extrahentis executivam potentiam ad agendum. Sed cum executiva potentia determinatione ulteriori non ageat, quamlibet partem contradictionis indifferenter habet in sua potestate, ita quod determinatur extrinsece ex plenitudine dominii, non autem intrinsece ex motione voluntatis conformari. Istam autem determinationem extrinsecam sequitur exterior effectus, quia talis determinatio non est aliud quam ipsamet operatio quae cum impediri non possit, manifestum est quod voluntas Dei efficax, hoc est plenitudo dominii in operationem prodiens impediri non potest quin impleatur semper. Et in hoc tertius articulus terminetur."

[60] *Ibid.*, ff. 513rb-va: "Ubi inferuntur multa ex praecedentibus, et primo quod Deus non vult aliquid extra se sic quod aliquid extrinsecum terminet ipsius voli-

trinsically move His will; God simply delights in His goodness and all things participating in His goodness.[61] Nor does the divine will, taken as executive power, will something on account of its goodness. An object need not have existence outside of the divine essence in order to participate in divine goodness:

> ...all creatures and divine operations in the created order have divine goodness as an end; they both exist towards that end and God produces them towards that end. Nevertheless, <God> is not determined to produce these sorts of things from the fact that He wills His goodness, because it does not matter to divine goodness whether they exist or not.[62]

Aureol's view is highlighted in his discussion of the problem of evil.[63] Although no Scholastic argued that God is the efficient and immediate cause of evil, experience and several Scriptural passages lead many theologians to say that God wills evil in some sense. As they noted, God seems to will evil in two ways. In some cases God seems to command things contrary to His own "previous" command; thus, God commanded that Abraham kill Isaac contrary to His "later" command in the Decalogue proscribing murder. God also seems to allow many of His commands to be broken, and in this way, too, He seems to permit evil.

Aureol denies that the command to kill Isaac makes God the cause of evil in any way. In the first place, one could argue that the command to kill Isaac was principally a command that Abraham be obedient to God.[64] Furthermore, the command to kill was not even evil in itself. Aureol claims that even if Abraham had actually killed Isaac, Abraham would not have been a sinner. He argues that Abraham would have been acting as a secondary cause in an operation which could have been carried out immediately by God, "who

---

tionem, licet complaceat in omni bonitate creata per modum eminentem, quia complacuit in sua bonitate."

[61] *Ibid.*: "Secundo vero sequitur ex praedictis quod Deus non movetur intrinsece a sua bonitate, tamquam a fine, nec motus a sua bonitate producit res exteriores, quamvis exteriores res et omnes operationes ad extra ordinentur in bonitatem Dei tamquam in finem."

[62] *Ibid.*, f. 513vb: "Hoc tamen non obstante omnes creaturae et operationes divinae ad extra habent pro fine divinam bonitatem, et ad illam sunt et ad illam Deus producit. Non tamen determinatur ad productionem huiusmodi ex hoc quod velit suam bonitatem, quia nihil refert ad ipsam sive sint res sive non sint."

[63] *Ibid.*, f. 514ra: "Quod Deus nullo modo vult mala. Quarto autem sequitur ex praedictis quod Deus nullo modo vult mala."

[64] *Ibid.*: "Non procedunt ergo instantiae. Prima siquidem non, ubi considerandum quod aliqui dicere voluerunt Deum, dum praecepit Abrahae ut Isaac immolaret, non voluisse fieri quod praecepit, quia factum non fuit, nec tamen propter hoc oportet ponere fictionem in Deo."

could have annihilated or killed Isaac <Himself> without any injustice".[65] Aureol makes no distinction between immediate divine operation and command in this case. Whatever God does is good, because He does it; whatever God commands is good, because He commands it.

Yet God's commands are not always fulfilled. This means that God permits sin to come about. Aureol is careful to draw a distinction here between two senses of "permission", such that it is revealed as not really the will of God, but the absence of God's will. Sin is that which is not the object of the divine will. Such a brief and simple explanation of divine permission is very different from the discussions of his contemporaries.[66] Nor does he explicitly account for the fact that an omnipotent God restricts His will in such a way as to allow evil. It seems to be the case that God restricts His will in order to allow for human free will. Human free will is responsible for sin, but it does not impede the divine will. Insofar as creatures do not participate in divine goodness, that is insofar as they sin, they have nothing at all to do with the divine will. God is not displeased with sin, He simply does not delight in it. Thus, we return to the connotative distinction between divine will and divine intellect. The intellect has all things as its object, the will has only good things as its object. As we shall see in the next chapter, such a reading of Aureol's implied account of evil is consistent with his understanding of the relationship between divine and human agency in the process of predestination.

On what basis then does God choose what will be an object of the divine will? Why does God delight in or bring about one thing rather than another? Aureol's answer at first glance seems to suggest that God's actions are simply arbitrary:

> ...if it is asked...why <God> determines Himself to willing when He is able not to will in the same instant...it is certainly responded that He thus determines Himself to will because He wills...Therefore, no cause is to be sought as to why <God> elicited such an act, except because He so willed, that is, because it was in His power and authority <to do so>.[67]

---

[65] *Ibid.*, f. 513rb: "Et est ulterius attendendum quod dato quod Abraham filium immolasset, non tamen peccasset, quia fuisset minister Dei, qui adnihilare potuit Isaac vel occidere absque iniustitia omni."

[66] Hervaeus Natalis O.P., *In libros Sententiae*, (Paris, 1647), I, d. 43, q. 2-4, ff. 182b-186b; Durand, I, d. 47, q. 3-5, ff. 122va-124va.

[67] *Borghese 329*, f. 510va: "...si quaeratur obiecto praesente quare determinat se ad volendum cum posset non velle in eodem instanti secundum illos qui ponunt eam simpliciter activam, respondetur utique quod ideo determinat se ad volendum, quia vult. Et tamen non est dubium quod illud vult, non importaret actum primum voluntatis, alioquin primum velle produceret velle et sic in infinitum. Exprimitur ergo

Taking into account, however, Aureol's understanding of evil, we can say that this arbitrariness is mitigated, at least insofar as the divine will pertains to human beings, by the ability of human free will to resist divine love. The most obvious example of this in Aureol's thought is his understanding of the relationship between God and humankind in the process of predestination.

per illud velle quoddam dominium et quidam modus potestativus, unde magis causa excluditur et quaestio repellitur quam causa detur, cum dicitur quod ideo vult quia vult, quasi dicere velit qui sic respondet quod actus ille est in pleno dominio et in plenaria potestate, et ideo non est quaerenda causa quare elicit talem actum, nisi quia ita vult. Hoc est quia illud est in suo dominio et in sua potestate."

CHAPTER THREE

QUI HOMINES VULT SALVOS FIERI: PREDESTINATION AND THE DOCTRINE OF GENERAL ELECTION

Predestination is a paradigm example of divine efficacy. Therefore, a doctrine of predestination depends upon a doctrine of the divine attributes and should be understood in that context. This is particularly the case with Aureol. From his unusual views on the divine attributes comes an equally unusual view of predestination. His conception of general election (i.e., that God does not have an intrinsic will to save or damn any particular person) exemplifies the intrinsic indeterminacy of divine love. This does not mean, however, that Aureol's doctrine of predestination is simply a footnote to his doctrine of the divine will. To understand Aureol's position on predestination one must examine it in both its internal and external contexts. The internal context for Aureol's doctrine of predestination is his doctrine of the attributes; thus, in developing the former, he applies the entire range of theological tools that he has used in his explication of the latter. Once again, he turns to semantics, using the connotative distinctions (a) among the will, intellect, and essence, and (b) among the intrinsic and extrinsic will, to redefine the concepts of "predestination", "reprobation", and "election". Aureol also utilizes his appreciation of the immediate, atemporal relation between Deity and the objects of the intellect and will. In addition, he proposes a theory of resistible grace, based on his doctrine of the divine will; and this in turn allows him to argue for a basis for both predestination and reprobation on the part of the predestined and reprobate without resorting to a doctrine of predestination based on human merit.

The external context is Aureol's complex relationship to his own theological tradition. While single-particular election had been the consensus opinion of the 13th century, there was disagreement over other issues involved with predestination. For instance, most theologians of the time attributed predestination primarily to the divine intellect. Aureol's formulation of a voluntarist understanding of predestination clearly puts him at odds with this trend. The relationship of his treatment to those of the major figures of his own order is more complicated. Aureol's goal was to maintain Scotus's voluntarism, while eliminating its purported heretical tendencies and logical inconsistencies. In order to do this, Aureol drew upon the methodological approach to predestination of 13th-century Franciscan theology. Nevertheless, the result, a doctrine of general election, falls well outside any previous Scholastic understanding of predestination.

Aureol's doctrine was a source of controversy because he attempted to develop a doctrine which would at the same time leave humans both entirely free and entirely dependent on the grace of God in every step of the process of salvation. For Aureol, any hint of divine causal determinism in the process would lead to either pride or despair in men and women, and would render the exhortation of Scripture and the passion of Christ useless.[1] On the other hand, he denies that human actions are a meritorious cause of predestination. Aureol's doctrine is more than a subtle version of a doctrine of predestination according to foreseen merits, but only by taking into account this two-fold context of his doctrine can this distinction be appreciated.[2]

Scholastic discussions of predestination are typically divided into two parts. The author explains what predestination and reprobation are; then he explains why they happen. Since historians dealing with these texts are usually concerned with the author's views about why someone is predestined or reprobate, the wide variation in the use of these technical terms is often neglected. For instance, "predestination" can refer to (a) the entire soteriological process, (b) God's eternal salvific election, (c) the divine giving of grace and eternal life, or (d) any combination of the above. Unless one recognizes how each particular author defines and uses "predestination", it is probably the case that any comparative analysis between two authors is a

---

[1] *Borghese 329*, f. 424ra: "Sed in oppositum videtur quod praedestinatus possit mutare et impedire ne salvetur, et reprobatus similiter ne damnetur. Illud enim nullo modo ponendum est, ex quo sequitur desperatio hominum vel praesumptio et in curia, seu negligentia omnium agendorum. Sed si praedestinatus non posset impedire seipsum a salute aeterna, merito in eo oriretur praesumptio; similiter si reprobatus immutare non posset, quin duceretur ad aeternum supplicium, oriretur in eo merito desperatio. In utroque autem contemptus et negligentia agendorum, quia quicquid agant homines, determinati sunt eorum fines quos impedire non possunt. Ergo id poni non potest. Praeterea, illud dici non debet, ex quo vana redditur omnis persuasio et omnis oratio et effectus scripturae sacrae, immo et Christi passio et quicquid sollicitudinis divinae, angelicae, vel humanae circa homines esse potest. Sed haec omnia vana essent, si ex aeterna praedestinaione iste immutabiliter salvaretur, et ille damnaretur ex reprobatione. Ergo hoc esse non potest."

[2] Vignaux, *Justification*, pp. 43-97, does not fully explore either context. Since he was concerned mainly with predestination as it pertained to the doctrine of justification, he saw Aureol simply as a critic of Scotus and a defender of the traditional understanding of divine acceptation. He does not take into account the 13th-century context at all. Vignaux does briefly explore Aureol's doctrine of the attributes, but not in any systematic way (pp. 61-79).

comparison of apples to oranges. Just as the doctrine of predestination depends on various other positions held by a theologian, the causal explanation of predestination depends on the meaning of terms like "predestination" and "reprobation". In the case at hand, this is especially important. Aureol's major break with his tradition occurs in the definitional stages of his argument. Therefore, we must examine what "predestination" is for Aureol and how his definition relates to the definitions of earlier scholastics before taking up the cause of predestination.

Predestination, Reprobation, Election

The first definitional issue for Aureol concerns assigning predestination to the proper divine attribute. The dominant trend at his time was to associate predestination with God's providence and knowledge. Not only was this the norm for theologians in both the Dominican and Augustinian orders, but Scotistic voluntarism was only one of several options in Franciscan theology.[3] Aureol's choice of opponents is illustrative of this situation: Thomas Aquinas represents the intellectualist position current in Parisian theology; Richard of Middleton stands for that trend within the methodological tradition of Aureol's own order.

Aureol attacks Aquinas's claim that predestination is the characteristic in the divine mind of the order (*ordo*) of a rational creature to eternal life.[4] Each of Aureol's replies rests on the assumption that

---

[3] McGrath, *Iustitia Dei*, pp. 163-166.

[4] *Summa,* q. 23, a. 2, (Leonine, vol. 1, p. 273): "Respondeo dicendum quod praedestinatio non est aliquid in praedestinatis, sed in praedestinante tantum. Dictum est enim quod praedestinatio est quaedam pars providentiae. Providentia autem non est in rebus provisis; sed est quaedam ratio in intellectu provisoris, ut supra dictum est. Sed executio providentiae, quae gubernatio dicitur, passive quidem est in gubernatis; active est in gubernante. Unde manifestum est quod praedestinatio est quaedam ratio ordinis aliquorum in salutem aeternam, in mente divina existens. Executio autem huius ordinis est passive quidem in praedestinatis; active autem est in Deo. Est autem executio praedestinationis vocatio et magnificatio, secundum illud Apostoli, ad Romanos VIII: 'quos praedestinavit, hos et vocavit; et quos vocavit, hos et magnificavit'."

Aureol misreads Aquinas on this point. The term in question is *"ratio"*. Aquinas probably means something like "basis", while Aureol takes it as "characteristic". This, however, does not mean that differences between the two theologians ought to be minimized. Aureol misunderstood Aquinas because of the vast conceptual gulf between them. Although using the same terms, they were using different languages to describe different conceptions of divine reality. The incommensurability of these two outlooks is even more pronounced in John Capreolus's 15th-century defense of Aquinas's doctrine of predestination against Aureol's critique. See chapter 6, p. 166-168, below.

knowledge is neither active, nor causal with respect to extra-mental reality, and thus only an act of the will can predestine. These replies, especially the first and third, provide an excellent example of Aureol's voluntarist assumptions.[5] Aureol perceived an equivocation in Aquinas's use of the word "*ordo*" to describe predestination: Aquinas seemed to conflate the act of ordering and the order itself. If "*ordo*" is taken as "an order", then it exists in the divine mind as a passive object. In this sense predestination cannot be an order, since things existing as objects—"subjectively" in modern terms—in the intellect are, for Aureol, effects not causes.[6] Instead, Aureol insists that predestination is not an order, but an ordering:

> The predestination which is assumed to be in God is not a passion, but rather an action. But a foreknown order is not an action, since it is the same as that order which is assumed to be in reality. Thus, actively to predestine is to destine or to ordain; it is not, however, the order itself, but rather <the act of> forming the order. But the formed order and the formation of the order are not the same..."[7]

Of course, based on Aureol's doctrine of the attributes, ordering belongs to the will, and not the intellect, since ordering involves causality and action extrinsic to Deity.[8]

Although Aureol's attack on Aquinas reveals the differences between Aureol and the majority opinion of his day, it is his attack on Richard of Middleton (who was active as a student and Master of Theology at Paris from 1278 to 1286) which serves as a key to understanding the more immediate context in which Aureol developed his own position.[9] At least since Pannenberg, scholars have generally

---

[5] *Borghese 329*, f. 424rb: "Sed hic modus dicendi non videtur conveniens, talis enim ordo creaturae rationalis in finem vitae aeternae aut accipitur aliquid existens in intellectu divino obiective aut accipitur pro actu voluntatis, cuius est ordinare in finem, ut non sit aliud praedestinatio quam velle divinum sive propositum conducendi aliquas creaturas rationales in finem vitae aeternae."

[6] This notion is consistent with Aureol's conviction that (mental) acts and their contents are distinct. See Tachau, *Vision and Certitude*, pp. 93-94, 100-101.

[7] *Borghese 329*, f. 424va: "Praeterea, praedestinatio quae ponitur in Deo, non est passio, sed potius praedestinatio actio. Sed ordo praecognitus non est actio, cum sit idem cum ordine illo qui ponitur in re. Unde praedestinare active est destinare vel ordinare, non autem ipse ordo, sed potius formare ordinem. Ordo autem formatus et formatio ordinis non sunt idem; ergo id quod prius."

[8] Aureol does note in his first reply that Aquinas may also be understood as using "*ordo*" in the sense of ordering. In fact, Aquinas uses the term "*ordinare*", in the passages immediately preceding the ones cited by Aureol (*Summa*, v. 1, q. 23, a. 1, p. 271). This reading is unacceptable to Aureol because Aquinas says that providence and predestination involve ordering to some future end. As I showed in the previous chapter, Aureol claims that God does not will towards an end, nor does God's will tend towards the future.

[9] Richard of Middleton is generally considered the last important figure in the

accepted that 13th-century Franciscan theology understood predestination as an act of the intellect.[10] The situation, however, was not so
simple. Pannenberg made this judgment using the *Summa* attributed
to Alexander of Hales, the authenticity of which had been called into
doubt a few years before Pannenberg's study.[11] Although all medieval
authors assumed the authenticity of the text, the *Summa* was not consistent on this point with Hales's authentic gloss on the *Sentences*.

In glossing Lombard's text, Hales frames the question of whether
predestination is an act of will or intellect on the basis of a necessary
distinction among various meanings of the term "predestination".
Insofar as predestination is the divine purpose for conferring mercy,
it is an act of the will, but insofar as it is the foreknowledge of this
giving, it is an act of knowledge.[12] Bonaventure frames the question
similarly, saying that although he prefers ascribing predestination to
the will, it can also be ascribed to the intellect.[13] Also like Alexander,

"old" Franciscan school (i.e., before Scotus). This view was first advanced in the
20th century by E. Hocedez, *Richard de Middleton: sa vie, ses oevres, sa doctrine*, (Paris,
1925). Frederick Copleston, *A History of Philosophy, Volume II: Augustine to Scotus*,
(Garden City, NY, 1944), pp. 454-456 concurs with Hocedez. McGrath, *Iustitia Dei*,
p. 163, argues similarly for Middleton's soteriology in particular. It is always dangerous to generalize, but the differences between Middleton's treatment of predestination and those of 14th-century Franciscans such as Scotus, Aureol, and Ockham
are significant. Even though all of them are indebted to the semantic approach of
Hales and Bonaventure, Middleton supports the conclusions of Hales and
Bonaventure, while the 14th-century Franciscans use the traditional methodology
to break new ground.

[10] Pannenberg, *Skotus*, pp. 30-33; McGrath, *Iustitia*, v. 1, p. 134.

[11] Victorin Doucet, "The History of the Problem of the Authenticity of the
Summa", *Franciscan Studies* 7, (1947), pp. 26-41, 274-311. Doucet does point out that
the authenticity of the text was unquestioned until the 19th century.

[12] Alexander of Hales, *Glossa in quattor libros Sententiarum*, (Bonaventure, 1951-7), b.
I, d. 40, n. 10, p. b, p. 405: "Et videtur quod secundum diversas definitiones poni
debet in diversis generibus. Invenientur enim quatuor rationes praedestinationis,
quarum una est: 'praeperatio gratiae in praesenti' etc.; alia est: 'propositum miserendi'; tertia: 'praescientia beneficiorum Dei'; quarta: 'praeordinatio alicuius ad
gloriam'. Ex tertia definitione habetur quod sit in genere scientia, et ex prima quod
sit in genere potentiae, et ex secunda quod sit in genere voluntatis."

[13] Bonaventure, *Commentarius in Primum Librum Sententiarum Petri Lombardi*, in *Opera
omnia*, (Quaracchi, 1883), vol. 2, b. 1, q. 40, a. 1, q. 2, p. 705: "Conclusio: Praedestinatio, quae est causa gratiae et gloriae, importat et scientiam et potentiam et voluntatem, sed principalius est in genere voluntatis.

"Respondeo: Dicendum, quod cum praedestinatio significet divina essentiam ut
causam gratiae et gloriae, et hoc secundum ordinatam distributionem gratiae et gloriae, quantum est de se, non tantum importat scientiam, sed etiam voluntatem et
potentiam. Sed quoniam causalitas gratiae et gloriae attribuitur proprie voluntati ut
efficienti, sed scientiae ut disponenti, et potentiae ut exsequenti; ideo, etsi praedestinatio importet illa tria, tamen principalius est in genere voluntatis.

"Voluerunt tamen aliqui dicere, quod principalius est in genere scientiae, eo
quod in ratione praedestinationis cadit scientia in recto, sed voluntas in obliquo; est
enim praedestinatio scientia beneplaciti. Uterque modus dicendi satis est probabilis,
sed primus magis."

Bonaventure points out that "predestination" can be taken in several ways. Based on Alexander and Bonaventure, one can say that there was a traditional Franciscan methodological approach to the issue of predestination, which focused on the semantics of the important terms normally associated with this topic. While this approach had been only embryonic in Alexander's *Glossa*, it was fully developed by the author(s) of the *Summa* attributed to Alexander[14] and by Bonaventure, both in his commentary on the *Sentences* and in his *Summa*.[15]

The Franciscan approach to the issue of predestination goes beyond the typical Scholastic methodology of drawing relevant distinctions. In Aquinas and others, the relevant distinctions are between the act of predestination and its effects.[16] On this account, the term "predestination" simply signifies the divine purpose to predestine particular individuals. For the Franciscans, the problem of predestination revolves around the multiple significations of the term "predestination". Such a difference in approach may be philosophically and, strictly speaking, theologically insignificant; Aquinas and Bonaventure both arrive at an SPE understanding of predestination. Historically, however, the difference between the two approaches is important. It is no coincidence that the two earliest defenders of GE, Aureol and Ockham, are Franciscans. Each of them uses the Franciscan notion that "predestination" is a complex sign to redefine the process of predestination in a manner impossible for those to whom "predestination" simply signifies eternal divine election. Moreover, GE, as held by Aureol, Ockham, Holcot, and Biel has been misunderstood by many historians, since these historians have missed the innovative way in which each of these theologians uses "predestination".

---

[14] (Pseudo-)Alexander of Hales, *Summa*, pars 1, i, 1, tract. 5, s. 2, q. 4, c. 1, (Quarrachi, p. 316): "In nomine praedestinationis duo sunt: antecessio et destinatio et in destinatione tria: oportet enim quod sit alicuius et de aliquo et ad aliquid. Et ideo in praedestinatione sunt tria: unum ut principium, scilicet 'praeparatio', quo est; quod dicitur 'gloriae in futuro', dicit ut terminum ad quem est; quod dicitur 'gratiae in praesenti', dicit ut medium per quod est...

"Electio vero dicitur secundum duos modos: uno modo, ut connotet effectum separationis boni a malo...alio modo, ut connotet effectum assumptionis a minus bono ad melius..."

[15] Bonaventura, *In libros Sententiarum*, b. 1, d. 40, a. 1, q. 1, (Quarrachi, p. 703): "Dicendum, quod in praedestinatione non sunt nisi duo, scilicet principale significatum et connotatum. Principale significatum est divina essentia, connotatum vero est creatura, ut gratia et gloria et persona salvandi. Et haec duo importat praedestinatio cum ordinem antecessionis unius ad alterum ratione praepositionis."

[16] See below, p. 95.

This, then, is the context within which Aureol attacks Richard of Middleton.[17] Both utilize semantics at various points, and are thus firmly within the Franciscan "tradition", but they come to opposite conclusions.[18] Middleton argues that predestination is primarily an act of God's knowledge and only secondarily an act of God's will or power. Middleton's conception of practical knowledge implies that God's knowledge is extra-mentally causal, and that God's will and power function as agents carrying out the determination of the intellect:

> For predestination is practical foreknowledge of the salvation of someone and of the ordination of that person to salvation. But there is no practical divine foreknowledge, except with respect to things that are going to be done <by God>, and whatever is going to be done has been proposed by Him in eternity to be done in time and proposed from eternity that it be accomplished in time. Therefore, although 'predestination' formally labels practical foreknowledge of someone's salvation and the ordination of that person to salvation, it nevertheless includes the purpose for saving and ordaining the predestined person to salvation, and the power for bringing this about.[19]

To Aureol, Richard's conception of practical knowledge was essentially confused. According to Aureol's doctrine of the attributes, practicality (i.e. efficaciousness) was one of the features which made the will distinct from the intellect. Richard's confusion, Aureol argues, stems from his assumption that God has knowledge with respect to things that He is going to do. If God's knowledge were of things that He is going to do, then not only would divine foreknowledge be efficacious, but it would impose necessity on events.[20] On

---

[17] *Borghese 329*, f. 424va: "Propterea, dixerunt alii quod praedestinatio formaliter non est aliud quam praescientia practica salutis alicuius et ordinationis ipsius ad salutem; praescientia autem practica non est, nisi respectu eorum quae Deus facturus est."

[18] Richard uses a semantic argument similar to the ones found in Bonaventure to draw a distinction between predestination and its effects. Richard of Middleton, *Supra quattuor libros Sententiarum*, (Bresciae, 1591), vol. I, I, d. 40, a. 1, q. 1, p. 354a: "Cuius ratio est, quia praedestinare et praedestinari quantum ad principalem significatum realiter idem sunt, sed secundum rationem et secundum modum significandi differunt. Connotat tamen praedestinatio aliquid futurum in praedestinato, scilicet effectum finalis gratiae et gloriae, quia qui praedestinatus est vere habebit finalem gratiam et gloriam."

[19] *Ibid.*, p. 353b: "Praedestinatio enim est praescientia practica salutis alicuius et ordinationis ipsius in salute, sed praescientia Dei practica non est, nisi respectu eorum quae facturus est, et quicquid facturus est, proposuit ab aeterno se facturum in tempore et proposuit ab aeterno illud operari in tempore. Ergo praedestinatio quamvis formaliter dicat praescientiam practicam salutis alicuius et ordinationis ipsius in salutem, includit tamen propositum salvandi et ordinandi in salutem illum qui praedestinatus est, et potentiam haec faciendi."

[20] *Borghese 329*, ff. 424va-vb: "Praeterea, si aliqua scientia ordinationis hominis in

the contrary, God knows things as they have been done and actually exist.[21] But in this case, since the extramental object of the intellect already exists, divine knowledge cannot be efficacious with respect to that extramental object. Therefore, the intellect must be secondary to the will in the process of predestination.

Returning to the connotative distinction between the will and the intellect and the further connotative distinction between will as intrinsic ultimate love and extrinsic executive power, Aureol argues on that basis that efficacy should be primarily attributed to the divine will. He compares predestination, an example of this efficacy, to a practical syllogism. The major premise, which in a practical syllogism is a willed end, is God's pleasure in the salvation of all humans. Aureol argues that this is God's will on the basis of *I Timothy* 2:4: "God wills that all men be saved".[22] Aureol does, however, realize that all humans are not saved, so he adds that God's universal will to save all men is conditioned by the presence or absence of an obstacle to His saving grace. Therefore, *I Timothy* 2:4, as the major premise of the syllogism, should be interpreted in this way: God wills that all men who do not possess an obstacle to grace be saved. The minor premise, that someone does not possess an obstacle to grace, is affirmed by God's foreknowledge. The conclusion of the syllogism is the divine operation carrying out the end willed in the major premise.[23] Take the example of Peter for instance:

---

salutem intelligitur practica esse in Deo, aut illa erit scientia qua novit Deus salutem talis hominis esse futuram, non quidem sibi, sed isti nunc, aut erit illa scientia qua indistanter novit determinationem salutis hominis quam actualitas salvationis dat sibi, quae proprie 'praescientia' appellatur. Sed non potest dici quod haec ultima practica sit, ut declaratum est; nec etiam potest dici de prima quia talis scientia dictans practice in futurum quod Petrus salvabitur daret huic propositioni determinatam veritatem, 'Petrus salvabitur', et sic esset immutabile nec posset <oppositum> evenire; quod omnino dici non potest ut inferius apparebit. Ergo non est verum quod Deus habeat aliquam scientiam practicam per istum modum."

[21] *Ibid.*: "Nulla enim scientia quae non praecedit rem nec est ipsius, ut futura."

[22] This is my own translation of the text as it appears in the Vulgate. This rendering best captures Aureol's understanding of the verse.

[23] *Borghese 329*, f. 424vb: "Ubi considerandum secundum Philosophum 7 Ethicorum quod in syllogismo practico maior est universalis et volita, minor autem sumitur sensu, et tunc sequitur conclusio, quae est operatio seu volitio ponens immediate operationem. Verbi gratia in animo alicuius potest haec propositio esse quieta et determinata: 'volo omni tempore occurrente gustare lac'. Tunc, si contingat quod sensus sumat minorem sub dicendo de aliquo occurrente quod sit lac, statim sequitur operatio, scilicet potus lactis vel volitio particularis quam concomitatur haec operatio. Consimiliter ergo sciendum est quod Deus habet quandam complacentiam generalem in salutem omnis rationalis creaturae, secundum illud Apostoli primae ad Timotheum 2 dicentis quod 'vult omnes homines salvos fieri et ad agnitionem veritatis venire', et illud Iohannem 6, 'Haec autem est voluntas eius qui misit me, ut omne quod dedit mihi, non perdam ex eo'. Existente ergo hac complacentia

God wills that all men be saved provided that they do not possess an
obstacle to grace at the moment they die.

God (fore)knows that Peter does not possess an obstacle to grace at
the moment he dies.

. . . .

Therefore, God wills grace and glory for Peter.

Reprobation can also be described as a logical process; indeed, it
can even be described by a logical process parallel to that of predestination. In this case God's foreknowledge affirms that Judas does
possess an obstacle to grace. Therefore, God does not give grace
and glory to Judas. But "reprobation" for Aureol does not mean
merely "not predestined", and thus reprobation is more properly described by its own practical syllogism:

> ...but the lack of this <predestination> with respect to Judas is called
> "reprobation". <Reprobation>, however, is not only the lack <of
> predestination>, but the volition of eternal punishment arising from a
> different syllogism. For God wills, and on account of His justice is
> pleased in, the due punishment of those who finally persevere in sin.
> But <divine> foreknowledge affirms that Judas finally dies in a state
> of sin. And thereupon a volition of eternal damnation arises for Judas,
> and this is reprobation.[24]

Although predestination and reprobation can be described using this
logical model, Aureol does not claim that predestination is all three
parts of the syllogism taken together. Besides defining predestination
in terms of which attribute is its primary locus, Franciscan theologians, as we have seen, were concerned with the complex meanings
of "predestination" and "reprobation". For Aureol, therefore, the
second definitional aspect of the discussion is the distinction between
the primary and secondary meanings of "predestination" and "reprobation". While his voluntarist definition of predestination puts
him in the minority, his further semantic analysis allows him to defend the concept, "general election". Using a semantic approach to
the problem fits well with Aureol's use of connotation theory, and

---

generali in voluntate divina qua complacet in salute omnium hominum et omnis rationalis creaturae, nisi tamen illa obicem ponat, statim praescientia sumit minorem
sub ista, ostendendo quod Petrus pro nullo instanti obicem ponit. Iudas vero finaliter obicem ponit, et tunc infertur specialis volitio respectus Petri, non infertur
autem respectu Iudae. Haec ergo volitio particularis respectu Petri, qua Deo complacet in salute ipsius Petri 'praedestinatio' dicitur."

[24] *Ibid.*, f. 525ra: "Carentia vero illius respectu Iudae dicitur 'reprobatio'. Nec
solum carentia, immo volitio poenae aeternae quae infertur ex alio syllogismo; vult
enim Deus et complacet ex iustitia in poena debita peccatori finaliter perseveranti.
Praescientia autem subsumit quod Iudas finaliter moritur in peccato, et tunc infertur volitio aeternae damnationis pro Iuda."

his logical analogy here is based on the connotative distinction between the attributes. Each term of the syllogism represents one of
the attributes. Thus, the major premise represents God's loving will;
the minor represents God's knowledge; the conclusion represents
God's efficacious will:

> ...then we do not have the understanding that this order exists be-
> tween the intrinsic characteristics of foreknowledge and volition, but
> only between their connotates. For Deity <as divine delight> first
> connotes the salvation of all men, unless an obstacle is maintained, as
> a willed object. Next <divine foreknowledge> connotes Peter-not-
> maintaining-an-obstacle as a known object. Then, in the third place,
> <divine executive power> connotes as a willed object the salvation of
> Peter. And so with this <third> connotate Deity <as divine will> is
> called "a special volition for the salvation of Peter" (as if it were the
> conclusion of the prior syllogism), and is the active predestination by
> which...Peter is denominated as predestined.[25]

Even though a semantic approach to predestination is consonant
with the tradition of his order, Aureol does not follow the conclusions of the 13th-century Franciscan masters. The *Summa* attributed
to Alexander of Hales had distinguished between three significates of
"predestination", the principle one being divine foreknowledge,
while its secondary significates are grace and glory in the predestined. Bonaventure had claimed that "predestination" primarily signifies the divine essence, while it connotes grace and glory in the
predestined. Aureol reverses the emphasis of the distinction. Bonaventure and the author(s) of the *Summa* had been concerned with a
semantic analysis of "predestination" and claim that it signifies
something intrinsic to God. Aureol, on the other hand, is still concerned with a semantic analysis of "Deity", and his doctrine of the
attributes implicitly underlies this entire discussion. Since predestination has to do with God's relation to humans, "predestination" must
refer to a concept of "Deity" which connotes. Aureol has already
eliminated the possibility that "predestination" refers to divine
knowledge. Therefore, "predestination" must refer either to God's
intrinsic will (*complacentia*) or to His extrinsic will (*potestas*).

Aureol chooses the latter, and argues that "predestination" primarily refers to the volition whereby Peter is granted grace, while "repro-

---

[25] *Ibid.*: "Tunc non intelligimus quod sit iste ordo inter rationes praescientae et
volitionis, sed tantum inter connotata. Connotat namque Deitas primo salutem omnium hominum ut volitam, nisi obex ponatur; deinde connotat Petrum ut cognitum
in non ponendo obicem; et tunc tertio connotat salutem Petri ut volitam, et ita
Deitas cum isto connotato dicitur volitio specialis salutis Petri, quasi conclusio prioris syllogismi, et est activa praedestinatio qua existente in Deo, denominatur Petrus
quasi praedestinatus."

bation" refers to the volition whereby Judas is punished. Aureol's choice to identify predestination with God's volition of giving grace and glory places him outside the theological trends of his period.[26] Following the Vulgate translation of Paul's letters, Latin theology had defined predestination as the divine purpose for election. So, besides leaving the 13th-century Franciscan tradition, Aureol positions himself to reject the dominant position held by such authors as Aquinas, Giles of Rome, Durandus, and Hervaeus that "predestination" simply signifies the eternal will of God and that the volitions of giving grace or glory are only effects of predestination. It is partly due to this break with tradition that Aureol's doctrine of predestination can be construed as Pelagian, since his position allows him to stress human free will in ways that previous positions would not allow. Indeed, Aureol adopts this position in order *to avoid* the determinism that he perceived in the traditional understanding of predestination.

The basis for Aureol's rejection of the Scholastic definition of "predestination" as "divine purpose" is his understanding of the divine will. "Purpose", Aureol notes, commonly refers to a desire or something which tends toward the future.[27] However, as we have seen, Aureol holds that objects of the divine essence, as they are known and willed, are not related to the divine essence as future. He reiterates this point as it pertains to predestination:

> ...the divine intellect is not more abstract than the divine volition, but the intellect abstracts <its object> from all linear succession, so that something not be understood as past or future with respect to itself, but rather as lacking any distance. Therefore neither does the divine will will something as future with respect to <the intellect>. And consequently <the divine will> does not desire, nor does it purpose, because purpose and desire are tendencies of the will towards something as if it were distant and future; but rather God will be pleased in something as if it were not distant. And consequently that will by which <God> wills salvation for Peter, insofar as <Peter> does not maintain an obstacle, is not the purpose for giving grace and glory to Peter, but rather pleasure in the giving of grace and glory, not even as <the grace and glory> are simultaneous and present <to God>, but lacking distance.[28]

---

[26] I am excluding the Oxford *pactum* doctrines of predestination, since Aureol does not seem to have had any knowledge of them. I will deal with the difficult case of Scotus's definition of predestination and reprobation below; Scotus does, however, seem to imply a definition of predestination similar to Aureol's. I devote chapter 4 to the Oxford context.

[27] *Borghese 329*, ff. 425ra-rb: "Secunda vero propositio est quod nulla volitio intrinseca Deo consequens praescientiam respectu salutis Petri potest esse desiderium aut propositum vel actus alius voluntatis tendens in obiectum ut in futurum."

[28] *Ibid.*: "Praeterea, non est magis abstractus divinus intellectus quam divina volitio, sed intellectus abstrahit ab omni linea successiva, ut non intelligatur aliquid ut

According to Aureol, if one were to hold that the divine purpose for election is intrinsic to God, then several absurd conclusions must follow. First, if God intrinsically wills that Peter be saved in the future, Peter would be saved in the future even if he tried to resist God's grace. Such a position would be unacceptable, Aureol points out, since it would eliminate any grounds on the part of the predestined for fearing God.[29] Second, any identification of the purpose of election with God's intrinsic will would impugn divine immutability. Once God has given the grace to the predestined person, He would no longer have a purpose of giving grace.[30]

Yet, in order to hold this position, Aureol still had to deal with the Pauline passages which use the term "*propositum*". According to his method for natural theology, all concepts attributed to God must be subjected to his law of attribution. This also holds true in revealed theology, and this law functions also as an exegetical tool. The words of Paul, Aureol stresses, must be read with this in mind,

> For the saints <i.e., Apostles and the Church Fathers> say one thing and mean another, since they attribute words to God which convey imperfection. For they do not intend that there be any imperfection in God, but they strive, as much as they can, to express something higher. Therefore, the purpose about which the Apostle speaks does not signify that there is some desire or any will in God other than

---

praeteritum vel futurum respectu sui, sed potius ut indistans. Ergo nec divina voluntas vult aliquid ut futurum respectu sui. Et per consequens non desiderat nec proponit, quia propositum et desiderium sunt tendentiae voluntatis in aliquid distans et quasi futurum, sed potius complacebit Deus tanquam in aliquid non distans. Et per consequens illud velle quo vult salutem Petri, obicem non-ponentis, non est propositum dandi gratiam et gloriam Petro, sed potius complacentia in datione gratiae et gloriae, non quidem simultanea et raesenti, sed tamen penitus indistanti."

[29] *Ibid.*: "Praeterea, si velle divinum quo vult salutem Petri esset desiderium vel propositum in futurum, impossibile esset quin Petrus salvaretur. Nam divinum propositum dat determinationem pro illo tunc pro quo est, et ita in tota linea futuritionis salus Petri esset determinata, et per consequens in tota illa futuritione haec esset vera, 'Petrus salvabitur'. Immo ab aeterno fuisset vera. Declaratum est autem in praecedentibus quod ista existente vera, impossibile est quin Petrus salvetur aut saltem inevitabile et immutabile, quantumcumque Petrus ad oppositum conaretur. Hoc autem absonum est et abiciens timorem divinum, cum tamen scriptum sit: 'beatus homo, qui semper est pavidus' (Proverbia 28). Ergo volitio de qua loquimur, non potest esse actus aliquis qui sit tendentia in futurum."

[30] *Ibid.*, ff. 425rb-va: "Praeterea, si praedestinatio esset actus voluntatis divinae tendens in futurum per modum propositi et expectationis cum hoc quod est inconveniens quod propositum et expectatio sit in Deo, sequeretur quod aliquis actus nunc sit in Deo qui alioquando excluderetur ab eo. Si enim habet nunc propositum dandi gratiam et gloriam alicui praedestinato in futurum, cum dedit, iam non manet propositum dandi, nullus enim proponit se fecisse. Unde nihil est dictu 'propono cucurrisse' nec 'propono currere', si actu currentis. Semper enim propositum aspicit futurum, sed impossibile est quod aliquis actus cesset esse in Deo, ergo nunquam fuit tale propositum in eo."

being pleased, since God wills nothing except through willing His own essence.[31]

Using such an exegetical principle, Aureol has turned a text which seems to support his opponents into an argument for his own position. "*Propositum*" as Paul uses it does not refer to God's intrinsic will, but it does refer to predestination; therefore Paul must be referring to the extrinsic operations of God carrying out His elective will. Insofar as the operation occurs in time and relates to creatures existing in time, one can understand the divine operation as happening in the future; insofar as divine operation is the divine will of operation, it is not a purpose for the future. "Purpose" and "predestination" do not refer to God directly, but to a particular *connotate* of the divine essence: the infusion of grace and the gift of glory to an individual as this operation is an object of the will and knowledge of God.[32]

Aureol gives the formal and complete definition of "predestination" as the divine "operation, foreknown from eternity, whereby God confers grace and glory upon the saved".[33] Aureol has thus defined the intrinsic will of God out of any concept of predestination. But predestination is not the only aspect of the soteriological process. Besides predestining and reprobating, God also elects (*electio, eligere*) and loves (*dilectio, diligere*) the person who is saved. Aureol explains the distinction between these acts by referring back to his previous logical analogy and its underlying semantic distinction. While predestination is represented by the conclusion of the practical syllogism, election is represented by the major and minor premises. The election of Peter is a combination of God's intrinsic will (*complacentia*) to save all men who do not maintain an obstacle to grace and His foreknowledge that Peter is among those who do not

---

[31] *Ibid.*, f. 426ra: "Non procedunt ergo instantiae. Prima siquidem non, sancti enim aliud dicunt et aliud intelligunt, cum verba imperfectionem importantia Deo attribuant, non enim intendunt quod aliqua imperfectio sit in Deo sed aliquid altius quod nituntur exprimere, sicut possunt. Propositum ergo de quo loquitur Apostolus non significat in Deo esse aliquod desiderium aut velle aliud, nisi complacere, cum nihil Deus velit nisi volendo suam essentiam."

[32] *Ibid.*, f. 426rb: "Non ergo praedestinatio dicitur causa gratiae et gloriae in praedestinato ratione volitionis complacentiae, sed quia includit voluntatem operationis ab aeterno praevisam in qua consistit completive ratio praedestinationis, ut in sequentibus apparebit."

[33] *Ibid.*: "Quod voluntas operationis divinae seu voluntas signi quae dicitur operatio gratiae et salutis praevisa ab aeterno respectu quorundam dicitur praedestinatio formaliter et completive. Tertia quoque propositio est quod voluntas signi quae dicitur operatio qua Deus confert gratiam et gloriam salvatis praevisa ab aeterno dicitur praedestinatio formaliter et completive, et ista est propositum miserendi, non aliquis actus alius intrinsecus voluntatis."

maintain an obstacle to grace. Divine love for the individual elect
and predestined person is His intrinsic and necessary love (*complacen-*
tia) for those who have been infused by grace.[34]

> ...the love (*dilectio*) of Peter is the pleasure (*complacentia*) of God in
> Peter having been infused by grace and saved, but election, as the
> taking up of Peter out of all others, is the application of that universal
> will, by which God wills that all men be saved, to Peter by virtue of
> foreknowledge. And according to this election precedes, predestina-
> tion follows, and then love (*dilectio*)—according to our way of under-
> standing, even though they are all the same from eternity. And this
> order should be understood connotatively, because Deity first con-
> notes Peter as elected and separated from others (by virtue of the syl-
> logism). Next <he should be considered> as predestined, and thus as
> justified and blessed, since that is the end of the divine operation.
> Next <he should be considered> as loved (*dilectum*) and as an end of
> divine pleasure.[35]

In light of Aureol's concern with determinism it may be surprising
that foreknowledge plays a role in his understanding of predestination, but according to the logical analogy that he has employed, one
of the premises is foreknowledge of the presence or absence of an
obstacle to grace. For Aureol, "foreknowledge" can be successfully
attributed to God. He explains that God knows things in two ways.
First, He knows actual things which have been brought about by
other causes. An example of this would presumably be culpable sin.
Second, He "fore"knows things as He Himself is the cause.[36] In both
cases God's "fore"knowledge depends on a will determining the actuality of the object. In the case of predestination God knows the determination of an actual infusion of grace. This knowledge is "from
eternity", since divine knowledge is abstracted from all time; this

---

[34] God necessarily loves those who have been infused by grace, because He necessarily loves those things participating in His goodness. Aureol argues this point
more thoroughly in his treatise on acceptation. See Vignaux, *Justification*, pp. 80ff.,
for the relevant texts.

[35] *Borghese 329*, f. 426va: "Complacentia vero Dei in Petro gratificato et salvato
est Petri dilectio, applicatio vero universalis voluntatis qua Deus vult omnem hominem salvum fieri ad Petrum virtute praescientiae appellatur electio, quasi aliis omis-
sis, Petri assumptio. Et secundum hoc praecedit electio, sequitur praedestinatio, et
deinde dilectio secundum nostrum modum intelligendi, quamvis omnia ista sint ab
aeterno. Et intelligatur ordo iste in connotando, quia Deitas primo connotat Petrum
ut electum et segregatum ab aliis, virtute illius syllogismi, deinde ut praedestinatum,
sic est ut iustificatum et beatum, quia ut terminum divinae operationis, deinde ut
dilectum et terminum divinae complacentiae."

[36] *Ibid.*, f. 426rb: "Sed quia non solum Deus novit actualitates rerum contingentium quae ponuntur in actu per causas alias, immo etiam praenovit illas quae ponuntur ab ipso, necesse est dicere quod novit ab aeterno illam collationem gratiae et
gloriae quam fecit in Petro in tempore."

knowledge is "fore"knowledge because, with respect to creatures in time, God seems to know the operation before it happens.

Aureol's definitions of "predestination", "reprobation", and "election" are not merely unusual, but are the crucial issues at stake in the later reaction of Rimini and the development of double-particular election. Although working from a mainstream theological tradition, Aureol has developed a doctrine of predestination unlike any in Latin theology. For Aureol there is no eternal or intrinsic will for the salvation or damnation of any particular individual. Instead, God's elective will is general, referring to types of people (i.e., those lacking an obstacle to grace). Furthermore, predestination and reprobation are not intrinsic to God, but are temporal actions extrinsic to Deity itself. In the entire process particular individuals are only objects of the intrinsic divine will as they are predestined or reprobate. God delights in the predestination of a person infused with grace and also delights in the damnation of a person resisting His grace.

The Cause of Predestination and Reprobation

Aureol claims that there is a cause on the part of the reprobate of their reprobation and, more importantly, that there is a cause on the part of the predestined of their predestination. Of course, Aureol does not mean that God elects some and not others on account of merit. According to his view of general election, God's election does not consider individuals, so it cannot be effected by the actions of individuals. However, by the same argument, the carrying out of God's general elective will for particular people must have some cause in the individual, since God wills all men to be saved, but not all men are saved. This leads Aureol to argue that there is some cause on the part of the predestinated and the reprobate for their respective states. Even on Aureol's definition of predestination, however, this position can easily be construed as Pelagian. For Aureol, "predestination" refers to the volition for giving grace; but if the volition for giving grace depends on something in the recipient, it does not seem to be grace at all. But this is not in any way Aureol's intention. As I will show, he vigorously attacks any position which implies a meritorious cause for predestination. Yet, he is not satisfied with the theory of single-particular election which had been developed to avoid Pelagianism. For Aureol, SPE was not sufficient for holding to the thin line between Pelagianism and determinism. For those theologians who identified predestination and reprobation with election, single-particular election leads to determinism. For those, such as Scotus, who define "predestination" and "reprobation" as Aureol does, the result is Pelagianism.

Although Aureol eventually argues for *some* basis in the predestined, he emphatically rejects any argument which holds that man can merit predestination.[37] By "merit" Aureol seems to mean any positive action on the part of the predestined. He reveals this attitude in his refutation of an anonymous opinion which seems to be Aureol's own construction of a stock Pelagian position.[38] This opinion rejects absolute predestination, in favor of one based simply on the foreseen good use of free will. On the face of it, there seem to be many benefits to such a position. In the first place, it preserves divine justice, since God does not seem to reprobate arbitrarily. It also preserves the contingency of predestination and reprobation and leaves mankind with some role in the justification process. Although these are advantages that Aureol will try to preserve in his own opinion, he rejects this version on three grounds. First, Aureol introduces the popular example of boys who die immediately after baptism. Doctrine holds that these boys will be saved. But if one holds a doctrine of predestination based on foreseen merits, one must say that these boys would be reprobate because they have no opportunity to exercise free will. Nor will Aureol accept the utterly ridiculous (*omnino absonum*) position that God predestines some of these boys on

---

[37] It should be noted that the examples of modern Pelagian opinions which Aureol singles out are the same (with the obvious exception of Aureol's own opinion) as the ones which Rimini attacks. Thus, according to the editors of Rimini's *Lectura* he knows Thomas of England's doctrine through his reading of Aureol's *Scriptum*. Rimini, *Lectura*, d. 40-41, a. 1, (vol. 3, p. 325).

[38] *Borghese 329*, ff. 436vb-437ra: "Propterea dixerunt alii quod bonus usus liberi arbitrii, ut praevisus a Deo, causa est praedestinationis illius qui bene usurus est gratia et libero arbitrio. Et per oppositum praescientia usus mali causa est reprobationis in aliis. Et secundum hoc salvatur melius divina iustitia et contingentia praedestinationis et reprobationis. Non erunt enim necessaria absolute, sed ex suppositione, scilicet supposito usu bono qui aeternaliter praevidetur. Sed hic modus dicendi non videtur posse stare. Constat enim quod pueri qui <sine> baptismo moriuntur reprobati sunt, qui vero statim baptizati decedunt, dicuntur praedestinati. Sed hos Deus non praevidit aeternaliter esse bene usuros libero arbitrio et illos male, quia non fuerunt usi. Ergo, talis praescientia non potuit esse causa quod isti essent praedestinati aeternaliter et illi reprobati. Et si dicatur, quod praevidit Deus, si vixissent, bene vel mali usuros, non valet, quia secundum hoc tantum haberet de merito puer, si vixisset baptizatus per unum annum tantum, quantum si vixisset per mille. Praevidisset namque Deus omnes bonos usus liberi arbitrii quos habiturus esset in millenario annorum, et secundum hos praedestinasset et maiorem gloriam praeparasset. Quod omnino absonum est. Praeterea, effectus praedestinationis non potest esse causa ipsius, sed bonus usus liberi arbitrii est effectus praedestinationis. Ergo, non potest esse quantumcumque praevisus bonus usus causa praedestinationis. Praeterea, Magister in littera reprobat illum modum, et Apostolus Ad Titum 3, ubi dicit quod 'non ex operibus iustitiae quae fecimus nos, sed secundum suam misericordiam salvos nos fecit'. Constat enim quod si usus, ut praevisus, esset causa praedestinationis, non solum salvi essemus secundum Dei misericordiam, immo secundum iustitiam aliqualem."

account of good works that they would have performed, had they lived. Second, good use of free will is an effect of predestination, and an effect of something cannot also be its cause. Third, citing *Titus* 3, Aureol claims that predestination is an effect of God's mercy, not of His justice; but if predestination were based on foreseen merits it would also be an effect of God's justice.

Henry of Ghent had presented an attempt to preserve God's justice and mercy along with human free will which is more sophisticated than the previous anonymous opinion.[39] Saying that God would be unjust to elect arbitrarily, Henry had postulated possible reasons why God predestines some and not others. He claims that man's good use of free will is a result of divine grace cooperating with man's free will. So, inasmuch as good use of free will proceeds from grace, it is an effect of predestination; inasmuch as it proceeds from the human will, it can be a reason for predestination. It is significant that Henry does not say that natural good use of the free will is a meritorious cause of predestination. He is not, after all, attempting to attribute temporal causes to the divine will, but merely postulating possible reasons for the choices that God makes in order to make those choices seem less arbitrary.

For Aureol this position raises more problems than it solves. Specifically, he does not think that this position successfully deals with the problem of children dying immediately after baptism; if they do not have the opportunity to have good use of free will, they cannot have cooperating grace.[40] Thus, for Aureol, the problem of

---

[39] *Ibid.*: "Opinio Henrici 6 quodlibeto, quaestio 18. Eapropter dixerunt alii praedictum modum exponentes quod aliqua causa quaerenda est ex parte praedestinati et reprobati. Tum quia in omnino aequalibus nulla videtur esse electio. Praedestinatio autem electionem includit: 'elegit enim nos ante mundi constitutionem', secundum Apostolum, quare oportet diversitatem aliquam reperiri inter electos et non electos. Tum quia in omnibus operibus Dei concurrit misericordia et iustitia. Non esset autem aliqua iustitia, si nulla alia ratio maior esset in praedestinato quam reprobato. Dixerunt ergo isti quod usus liberi arbitrii bonus non solum est ex gratia, immo liberum arbitrium cooperatur active, et non solum passive acceptus. Ergo, talis usus, in quantum est a gratia, effectus est praedestinationis; in quantum vero a libero arbitrio, potest esse ratio aliqualis de congruo respectu praedestinationis. Ita quod bonus usus praevisus in aliquo perseverare usque in finem ab ultima iustificatione potest esse causa in generali, quare aliqui eliguntur, quamvis de hoc particulari vel illo iudicare temerarium sit, quia nemo novit bonum usum finalem alicuius in particulari. Et sic intellegitur verbum Augustini super Iohannem, cum ait, 'noli iudicare, si non vis errare'. Sed hic modus dicendi non evadit difficultatem de parvulis qui non sunt usum liberi arbitrii habituri, nec cooperabuntur gratiae, ut talis cooperatio possit assignari pro causa praedestinationis eorum."

[40] *Ibid.*: "Sed hic modus dicendi non evadit difficultatem de parvulis qui non sunt usum liberi arbitrii habituri, nec cooperabuntur gratiae, ut talis cooperatio possit assignari pro causa praedestinationis eorum."

children dying immediately after baptism not only negates the possibility of meritorious causes on the part of the predestined of their predestination, but also any possible non-causal reason on the part of the predestined that would serve to reveal the compatibility of God's will and His justice in His election.

Aureol's refutation of Thomas of England[41] rejects yet another attempt at preserving man's free will, God's mercy, and God's justice.[42] Thomas distinguishes between two kinds of good use of free will. By his own natural ability (*ex puris naturalibus*) man is capable of performing a morally good act. This is due to the general influence of God which is natural to all men.[43] This type of good use of free will is a meritorious cause of predestination *de congruo*. The second use of free will, which is meritorious *de condigno*, can be performed only in a state of grace and is an effect of predestination. For Thomas, as Aureol cites him, this distinction solves the problem of boys who die immediately after baptism, because God rewards according to the quantity of works done. Thus God could give a lesser reward than would be given for works that would have been done had they lived.

This does not, however, solve the problem for Aureol, who draws a distinction between unconditional (*absolute*) causes and effects and conditional (*ex suppositione*) causes and effects. An unconditional effect cannot have a conditional cause, because,

> whenever something is a cause of some effect, the effect ought to be considered in the same way that the cause is considered, so that, if a

---

[41] I have not yet identified this person. The most likely candidate is Thomas of Wilton, who seems to have influenced Aureol in other areas. See McGrath, *Iustitia Dei*, vol. 1, p. 149.

[42] *Borghese 329*, f. 437rb: "Opinio Thomae Anglicae. Et ideo dixerunt alii quod usus liberi arbitrii potest intelligi quod sit bonus dupliciter. Primo quidem bonitate moris qui est in potestate nostra supposita influentia generali Dei, qua bonitate operationes virtutum moralium de quibus tractat Philosophus bonae sunt; et in illam potest homo ex puris naturalibus. Secundo vero bonitate supernaturali et gratuita per quam aliquis dicitur Deo gratus, dilectus, et acceptus. Loquendo, ergo, de bonitate prima bonus usus praedestinationis esse causa potest, non quidem de condigno, sed de congruo et dispositione. Loquendo vero de bonitate secundo modo, sic bonu usu, est praedestinationis effectus; et ad hunc intellectum currunt auctoritates. Instantia vero de parvulis solvitur secundum istos, quia licet praedestinatio vel reprobatio finalis habeat pro causa congruente bonam vel malam voluntatem praevisam ipsius praedestinati vel reprobati, quantitas tamen praemii non solum attenditur penes voluntatem, sed penes continuitatem boni operis et quantitatem laboris. Licet, ergo, puer praedestinatus sit propter bonum usum quem habiturus esset, non tamen aequaliter praemiabitur, sicut si tempore multo cum illo bono usu vixisset."

[43] While late-medieval theologians disagree as to the level of benefits received in God's general grace, all admit that humans as creatures receive the general preserving grace by which God maintains His creation. For a discussion of the 14th-century debate, see Burger, "Der Augustinschueler".

'cause is considered unconditionally (*absolute*), then the effect is considered unconditionally, but if <the cause is considered> from a supposition, then the effect will be from the supposition. But good use of free will is considered a cause of predestination according to some. In children who have died after baptism, however, this use is not considered unconditionally, but from a supposition, because, supposing that he had lived, he would have had use of this sort. Therefore, he is to be considered predestined with this condition, namely, supposing that he had lived into the future, God would have predestined him... Likewise, therefore, if he had lived and had good use <of free will>, he would have been predestined, but since he did not live, nor did he have <good use of free will>, he was not predestined.[44]

Aureol's analysis rests on a logical distinction captured in the use of the indicative and subjunctive moods. In a hypothetical claim conveyed by the structure "if...then", the consequent to a contrary-to-fact antecedent must be stated in the subjunctive. For example, this statement's grammatical construction correctly captures the logical distinction Aureol is drawing: "if he had lived and done good works, (then) he *would* have been predestined". We are entitled to state the consequent in the indicative ("he is predestined"), only if the situation stated by the antecedent comes about (i.e, that he actually lives after baptism and does good works). In the instance at issue, however, the boys did not live, so they cannot be predestined to any degree of reward.

Aureol next turns to the conception of SPE, specifically the versions held by Thomas Aquinas and John Duns Scotus. This is a switch in emphasis that should not go unnoticed. Although Aureol would not argue for a predestination based on merit, he considers the ability of humans to reject grace to be crucial for the preservation of free will. Therefore, there must be more to reprobation than the lack of a will to save on God's part. Aureol rejects Aquinas's view entirely. Scotus's position, on the other hand, provides a basis, along with older Franciscan assumptions, for a doctrine which de-

---

[44] *Borghese 329*, f. 437va: "Praeterea, quandocumque aliquid est causa effectus alicuius, eo modo quo ponitur illa causa, poni debet effectus, ut si absolute ponitur causa, ponetur absolute effectus. Si vero ex suppositione et effectus erit ex suppositione, sed bonus usus liberi arbitrii ponitur causa praedestinationis secundum istos. In parvulo, autem, post baptismum defuncto ponitur usus iste non absolute, sed ex suppositione, quia, si vixisset, usum huiusmodi habuisset. Ergo, et ipsa praedestinatio ponenda est circa ipsum cum ista conditione, quod scilicet, si viveret in futurum, Deus ipsum praedestinasset. Et confirmatur, quia certum est quod, si vixisset et plura bona fecisset, maiorem gloriam habuisset quam tamen modo non habet. Pari, ergo, ratione, si vixisset et bonum usum habuisset, praedestinatus fuisset, sed quia nec vixit, nec habuit, praedestinatus non fuit."

parts significantly from both the 13th-century and contemporary Scotist trends in his order.

Aquinas's position is an example of SPE account on which predestination and reprobation are intrinsic to God. As we have seen, Aquinas considered predestination to be something intrinsic to God; reprobation is also intrinsic to God. They differ, however, in that predestination is a positive act, while reprobation is not a positive act. Aquinas defines "reprobation" as an example of God's permissive will by which God does not impede the actions of creatures.[45] In the case of reprobation this means that God allows some to fall into sin, rather than order them to eternal life and give them grace and glory.[46] The reprobate are not objects of election; they are left out of the soteriological process.

For Aquinas, then, any explanation of the causes of predestination and reprobation depends on a distinction between predestination and its effects. There is no cause on the part of the predestined for their predestination or on the part of the reprobate for their reprobation.[47] Causes, however, can be attributed to effects of predestination, provided a further distinction is made. There are two kinds of effects of predestination: particular and general. A particular effect of predestination can be the cause of another particular effect of predestination. For instance, glory is the *final* cause of grace and merit, because God's glory revealed in saving the elect is an end to which God's will is directed, and grace and merit are means by which this end is brought about. Thus, merit and grace are the *material* causes of glory, because God saves and glorifies the elect on account of the presence of grace and merit in them. In general (i.e., in taking all ef-

---

[45] *Summa*, q. 19, a. 12, (Leonine, vol. 4, p. 250): "...quod huiusmodi signa voluntatis dicuntur ea, quibus consuevimus demonstrare nos aliquid velle. Potest autem aliquis declarare se velle aliquid, vel per se ipsum, vel per alium. Per se ipsum quidem, inquantum facit aliquid, vel directe, vel indirecte et per accidens...Indirecte autem, inquantum non impedit operationem; nam removens prohibens dicitur movens per accidens, ut dicitur in VII Physicorum Et quantum ad hoc dicitur signum permissio."

[46] *Ibid.*, a. 3, p. 274: "Sic igitur, sicut praedestinatio est pars providentiae respectu eorum qui divinitus ordinantur in aeternam salutem; ita reprobatio est pars providentiae respectu illorum qui ab hoc fine decidunt. Unde reprobatio non nominat praescientia tantum: sed aliquid addit secundum rationem, sicut et providentia, ut supra dictum est. Sicut enim praedestinatio includit voluntatem permittendi aliquem cadere in culpam, et inferendi damnationis poenam pro culpa."

[47] *Ibid.*, a. 5, pp. 276-277: "Nullus ergo fuit ita insanae mentis, qui diceret merita esse causam divinae predestinationis, ex parte praedestinantis. Sed hoc sub quaestione vertitur, utrum ex parte effectus, praedestinatio habeat aliquam causam. Et hoc est quaerere, utrum Deus praeordinavit se daturum effectum praedestinationis alicui, propter merita aliqua..."

fects in common), however, the effects of predestination have no temporal, created cause.[48]

Yet God does predestine and reprobate for a reason, according to Aquinas. Both predestination and reprobation represent divine goodness: predestination represents the mercy of God, while reprobation represents His justice. Aquinas argues that God permits evil to happen in order that more good may result, so that He may reveal His just goodness by reprobating sinners.[49]

In Aureol's response to Aquinas we have an example of two theologians operating on different assumptions. Those things which Aquinas calls the effects of predestination Aureol calls predestination itself. The goal of each of Aureol's replies to Aquinas is to deny any divine cause for reprobation and assign a human cause to it—without, however, arguing that the divine will depends on human action. If we are to understand Aureol's arguments here against Aquinas we must remember that concerning the most basic points at issue, the two theologians argue from incommensurable positions. For Aquinas, reprobation is part of the *intrinsic* will of God, and therefore it can have only a divine cause; for Aureol, reprobation is an *extrinsic* operation of the divine will occurring in time, and therefore it can have a created cause without that cause determining God's intrinsic will.

Furthermore, in responding to Aquinas, Aureol is addressing a position held by other important authors, notably Giles of Rome and Durand de Saint-Pourcain, who shared similar understandings

---

[48] *Ibid.*: "Dicendum est ergo quod effectum praedestinationis considerare possumus dupliciter. Uno modo, in particulare. Et sic nihil prohibet aliquem effectum praedestinationis esse causam et rationem alterius: posteriorem quidem prioris, secundum rationem causae finalis; priorem vero posterioris, secundum causae meritoriae, quae reducitur ad dispositionem materiae. Sicut si dicamus quod Deus praeordinavit se daturum alicui gloriam ex meritis; et quod praeordinavit se daturum alicui gratiam, ut mereretur gloriam. Alio modo potest considerari praedestinationis in communi. Et sic impossibile est quod totus effectus in communi habeat aliquam causam ex parte nostra."

[49] *Ibid.*, pp. 277-278: "...dicendum quod ex ipsa bonitate divina ratio sumi potest praedestinationis aliquorum, et reprobationis aliorum. Sic enim Deus dicitur omnia propter suam bonitatem fecisse, ut in rebus divina bonitas repraesentatur. Necesse est autem quod divina bonitas, quae in se est una et simplex, multiformiter repraesentatur in rebus; propter hoc quod ad completionem universi requiruntur diversi gradus rerum, quarum quaedam altum, et quaedam infimum locum teneat in universo. Et multiformitas graduum conservetur in rebus, Deus permittit aliqua mala fieri, ne multa bona impediantur, ut supra dictum est.

"Sic igitur consideramus totum genus humanum, sicut totam rerum universitatem. Voluit igitur Deus in hominibus, quantum ad aliquos, quos praedestinat, suam repraesentare bonitatem per modum misericordiae, percando; et quantum ad aliquos, quos reprobat, per modum iustitiae, puniendo. Et haec est ratio quare Deus quosdam eligit, et quosdam reprobat."

of SPE.[50] Both authors had distinguished between the divine will and its object or effect;[51] moreover, like Aquinas, they had claimed (a) that the divine will has no exterior cause, (b) that the divine will is the only cause of its effects taken together, and (c) that the particular effects of the divine will can be in a causal relationship to one another. While these authors had not maintained identical positions, from Aureol's standpoint they are of a kind, differing only in degree. By rejecting Aquinas's understanding of the causes of predestination, Aureol has rejected what was probably the most popular position on predestination then current, one defended by the most influential theologians of two of the three major mendicant orders. This was one position that the Dominican Order's most prominent Thomist (Hervaeus) and its most prominent black sheep (Durandus) held in common; both were less influential than Giles of Rome, whose theology dominated the Augustinian order.

Aureol rejects the argument that the divine decision to predestine and reprobate is caused by the pleasure of God's will to reveal His justice. Aureol cites Biblical texts which support his claim that predestination alone reveals both mercy and justice:

> But even if no one were damned, still the mercy and justice of God would be sufficiently revealed. For in the glory of the elect both are revealed. Mercy, of course, <is revealed>, because it is written that according to His mercy He makes us saved (*Titus* 3); but justice too <is revealed>, because the Apostle (*II Timothy* 4:8) says that the crown of justice which God the just judge will give to him, has been reserved for him on the day <of judgment>. Therefore, the revealing of <mercy and justice> does not seem to be the cause whereby some are elect and some are reprobate.[52]

When Aureol's reading of *I Timothy* 2:4 is taken into account this position becomes even clearer, since on his interpretation, God's elective will refers only to types of people. Moreover, His elective will allows for the possibility that all people may be of the type that

---

[50] Giles of Rome, *In libros Sententiarum*, (Frankfurt, 1969), I, d.41, pp. 215-219; Durandus, I. d. 41, pp. 109-111.

[51] Giles distinguishes between "*velle*" and "*volitum*", while Durand uses the terms "*actus volitatis seu actus volendi*" and "*ipsius rei volitae*" to make the same distinction. See Giles, *op.cit.*, p. 217; for Durand, see *op.cit.*, p. 110.

[52] *Borghese 329*, f. 437vb: "Sed dato quod nullus esset damnatus adhuc sufficienter Dei misericordia et iustitia relucerent. Nam in gloria electorum utramque relucet. Misericordia quidem, quia scriptum est quod 'secundum suam misericordiam salvos nos fecit', Ad Titum 3; iustitia vero, quia II Timotheum 4 dicit Apostulus quod 'reposita est sibi corona iustitiae quam reddet ei Dominus in illa die iustus iudex'. Ergo, relucentia istorum non videtur esse causa, quod aliqui sint electi et alii reprobati."

are saved. The types are made distinct, not through divine election, but through human free will. Hence, Aureol argues further that, if the only cause of reprobation were God's will to reveal His justice, then God would be the cause of evil because He ordains some to sin. If God's justice is to be preserved (as well as human free will), God must reprobate on account of some culpability on the part of the reprobate.[53]

If Aureol's views are shaped in part by the deficiencies he perceives in the dominant response of his day, his relationship to his own Franciscan tradition is, as we have seen, even more complex. The Franciscan discussion of the causes of predestination and reprobation depends on the aforementioned semantic approach to the issue.[54] We recall that the author(s) of the *Summa* attributed to Alexander of

---

[53] *Ibid.*, ff. 438ra-b: "Secundo vero deficit in eo quod ait non esse aliquam causam in speciali, quare iste praedestinatus sit et ille reprobatus, sed hoc esse solum ex simplici voluntate divina et pro libito eius. Omnis enim qui pro libito voluntatis aliquem affligit et punit et in peccatum labi permittit, ad hoc solum ut puniat et affligat, crudelis est et iniustus, delectatur enim per se in poenis. Sed si pro libito voluntatis Deus aliquem reprobaret, sequeretur quod delecteretur per se in poena et pro suo libito vellit affligere et punire. Et ad hunc finem permitteret de hominibus quod peccarent, ut fatiaretur poenis eorum. Ergo, erit Deus crudelis et iniustus, et cum hoc absonum, sit magis absonum fuerit dicere quod aliquem reprobet pro libito voluntatis. Praeterea licet in carentibus sensu et experientia mali possit artifex disponere pro libito voluntatis absque nota credulitatis et iniustitia, utpote aedificator potest lapides ponere istum inferius, et illum superius in loco magis honorabili vel minus absque nota iniuriae. Et similiter figulus ex eadem massa potest facere vas in honorem et vas in contumeliam absque hoc quod iste iniurietur; et similiter Deus absque iniuria potest ponere unam partem materiae sub forma ignis et aliam sub forma terrae. Nihilominus in habentibus experientiam boni et mali, honoris et contumeliae, istud fieri non potest absque iniuriae, debitum est naturae, ut fiat sub perfectione qua aperte nata est sibi inesse. Et ideo non est absque iniuria facere hominem in sempiterna tristitia et miseria absque eius demerito pro solo libito facientis. Sed sic esset in proposito secundum istum modum dicendi. Ergo, non est verum quod Deus sic reprobet et eligat pro libito voluntatis. Et si dicatur quod Apostolus utitur exemplo illo de figulo, non valet utique, quia loquitur de massa corrupta per peccatum originale quo supposito nulla iniuriatur, si eo non redempto ab originali, alium misericorditer purget et redimat, nec per hoc sequitur quod reprobet absque culpa pro libito voluntatis, sicut fingunt positores praedicti. Praeterea, licet in gratuitatis possit tribuere plus vel minus cui vult distributor absque ullo praeiudicio iniustitiae. Non tamen verum est, quia possit cui vult poenam infligere absque iniuria, et sic intelligitur verbum patrisfamilias, 'an non licet mihi quod volo facere, plus scilicet minusve cui voluero tribuendo'. Non, autem, cui voluero poenam pro libito infligendo, sed in reprobatione poena infligitur. Ergo, no potest esse absque iniuria quod fiat reprobatio absque causa pro solo libito voluntatis."

[54] The failure to note the significance of the semantic approach is probably the greatest flaw in Pannenberg's otherwise fine analysis of Franciscan theology (Pannenberg, *Skotus*, pp. 77-81). His claim that Franciscan theology before Scotus argued for a predestination based on foreseen merits is not true if by "predestination" one means the elective will or knowledge of the divine essence. The major Franciscan sources all deny that God is intrinsically motivated to predestine or reprobate on account of merit.

Hales claims that the terms "predestination" and "reprobation" can signify three different things. The principal significate of both "predestination" and "reprobation" is God's foreknowledge of and preparation for the giving or withholding of grace. The terms can also signify the two secondary or additional significates of "predestination" (grace and glory) and "reprobation" (iniquity and punishment). While there is no meritorious cause of God's foreknowledge, meritorious causes can be attributed to the secondary significates of "predestination" and "reprobation", even though, according to the *Summa*, causes do not play the same role in reprobation as they do in predestination. For instance, the term "predestination" can also signify the two effects of its principal significate: the infusion of grace and glory. While the infusion of grace does not have a meritorious cause, that very infusion of grace is itself a meritorious cause of glory. Likewise, the term "reprobation" can also signify the two effects of its principal significate, namely, the present sinful state of the reprobate and his impending punishment. But unlike the secondary significates of "predestination", both secondary significates of "reprobation" have meritorious causes on the part of the reprobate.[55]

Bonaventure had come to a similar conclusion. He, too, claims that one must distinguish among three different significates of the terms "predestination" and "reprobation".[56] The first is the eternal

---

[55] Alexander of Hales, *Summa*, pars I, inq. I, tract. 5, q. 4, tit. 1, pp. 228-229: "In nomine praedestinationis et reprobationis intelliguntur plura. In praedestinatione enim intelligitur praescientia et gratia et gloria respectu quorum est praedestinatio. Similiter in reprobatione sunt tria: praescientia et praesens iniquitas et poena futura. Cum ergo invenitur in auctoritatibus Sanctorum quod praedestinatio vel reprobatio sit ex meritis, respondendum quod si hic dicatur quantum principale significatum, sic non sunt ex meritis; si quantum ad connotatum, sic sunt ex meritis, sed differenter ex parte praedestinationis et reprobationis. Nam ex parte praedestinationis nec ex meritis, nec etiam primum connotatum, quod est 'infusio gratiae', sed 'collatio gloriae' ex meritis est. Ex parte autem reprobationis aliter est: nam principale significatum est 'praescientia et praeparatio', connotatum 'praesens iniquitas et futura poena'. Patet ergo quod reprobatio quantum ad principale significatum non est ex meritis, sed quantum ad connotata potest dici quod est ex meritis."

[56] Bonaventure, *Commentarius*, I, d. 41, a. 1, q. 1, (vol. 2, pp. 728-729): "Ad hoc intelligendum notandum, quod in praedestinatio tria intelliguntur: primum est propositum aeternum; secundum est temporalis gratificatio; tertium vero aeterna glorificatio. Similiter in reprobatione intelliguntur tria, scilicet propositum aeternum, et temporalis obduratio, et aeterna damnatio. Quantum ad primum et ultimum similiter iudicandum: nam ultima, scilicet poena et gloria simpliciter cadunt sub merito; primum vero, scilicet propositum aeternum, eo ipso aeternum est, meritum non habere potest. Quantum vero ad medium, quod est gratificatio et obduratio, differenter iudicandum. Nam obduratio simpliciter cadit sub demerito, sive sub malo merito, gratificatio vero nec simpliciter sub merito, nec simpliciter extra."

Bonaventure does not use the term "*principale significatum*", but he does use the term "*connotatum*". Given how closely he follows Alexander, I am assuming that "*connotatum*" stands in opposition to an assumed "*principale significatum*".

purpose of God to predestine and reprobate; the two additional significates are the mediating and ultimate effects of predestination and
reprobation. For Bonaventure, the mediating effect of predestination
is the infusion of grace (*gratificatio*), while its ultimate effect is eternal
glorification. The mediate effect of reprobation is the hardening of
the sinner's heart (*temporalis obduratio*); its ultimate effect is eternal
damnation. Thus, if the terms are taken as signifying the eternal
purpose to predestine and reprobate, then one must say that predestination and reprobation have no cause. If, however, the terms are
construed as signifying the effects of God's eternal purpose, then one
can indeed attribute causes. But, as in the *Summa* attributed to
Alexander of Hales, on Bonaventure's view, the effects of predestination and the effects of reprobation do not admit meritorious causes in the same way. While the final effects of both predestination
and reprobation have meritorious causes, such correspondence does
not hold for mediating effects, for the mediating effect of predestination does not have a meritorious cause, but reprobation's mediating
effect does.

In light of the tradition in which Aureol is operating, his insistence
that there is some basis on the part of the predestined and reprobate
for their respective states clearly does not entail that the eternal, intrinsic divine will is caused. On this point he is in agreement with
Bonaventure. Yet, they differ in the meanings that they ascribe to
"predestination" and "reprobation", since for Aureol, predestination
and reprobation are both positive divine acts. Moreover, neither can
be caused solely by the intrinsic divine will; there must be a something in the predestined, as well as the reprobate, which explains
why that person is saved or not. So Aureol argues for a basis on the
part of the predestined for the divine gift of grace.

Aureol develops this position not in direct debate with earlier
Franciscan theology, but rather as it has been reworked by Scotus.
This discussion of Scotus's teaching of predestination is the only aspect of Aureol's doctrine of predestination to have received any detailed attention, and then only as it pertains to defense of the necessity of habits of grace.[57] Moreover, these studies of Aureol, like most
studies of predestination and justification, ignore his doctrine of
reprobation and the importance of his doctrine of the divine attributes. But the most serious problem posed by historians' approach to

---

[57] See Vignaux, *Justification*, pp. 43-96; G. Etzkorn, "Walter Chatton and the
Controversy on the Absolute Necessity of Grace", *Franciscan Studies*, 37 (1977), pp.
32-75.

Aureol stems from their assumption that his critique of Scotus's doctrine of predestination constitutes Aureol's own doctrine. As a result, Aureol's position has been significantly distorted in the secondary literature.[58]

Even so, it must be admitted that Aureol's position cannot be understood except in light of the contribution of John Duns Scotus. Like the vast majority of Scholastics, the Subtle Doctor argues for SPE. He holds that there is no cause of predestination on the part of the predestined, but that God predestines on account of His elective will. Divine reprobation is a lack of elective will for the damned. Scotus explains the logical sequence of predestination by depicting the process as occurring over four *instants of nature*.[59] In the first instant, Peter and Judas are considered as equals by God. In the second instant, where election occurs, God freely wills that Peter be elevated to a state of glory, but does not will (*non vult*) anything for Judas. In the third instant, God wills grace to Peter so that he may be glorified. Since Judas, however, is not ordained to glory, he does not receive grace and proceeds to fall into mortal sin through evil use of his free will. In the fourth instant, Peter receives final glory on account of grace, but Judas is consigned to eternal punishment on account of his evil use of free will.[60]

---

[58] Some notable examples besides Vignaux: Oberman, *Harvest*, pp. 212-215; McGrath, *Iustitia Dei*, p. 150; Pannenberg, *Skotus*, pp. 141-142.

[59] For more on the 14th-century language of *instants of nature* (as opposed to temporal instants), see Simo Knuutilla, "Change and Contradiction: A Fourteenth-Century Controversy", *Synthese* 40, (1979), 189-207; Norman Kretzmann, "Continuity, Contrariety, Contradiction, and Change", *Infinity and Continuity in Ancient and Medieval Thought*, ed. idem, (Cornell, 1982), 270-296; Paul Spade, "Quasi-Aristotelianism", in idem, 297-307.

[60] *Reportata*, d. 41, q. 1, (Vives, vol. 6, p. 334): "<contra Scotum>" Petrus et Iudas aequales in naturalibus, voliti a Deo in esse existentiae, in illo instanti in quo offeruntur voluntati divinae in existentia naturali et aequales: Deus—per te <Scotum> primo vult Petro beatitudinem; quaero tunc quid velit Iudae? Si damnationem, habeo propositum 'ergo reprobat sine omni ratione',—si beatitudinem, ergo praedestinat Iudam.

"Dici <Scotus> potest quod in illo instanti nihil vult Iudae; tantum est ibi negatio volitionis gloriae. Et similiter quasi in secundo instanti naturae, quando vult Petro gratiam, adhuc nullus actus positivus voluntatis divinae est circa Iudam, sed tantum negativus. In tertio instanti, quando vult permittere Petrum esse de massa perditionis sive dignum perditione (et hoc propter peccatum originale sive propter actualem), tunc vult permittere Iudam simili modo esse filium perditionis; et hic est primus actus positivus—uniformis quidem—circa Petrum et Iudam, sed ex isto actu est istud verum 'Iudas erit finaliter peccator', positis illis negationibus, scilicet quod non vult sibi dare gratiam et gloriam. In quarto ergo instanti offertur Iudas ut peccator finaliter, voluntati divinae, et tunc ipse vult iuste punire et reprobare Iudam."

Though he does not equate his logical schema of instants of nature to the Franciscan semantic methodology, the semantic argument is implicit in Scotus's analysis. Thus, just as an order of signification and connotation is a logical sequence in which meaning is explicated, so the move from one "instant" (or "sign") of nature to another is a logical progression. Like Aureol, however, Scotus does not use the term "reprobation" to signify God's elective will, but to signify the effects of that will only. But unlike Aureol, this change in the meaning of "predestination" and "reprobation" does not alter the causal argument of earlier Franciscan doctrine.[61] This is because Scotus operates with a definition of "election" that is different from Aureol's. Aureol avoids attributing reprobation to the intrinsic will of God by arguing that the divine elective will does not regard particular people; by contrast, Scotus, instead of arguing for a general elective will, proposes a particular election which refers only to predestined individuals. Therefore, predestination is caused by God's elective will, but since there is no elective will for the reprobate, their reprobation is caused by their own sin. Granting the semantic differences, Scotus's instants of nature schema provides a logical framework for the Franciscan understanding of merit and predestination. In the second instant, when God wills glory for Peter and not for Judas, what Bonaventure would call the principal significates of "predestination" and "reprobation" occur. In the third instant, when grace is conferred on Peter and not on Judas, the mediating effects of predestination (i.e. grace) and reprobation (i.e. obduration) occur. Thus, in the fourth instant the ultimate effects of predestination (i.e. glory) and reprobation (i.e. punishment) occur. Like Bonaventure, Scotus claims that grace is conferred solely on account of God's mercy, while obduration is merited by Judas on account of sin.

Rejecting Scotus's logical formulation of this position allows Aureol to put forth a doctrine which is contrary to tradition without baldly abandoning it. Instead of dismissing the traditional position wholesale, he points out that, as Scotus explains it, the position leads to Pelagianism. Aureol argues that Scotus's explanation fails at two points.[62] For Aureol the instants of nature explanation is analogous

---

[61] This conclusion is contrary to recent scholarly tradition which sees Scotus as making a radical break from Franciscan predestinarian teaching. For introductory and bibliographical information on this topic, see Courtenay, *Schools and Scholars*, p. 186; and McGrath, *Iustitia Dei*, pp. 163-166.

[62] *Borghese 329*, f. 438va: "Sed nec iste modus dicendi videtur rationalis. Primo quidem, quantum ad illam differentiam quam ponit pro secundo instanti. Constat enim secundum Apostolum 1 Ad Timotheum 2 quod Deus 'vult omnes homines salvos fieri et ad agnitionem veritatis venire'."

to his own practical syllogism analysis. The second instant for Scotus (the major premise for Aureol) represents election, while the third instant (or the conclusion) represents predestination.[63] In the first place, Aureol argues that Scotus's doctrine of election is flawed. Second, since there is no particular election in the second instant, Scotus's account of the causality of predestination and reprobation in the third instant is flawed.

The crux of the attack on Scotus is Aureol's doctrine of general election based on *I Timothy* 2:4:

> But, in the first place certainly, this way of speaking does not seem reasonable, as to the difference that <Scotus> holds as the second instant. For it remains that according to the Apostle (*I Timothy* 2) that "God wills that all men be saved and attain recognition of the truth". But it is manifest that this will cannot be understood with respect to Judas except as the second instant. In the first <instant> certainly Peter and Judas are not different. In the second <instant>, however, if <God> wills glory to Peter and not to Judas, <then> He does not will that all men be saved. Therefore, it is necessary that in this <second> instant God should will such glory to Judas no differently than to Peter...It is manifestly concluded that in the second instant God equally wills glory to Judas as <He does> to Peter.[64]

If divine election is not the cause of predestination or reprobation, then Scotus's account of the third instant becomes problematic: God wills all men to be saved in the second instant and then damns Judas in the third instant. There must be some cause on the part of Judas which differentiates him from Peter. Moreover, if God's election is

---

[63] *Ibid.*: "Praeterea, numquam ex aliqua propositione universali concluditur differenter, nisi per assumptionem differentis minoris. Sed Deus habet hanc propositionem penes se quod 'vult omnes homines salvos fieri', quantum in se est et ex sua voluntate et beneplacito; ita erit, ergo, in secundo insanti. Non concludeteur pro Petro excludendo Iudam, nisi per praescientiam operum Iudae illa voluntas excludatur, et econverso ex praescientia alicuius de Petro determinetur ad ipsum. In secundo, autem, instanti nondum assumitur praescientia, sed tantum in tertio. Non, ergo, in secundo instanti vult Deus Petro gloriam, Iudae autem nec gloriam, nec miseriam, sed vult gloriam uniformiter pro utroque."

[64] *Ibid.*: "Primo quidem, quantum ad illam differentiam quam ponit pro secundo instanti. Constat enim secundum Apostolum 1 Ad Timotheum 2 quod Deus 'vult omnes homines salvos fieri et ad agnitionem veritatis venire'. Sed manifestum est quod haec voluntas respectu Iudae non potest intelligi, nisi pro secundo instanti. In primo quidem Petrus et Iudas sunt indifferentes. In secundo vero, si vult gloriam Petro et non Iudae, non vult omnem hominem salvum fieri. Ergo, necesse est quod in illo instanti velit indifferenter gloriam ita Iudae, sicut Petro. Et confirmatur, quia omnes doctores exponunt hoc de voluntate antecedente omnem operationem Petri et Iudae. Sic enim aequaliter 'vult omnes homines salvos fieri', quamvis non velit hoc voluntate consequente praescientiae operum diversorum. Cum, ergo, illud instans secundum praecedat visionem huiusmodi operum, nam illa ponitur in tertio instanti, secundo istos. Manifeste concluditur quod in secundo instanti aeque vult Deus Iudae gloriam, sicut Petro."

general, and if there is some cause on the part of Judas for his reprobation, then there must be some cause on the part of Peter for his
predestination. Once the will of God is eliminated as a cause of
reprobation, Scotus's position is reduced to a Pelagian doctrine of
predestination based on foreseen merits.

> ...predestination, since it is the will to give grace to someone, either is
> a will preceding foreknowledge, or following <foreknowledge>. But
> one cannot say that it precedes <foreknowledge>, because by such an
> <antecedent> will God wills that all men be saved, and according to
> this all men would be predestined. Therefore, it is necessary that it be
> a will following foreknowledge, and consequently foreknowledge of
> something appearing in the predestined is the cause of this will. And
> thus predestination has a cause.[65]

Aureol's own position looks much like this conclusion except for the
introduction of the term "*obex gratiae*". He explains that foreknowledge of an obstacle or impediment to grace on the part of the reprobate is the cause for their reprobation.[66] In children this obstacle is
original sin, in adults it is actual sin.[67] Conversely, the cause of predestination is the foreknowledge of an absence of such an obstacle.
Aureol describes this using the analogy of the sun shining on the
earth. The sun shines wherever its rays are not impeded.[68] In a like
manner God's gracious will is effective wherever it is not impeded.

---

[65] *Ibid.*, f. 438vb: "Praeterea, praedestinationis, cum sit velle alicui gratiam et salutem, aut est velle praescientiam antecedens aut consequens. Sed non potest dicit
quod sit antecedens, quia tali voluntate vult omnem hominem salvum fieri, et secundum hoc omnes homines essent praedestinati. Ergo, necesse est quod sit velle
praescientiam consequens. Et per consequens praescientia alicuius reperibilis in
praedestinatio causa fuit illius voluntatis, et sic praedestinatio habet causam."
[66] *Ibid.*: "Quid dicendum secundum veritatem, et primo quod reprobationis est
causa positiva, scilicet intentio finalis obiicis gratiae, ut praevisa; praedestinationis
vero negativa, scilicet non obiicis intentio. Restat ergo nunc dicere quod videtur sub
triplici propositione. Prima quidem quod Deus nullum reprobat sine causa affirma-
tiva, nec praedestinat absque causa negativa. Ubi considerandum quod pro primo
instanti quo offertur divino conspectui omnis homo, vult Deus illi gratiam et salutem. Immo, et omnes creat ad istum finem, nisi tamen obicem gratiae reperiat per
quem homo reddatur indignus. Tunc, ergo, praescientia sumente sub illa generali
volitione, offeruntur in Dei praescientia aliqui cum obice gratiae et indignitate."
[67] *Ibid.*, f. 439ra: "Unde reperit in eis praescientia resistentiam gratiae vel habi-
tualem, sicut in parvulis in quibus est originale peccatum, vel actualem (ut malum
usum liberi arbitrii) in adultis."
[68] *Ibid.*: "Quod, ergo, hoc sit verum multipliciter patet. Agens enim universale in
omne illud agit quod non habet impedimentum; si vero non agit in aliquid, illud
habit impedimentum, sicut patet de sole qui, quantum est ex se, in tantum aeram
claritatem radiorum diffundit. Si enim aula aliqua opposita fuerit ipsi soli, et quaeratur, quare non sit interius radiosa, invenietur causa positiva, videlicet impedimentum parietis vel clausio fenestrarum. Si vero fuerit radiosa interius, non invenietur
causa alia, nisi negatio omnis impedimenti, utpote non interpositio fenestrarum aut
parietis inter domum et solem. Sed constat quod Deus ex sua bonitate universale

But it remains that God is a universal agent from His goodness, willing grace and salvation to all rational creatures. For, insofar as it is from Him, He who makes His sun rise over the good and the evil offers grace to all. Therefore, any who lack grace and salvation lack these things on account of their own impediment and obstacle which God perceives in him; but he who has grace and salvation lacks such an impediment. The former, however, is reprobate and the latter is predestined. Therefore, the cause of reprobation is the maintenance of an impediment foreseen from eternity; but the cause of predestination is the foreknowledge and foresight of the absence of any impediment with respect to he who is called predestined.[69]

The immediate problem with this argument is that it looks like a distinction without a difference. If the obstacle to grace is sin, then it seems to follow that the absence of such an obstacle is the avoidance of sin on the part of the human will. But Aureol stresses that all meritorious acts are effects of predestination; nor can an individual from his natural ability (*ex puris naturalibus*) prepare for or dispose himself to final grace. Aureol draws a distinction common in Medieval soteriology to explain the relationship between man's ability and God's grace. The preparation for grace that a man cannot accomplish *ex puris naturalibus* is made possible by prevenient grace (*gratia gratis data*) which is an effect of God's will extrinsic to man. Aureol insists that the preparation possible through prevenient grace is not meritorious, since it is not a positive act of the free will;[70] meritorious acts are possible only when one is in a state of sanctifying grace (*gratia gratum faciens*) which inheres in a person as a habit of the soul.[71]

---

agens est, volens omni creaturi rationali gratiam et salutem. Offert enim, quantum est ex se, omnibus gratiam qui solem suum facit oriri, super bonos et malos. Ergo, omnis qui caret gratia et salute, caret ea propter suum impedimentum et obicem quam Deus reperit in eodem."

[69] *Ibid.*: "Sed constat quod Deus ex sua bonitate universale agens est, volens omni creaturi rationali gratiam et salutem. Offert enim, quantum est ex se, omnibus gratiam qui solem suum facit oriri, super bonos et malos Ergo, omnis qui caret gratia et salute, caret ea propter suum impedimentum et obicem quam Deus reperit in eodem. Qui vero habet salutem et gratiam, caruit huiusmodi impedimento. Ille, autem, reprobatus est et iste praedestinatus. Ergo, reprobationis causa est positio impedimenti ab eterno praevisa. Praedestinationis vero causa est praescientia et praevidentia carentiae omnis impedimenti circa illum qui dicitur praedestinari."

[70] Aureol's concept of preparation should not be confused with other doctrines of preparation. First, it is not like the *pactum* theologian's concept of *meritum de congruo*, because preparation for Aureol is not an act on the part of the human. This is why he does not use their formula: *facientibus quod in se est Deus non denegat gratiam.* Nor is his doctrine like post-Reformation concepts of preparation. While Aureol does say that God is inclined to have mercy on those who have this preparation, one must understand this statement in its context. According to Aureol, God is inclined to have mercy on everyone, however, this grace is not efficacious *in se*, but only applied to those who do not resist.

[71] *Borghese 329*, ff. 439ra-b: "Praeterea, tale quid oportet assignari pro causa prae-

What does Aureol mean by saying that preparation is not an act? For Aureol the sin which creates the obstacle to grace is a resistance to that grace on the part of the person. God offers grace to all humans solely out of His own mercy. A particular individual can either *actively* resist this grace or *passively* accept it. There is no good use of free will on the part of the predestined, merely a lack of any action whatsoever. According to this way of understanding the process the cause of predestination is negative, but on the part of the reprobate there is an active resistance to grace, and thus a positive cause of reprobation.

Aureol describes passive non-resistance to grace using two examples, which pertain to the differing cases of (a) an individual possessing rational and volitional capacity (an adult) and (b) an individual who does not possess such capacities (a child). For Aureol, it must be the case that any human cause of predestination must apply to both cases. Clearly, there can be no good use of free will on the part of an individual lacking volitional capacity, so Aureol argues that children who die after baptism, but still before the age of reason, are predestined because original sin as an obstacle to grace has been deleted due to baptism.[72] In like fashion, the real cause of predestination in

---

destinationis quod non sit effectus proveniens ex ipsa praedestinatione et eam sequens. Sed constat quod nihil aliud potest poni subterfugiens causalitatem gratiae et praedestinationis, nisi quod dictum est. Omne enim positivum, utpote bonus usus liberi arbitrii, aut quaecumque dispositio ad gratiam, est a Deo. Unde ex puris naturalibus non sumus sufficientes cogitare aliquid ex nobis, quasi ex nobis, sed omnis sufficientia nostra ex Deo est. Licet enim sine gratia gratum faciente, possit homo aliquos motus habere disponentes ad gratiam, nihilominus tales motus sunt ex gratia gratis data. Et propter hoc dicitur 'gratiae praevenire' iuxta illud Prophetae, 'misericordia eius preveniet me'. Potest autem homo ex puris naturalibus non-ponere obicem, quia in hoc nullus est actus positivus, sed mera negatio. Unde hac negatione reperta Deus, qui ad miserandum pronus est, gratiam confert, ex quo oritur omnis bonus usus liberi arbitrii et omnis bona dispositio positiva. Ergo, praedestinationis non oportet quaerere causam aliam. Non enim exigit Deus dispositionem aliquam positvam. Immo, sufficit sibi non resistentia, sicut dictum est."

[72] *Ibid.*, f. 439rb: "Praeterea, causa talis debet assignari praedestinationis quae communis sit omni praedestinato, tam parvulo quam adulto. Sed nulla alia potest esse communis, nisi quae dicta est. Et in adultis quidem patet quod non semper exigitur praecedens dispositio positiva. Immo, de Apostulo Paulo dicit Augustinus quod non solum cum multis meritis, immo cum multis demeritis, elegerit eum Deus propter hoc quod non resitit gratia, sed statim dixit, 'domine, quid me vis facere'. Unde, Actus 26, cum narrasset apparitioenm sibi facta in qua conversus fuit ad Deum concludit quod non fuit incredulis caelesti visioni, per hoc innuens quod non resisterat gratiae, et ideo erat electus. In parvulis vero patet quod nulla ratio esse potest, quare unus praedestinatus est qui moritur baptizatus, alter vero non, nisi, quia Deus praevidit unum pro instanti mortis suae habere obicem gratiae, scilicet originale peccatum, alium vero non habere, tamquam deletum per baptizmum. Ergo, ista carentia impedimenti gratiae, ut praevisa, est generalis ratio omnium praedestinatorum quod sint praedestinati. Et econverso positio impedementi est causa generalis ipsius reprobationis.

adults can be found in those cases where good use of free will does not precede predestination. As an example of such a case, Aureol refers to the conversion of Paul. Aureol specifically points out the phrase Paul uses in *Acts* 26:19 when the Apostle recounts his reaction to the divine vision to his captor King Agrippa. According to the Vulgate version, Paul tells Agrippa: "I did not disbelieve this heavenly vision."[73] Aureol takes Paul's use of a double negative to mean that his initial reaction to the offer of grace contained in this divine revelation was passive.[74] The implication is that of his own free will Paul could have resisted Jesus's call to become an apostle and remained in his impenitent state; but Paul could not of his own free will believe or do anything meritorious until grace had been (a) offered by God, (b) passively accepted by him, and (c) *only* then given by God. According to Aureol, Paul was not presented with an initial choice between believing (good use of free will) and disbelieving (evil use of free will), but rather between *not* disbelieving (*no* use of free will) and disbelieving. Furthermore, in those who seem to have a positive disposition towards grace, it is in fact the case that this disposition is a gift of grace given on account of God's general offer of grace coupled with that individual's passive non-resistance to the offer.[75]

Aureol's doctrine of predestination is an attempt to accommodate several conflicting assumptions. First, in order to preserve human

---

"Et si dicatur quod puer qui baptizatus est habet a praedestinatione sua quod fuerit baptizatus, et per consequens carentia obicis est effectus praedestinationis, non causa, non valet quidem, quia hoc potius sequitur cursum naturae. Si enim puer, ex complexione mori debeat statim natus, non preveniet ad baptizmum, nec erit hoc ex alia reprobatione, sed quia non vult Deus facere propter ipsum novum miraculum. Immo, ipsum relinquit cursum naturali. Similiter, etiam si natus fuerit ex parentibus infidelibus, non baptizabitur, si vero ex fidelibus, baptizabitur. Hoc, autem, non habet alteri imputari, nisi ordini naturali secundum quem iste nascitur ex istis, ille ex illis. Nec propter hoc, ut iste baptizetur, debuit Deus ordinare, ut ex aliis parentibus nasceretur."

[73] *Vulgate, Actus Apostulorum* 26:19: "unde rex Agrippa non fui incredulus caelestis visionis…".

[74] *Borghese 329*, f. 439rb: "Unde, Actus 26, cum narrasset apparitionem sibi facta in qua conversus fuit ad Deum concludit quod non fuit incredulis caelesti visioni, per hoc innuens quod non resisterat gratiae, et ideo erat electus."

[75] *Ibid.*: "Unde ex puris naturalibus non sumus sufficientes cogitare aliquid ex nobis, quasi ex nobis, sed omnis sufficientia nostra ex Deo est. Licet enim sine gratia gratum faciente, possit homo aliquos motus habere disponentes ad gratiam, nihilominus tales motus sunt ex gratia gratis data. Et propter hoc dicitur 'gratiae praevenire' iuxta illud Prophetae, 'misericordia eius preveniet me'. Potest autem homo ex puris naturalibus non-ponere obicem, quia in hoc nullus est actus positivus, sed mera negatio. Unde hac negatione reperta Deus, qui ad miserandum pronus est, gratiam confert, ex quo oritur omnis bonus usus liberi arbitrii et omnis bona dispositio positiva."

free will, God's intrinsic, elective will must not refer to specific people. Given this, there must be a cause for both the giving of grace
and glory (predestination) to some and the obduration and punishment (reprobation) of others on the part of the predestined and
reprobate. But although both have a cause, they do not have the
same kind of cause. The cause of reprobation must be meritorious,
or else God would be unjust; in order to avoid the Pelagian heresy,
the cause of predestination cannot be meritorious. Aureol summarizes his position using his analogy to the practical syllogism.

> ...although, like reprobation, predestination has a cause, nevertheless it
> does not have, as reprobation does, a meritorious cause. Where it must
> be considered that in a conclusion willed from any premises, it is neces-
> sary to observe how it is willed from the premises, since the conclusion
> is willed through this way. But now in predestination God wills grace
> and glory to the predestined from the fact that <He> wills that all men
> not maintaining an obstacle <to grace> be saved. For when foreknowl-
> edge offers Peter-not-maintaining-an-obstacle, a volition for grace and
> glory is immediately concluded for Peter. It remains, however, that the
> first volition proceeds from the grace and life <of God> alone. For to
> will that all men who do not themselves impede <grace> be saved is a
> will of kindness without any merit on the part of him to whom this sort
> of will refers. On the contrary, however, in reprobation the <syllo-
> gism> is advanced from this proposition: "I will eternal punishment to
> anyone who finally remains in <a state of> sin". But this volition is just
> on account of the fact that when the foreknowledge <of God> offers
> Judas-persevering-in-<a-state-of->sin, <the syllogism> is justly conclud-
> ed against him. And in this way reprobation belongs to justice and has
> demerit as a cause, but predestination is mercy alone. Nor is merit the
> cause of <predestination>, but only the universal will which pertains to
> all men as it is applied to this or that <individual> in particular. This
> cause, however, is the privation of any obstacle or impediment with re-
> spect to final grace, as has been said.[76]

---

[76] *Ibid.*, f. 439va: "Secunda vero propositio est quod licet causam habeat praedestinatio (sicut et reprobatio), non habet tamen meritoriam (sicut illa). Ubi considerandum quod in conclusione volita ex aliquibus praemisis, intueri oportet de praemisa
quomodo volita sit, quia per illum modum est volita conclusio. Nunc, autem, in praedestinatione vult Deus gratiam et gloriam praedestinato, ex hoc quod 'vult omnem
hominem salvum fieri' obicem non-ponentem. Offerente namque praescientia
Petrum, ut non ponentem, statim concluditur pro Petro volitio gratiae et salutis.
Constat, autem, quod prima volitio procedit ex mera gratia et anima. Velle enim
omnem hominem salvum fieri qui se ipsum non impedit, est velle pietatis absque ullo
merito ex partis illius, superquem transit huiusmodi velle. Econverso autem in reprobatione proceditur ex ista propositione: 'volo poenam aeternam cuilibet in peccato finaliter remanenti'. Haec autem est iusta volitio, propter quod praescietia offerente
Iudam et remanente finaliter in peccato iuste concluditur contra ipsum. Et sic reprobatio est ex iustitia et habet causam demeritum; praedestinatio vero sola misericordia,
nec habet causam promerentem, sed solummodo applicantem voluntatem universalem respectu omnis hominis ad istum vel illum in particulari. Haec autem causa est
privatio omnis obicis et impedimenti respectu finalis gratiae, sicut dictum est."

PART TWO

AUREOL'S IMPACT ON LATE MEDIEVAL
SOTERIOLOGY

CHAPTER FOUR

GENERAL ELECTION AND ANTI-PELAGIANISM
AT OXFORD, 1317-1339

Aureol's doctrine of predestination would become a focus of soteriological controversy at his own University of Paris in the 1340s. But before this, his ideas were incorporated into the soteriological controversies which erupted at Oxford in the 1320s and 1330s. William Ockham O.F.M. and Robert Holcot O.P. seem to incorporate GE into their soteriology.[1] Ockham restricts his discussion to the temporal operations of saving and damning; he refers to eternal election only obliquely. When he does, however, his statements can best be understood in a GE context. Ockham's reticence in discussing the divine salvific will does not allow a claim that he fully endorses GE. But the assumption that Ockham is familiar with GE and has it in mind provides a more satisfactory explanation of his soteriology than those of previous scholars who were not aware of GE. Holcot, too, presents an interesting case, for although soteriology and moral theology occupy a central place in his theological works, predestination plays a minor role in his soteriological discussions. In his lectures on the *Sentences* only two columns of the printed edition are devoted to the doctrine of predestination and repro-

---

[1] Ockham lectured on the *Sentences* at Oxford from 1317-1319 and revised them in an *ordinatio* version between 1320-1324. References to Ockham are to the critical edition, *Guilleli de Ockham Opera philosophica et theologica ad fidem codicum manuscriptorum edita*, (St. Bonaventure, NY, 1976-1985, especially the *ordinatio* version of *I Sentences*, in *Opera Theologica. Scriptum in Librum Sententiarum. Ordinatio*, eds. Gideon Gal, Stephen Brown, G. Etzkorn, and F. Kelly (hereafter referred to as OTh vols. I-IV) and his treatise on future contingents in *Opera Philosophica, De praedestinatio et de praescientia Dei respectu futurorum contingentibus*, ed. Philotheus Boehner (hereafter referred to as OPh II). For more on the dating of Ockham's work see: OTh I, pp. 34-36: and William J. Courtenay, "Ockham, Chatton and the London Studium: Observations on Recent Changes in Ockham's Biography", *Die GegenwartOckhams*, ed. W. Vossenkhul and R. Schoenberger (Weinheim, 1990), pp. 327-337.
    Katherine H. Tachau, "Introduction", *Seeing the Future Clearly: Questions on Future Contingents by Robert Holcot*, eds. idem, Paul Streveler, et al., (Toronto, 1995), provides a detailed discussion of Holcot's career, including the historical controversies over the dating of Holcot's works. According to Tachau, Holcot lectured on the *Sentences* at Oxford in 1331-1333 and produced his *Wisdom* commentary, along with his other Biblical commentaries and *Quodlibetal* questions, during the 1333-1334 academic year.

bation.[2] He maintains SPE, but seems to distance himself from it by presenting it as the position held by "*doctores*". In his lecture on the book of *Wisdom*, delivered the year after he lectured on the *Sentences*, there is evidence that he has moved to a position resembling GE.

At the time Ockham and Holcot were already embroiled in a soteriological controversy that had begun at Oxford before either of them began to teach there. Yet, surprisingly this controversy had little to do with predestination. Whatever use they made of GE was ignored by Oxford anti-Pelagians. John Lutterell attacked Ockham's doctrine of acceptation in the early 1320s; in the mid-1330s Robert Halifax attacked Ockham and Holcot's contemporary, Adam Wodeham, for what Halifax perceived as Pelagian tendencies of his doctrine of fruition.[3] Bradwardine, too, criticized Holcot's doctrines as a variant of the Pelagianizing anthropological doctrines which he considered to be endemic in Latin theology, and not as a predestinarian heresy *per se*. Bradwardine's monumental anti-Pelagian treatise, *De causa Dei*, (composed at the end of the 1330s) devotes little space to predestination and there is no evidence that the opponents addressed in the sections concerning predestination include his Oxford opponents (Ockham, Wodeham, Holcot) or Parisian supporters of GE (Aureol, Strassbourg).

As for the accused parties, neither Ockham, Wodeham, nor Holcot deals with the problem of the *causes* of predestination at any length.[4] When Ockham and Holcot do address divine election, they approach the problem from the point of human ability and argue that grace, although *offered* to all, is *received* on account of a positive human act. Ockham and Holcot appropriated GE in terms of the ongoing Oxford soteriological debate, which was especially divided over the use of two distinctions—one between God's power taken absolutely and as God has limited His own range of operaton through His ordination of a certain state of affairs, the other be-

---

[2] *Roberti Holkot in quattor libros Sententiarum quaestiones argutissime*, (Lugdini, 1497), B. II, q. 1, U.

[3] Courtenay, *Schools and Scholars*, p. 296.

[4] Wodeham does not take up the issue of predestination at all. By Wodeham's time it was common for those lecturing on the *Sentences* at Oxford to take up only a few questions and deal with them at great length. Wodeham does not comment on those of Lombard's distinctions pertaining to predestination. Even so, Oberman claims that in Wodeham's "doctrine of predestination also the whole stress is on God's prescience" (Oberman, *Bradwardine*, p. 48) but without citing any supporting texts. This claim rests, rather, on an inference drawn from Wodeham's doctrine of fruition and his doctrine of Christ's foreknowledge. For a list of the *quaestiones* in the various redactions of Wodeham's commentaries on the *Sentences*, see William J. Courtenay, *Adam Wodeham: His Life and Writings*, (Leiden, 1979), pp. 183-234.

tween simple (*de condigno*) and appropriate (*de congruo*) merit—to allow a role for human free will in the process of salvation. Although both of these distinctions are common in late Medieval theology, they were not central to Parisian soteriological discussion.

Viewed against the backdrop of Oxford (rather than Parisian) debates, it is not surprising that Bradwardine did not focus more on predestination. Like Gregory of Rimini, he did not see a threat to the orthodox doctrine of predestination in the ideas of Scotus and the Oxford theologians. Unlike Rimini, Bradwardine seems not to have been aware of Aureol's challenge to SPE. Therefore, there was no reason for Bradwardine to move from the generally accepted consensus position. In most discussions, Bradwardine's text is ambiguous as to whether God actively elects humans to damnation or merely does not elect them to salvation. Bradwardine's doctrine should not be understood as a rejection of SPE. At the very most, Bradwardine's ambiguity merely suggests the possibility of DPE— and here the difference between Oxford and Paris soteriology is most pronounced. Unlike Rimini, who would make DPE the cornerstone of his anti-Pelagian doctrine of predestination, Bradwardine, in the very different Oxford milieu, was not sensitive to challenges to the accepted doctrine of election.

William Ockham

The claim that Ockham holds a doctrine of predestination which defends the divine will as the only cause of election is not new. In this century until the 1960s, the most prominent students of Medieval theology, including Reinhold Seeberg, Wolfhart Pannenberg, and Paul Vignaux, argued that Ockham held a traditional (SPE) doctrine of predestination.[5] Recently, however, Ockham's view of predestination has been interpreted as a variation of a doctrine of predestination (i.e. election) based on foreseen merits.[6] Unlike a doctrine which claims that God's elective will has no external cause (i.e. SPE, DPE, GE), predestination based on foreseen merits maintains that God's eternal, elective will is externally determined by the actions of human free will. This doctrine was condemned in the 5th century as a mitigated form of Pelagianism

---

[5] Reinhold Seeberg, *Lehrbuch der Dogmegeschichte*, (Leipzig, 1953), vol. 3, pp. 769ff; Pannenberg, *Skotus*, pp. 142-143; Vignaux, *Justification*, pp. 135-145.

[6] Oberman, *Harvest*, pp. 206-212; Harry McSorley, *Luther: Right or Wrong?*, (Minneapolis, 1969), pp. 199-215; Courtenay, *Schools and Scholars*, p. 318; Marilyn McCord Adams, *William Ockham*, (Notre Dame, 1987), vol. II, pp. 1327-1347. One recent scholar who dissents from this view is McGrath, *Iustitia Dei*, pp. 137-140.

called semi-Pelagianism.[7] Thus, if Ockham did hold this position, then his doctrine of predestination, as well as his doctrines of fruition and acceptation, would have challenged traditional Latin soteriology. But he does not in fact do so. An examination of his doctrine of predestination in the context of his own theological tradition, as well as its relation to other soteriological positions that he holds, leads to the conclusion that Ockham does not hold a doctrine of predestination based on foreseen merits, but rather is sympathetic to a GE account.

Ockham discussed the causes of predestination and reprobation in two places: distinction 41 of his lectures on the *Sentences*,[8] and his treatise *De praedestinatione et de praescientia Dei respectu futurorum contingentium*.[9] His approach to the problem betrayed his Franciscan roots. In both these works, the question concerning the cause of predestination rests on a semantic analysis of the terms "*praedestinatio*", "*reprobatio*", and "*causa*";[10] hence, any understanding of Ockham's claim that there is a "cause" for predestination in the predestined, must take into account the way in which Ockham uses these terms.

In lecturing on the *Sentences*, Ockham distinguishes between two significations of "*praedestinatio*" and "*reprobatio*":

> I say that predestination is not something conceivable in God distinct in any way from God, either from the persons or from Deity. Therefore <I say> that it is not some secondary actuality happening to God, but <that it> conveys God Himself who will give eternal life to someone, and therefore it conveys <God> Himself and the eternal life which will be given to someone. And it is the same way concerning "reprobation", which conveys God who will give eternal punishment to someone, and not anything happening to God.[11]

In the later treatise he adds a third signification:

> But the noun "predestination" (or the concept), whether taken in the active or in the passive sense, signifies not only God Himself who will give eternal life to someone but also the person to whom it is given. Thus it signifies three things: God <who will give eternal life to someone>, eternal life, and the person to whom it is given. Similarly,

---

[7] Pelikan, *Christian Tradition*, vol. 1, pp. 318-329.
[8] OTh IV, pp. 595-610.
[9] OPh II, pp. 507-542, esp. p. 536; William of Ockham, *Predestination, God's Foreknowledge and Future Contingents*, trans. Marilyn McCord Adams and Norman Kretzmann, (New York, 1969).
[10] OTh IV, p. 605: "Ideo sine praeiudicio et assertatione temeraria potest aliter dici ad quaestionem. Et primo videndum est de terminis quid per eos intelligatur; secundo ad quaestionem. Circa primum, primo videndum est quid sit 'reprobatio' et 'praedestinatio'; secundo quid intelligitur per 'causam'."
[11] OTh IV, p. 605.

"reprobation" signifies God who will give eternal punishment to some-
one<, eternal punishment, and the person to whom it is given>.[12]

Although this definition is somewhat different from Bonaventure's, it
is clearly within the Franciscan tradition. Like earlier Franciscans,
Ockham argues that God is the primary significate of "predestination", while the granting of eternal life is only a secondary significate.[13] Earlier Franciscans, too, had used the semantic distinction in
order to allow for human causality in the secondary significates of
these terms, but to deny that the principle significate (God, Deity,
the divine essence) was in any way determined by creatures. In this
way they avoided a doctrine of predestination based on foreseen
merits, and still allowed some role for creatures in the process.
Ockham's use of the distinction is consonant with theirs.

But before turning to the question at hand, Ockham draws another semantic distinction. Just as he is using "predestination" and
"reprobation" in a precise way, he is also using "cause" precisely:[14]

> ...concerning "cause", I make the distinction that it is accepted in two
> ways. In one way <it is accepted> as some thing having another thing
> as an effect. And in this way a cause is called: "that which when it is
> posited, the other is posited, and when it is not posited, the other <is
> not posited> without it". Cause is accepted in another way, not as
> some thing with respect to another thing, but rather a kind of priority
> of one proposition to another according to inference, just as if we
> would say that the reason why fire does not heat is because it does not
> have heat or because it is not close to that recipient. And thus it is fre-
> quently said that an antecedent is the cause of a consequent, and nev-
> ertheless <the antecedent> is properly neither an efficient cause, nor
> a material <cause>, nor a formal <cause>, nor a final <cause>.
> Thus, when there is a natural inference from one proposition to an-

---

[12] Adams and Kretzmann, *Ockham*, p. 45; OPh II, p. 514: "Sed hoc nomen 'praedestinatio' vel conceptus, sive accipiatur active sive passive, et significat ipsum
Deum qui daturus est vitam aeternam alicui et illum cui datur, ita quod tria significat, scilicet Deum, vitam aeternam, et illum cui datur. Et similiter 'reprobatio' significat Deum daturum alicui poenam aeternam."

[13] OPh II, p. 511: "Dico quod praedestinationem esse necessariam potest intelligi dupliciter: uno modo, quod illud principaliter significatur per hoc nomen 'praedestinatio' sit necessarium; et sic concedo, quia illud est essentia divina quae necessaria est et immutabilis. Alio modo, quod aliquis a Deo praedestinatur; et sic non
est necessaria, quia sicut quilibet contingenter praedestinatur ita Deus quemlibet
contingenter praedestinat." See also, Adams and Kretzmann, *Ockham*, p. 41.

[14] Ockham's distinction between two ways of considering "cause" as it pertains
to predestination is crucial for an understanding of his doctrine. It is no coincidence
that those who consider Ockham to hold a doctrine of predestination on account of
foreseen merits ignore these passages (Oberman, *Harvest*, pp. 206-212; Adams,
Ockham, pp. 1299-1348), while those who see Ockham as adhering to common
opinion stress these passages (Vignaux, *Justification*, pp. 127-140; McGrath, *Iustitia*,
pp. 137-140).

other, and not vice-versa, then it can in some way be said that the antecedent is the cause of the consequent, and not vice-versa. Nevertheless, this rarely or never happens, unless in reality something
<either> is, or can be, or was the cause of another.[15]

Given these definitions, Ockham can now turn to the question of
causality. He first takes up the causes of reprobation, arguing that
reprobation does have a cause, if "cause" is taken in the sense of
propositional priority. This is because the proposition "'A' will die in a
state of sin" causes the inference "therefore 'A' will be damned".[16]
This does not mean that sin causes damnation in the sense that there
is something intrinsic to sin which brings about damnation. According
to God's power considered absolutely, He could save a person who
dies in a state of mortal sin.[17] According to how God has revealed His
will, however, it always happens that someone who dies in a state of
mortal sin will be damned.

Furthermore, Ockham is not referring to the primary significate
of "reprobation"; here he is talking about damnation, the granting
of eternal punishment, which is only a secondary significate of
"reprobation". Ockham's doctrine is not *reprobation* on account of
foreseen demerits, but rather *damnation* on account of a person's sinful nature at the time of death—hardly a controversial position.
Even if Ockham had not distinguished between two types of causes,
he would not have been breaking new ground. In fact, his distinction between the two types of causes stresses God's will in the act of
damnation more than does the prevailing Scholastic opinion.

While concerning reprobation it is the rule that all who die in sin
are damned, an explanation of predestination is not so simple.

---

[15] OTh IV, pp. 605-606: "...de 'causa', distinguo quod dupliciter accipitur. Uno
modo pro re aliqua habente aliam rem tamquam effectum, et isto modo potest dici
causa 'illud quo posito aliud ponitur, et non ponitur illud aliud sine eo'. Alio modo
accipitur causa, non pro re aliqua respectu alterius rei, sed magis denotat quamdam
prioritatem unius propositionis ad aliam secundum consequentiam. Sicut si dicamus
quod causa quare ignis non calefacit est quia non habet calorem vel quia non est
approximatus passo. Et sic dicitur frequenter quod antecedens est causa consequentis, et tamen non est proprie nec causa efficiens nec materialis nec formalis nec finalis. Unde quando ab una propositione ad aliam est consequentia naturalis et non
e converso, tunc potest aliquo modo dici quod antecedens est causa consequentis et
non e converso. Verumtamen hoc vel raro vel numquam contingit nisi quia in re
aliquid est causa alterius, vel potest vel fuit."

[16] OTh IV, p. 606: "His dictis, dico ad quaestionem quod reprobationis est aliqua causa, accipiendo saltem secundo modo causam. Nam ista causalis est vera
'quia iste peccabit finaliter, ideo damnatur'."

[17] That is, according to His absolute power, God could save someone who does
not posses an infused habit of grace. See Adams, *Ockham*, pp. 1257-1299; Vignaux,
Justification, pp. 118-127; Etzkorn, "Necessity of Grace".

Ockham distinguishes between two accounts of predestination.[18] In most cases there is a cause for predestination,

> because just as the damned are reprobate because they are foreseen to die in sin...so it is concerning certain predestined that they are foreseen to persevere finally in love, and God does not confer eternal life upon them unless they first merit eternal life.[19]

But in certain cases, as for instance Mary and Paul, God seems to predestine for no reason except His own will. The distinction between those who receive eternal life on account of merits, and those who receive eternal life without respect to merits is left to the will of God.[20]

Ockham's account of the *first* type of predestination is what brings on the accusation of semi-Pelagianism. Even though God makes exceptions in certain cases, for the most part predestination seems to be based on human actions. Like Aureol, Ockham claims that predestination, at least in most cases, has a causal process parallel to that of reprobation. Such is the case in both a *post praevisa merita* account and a GE account of predestination. Yet, in the context of Ockham's entire discussion of grace and predestination, it appears that, by attributing a GE account to Ockham, we can achieve a more satisfactory reading of his views. This is because, first of all, there are several passages which contradict a *post praevisa merita* reading. Moreover, there are several passages which support a GE reading.

Ockham's use of the term "predestination" exemplifies the passages which will not support a *post praevisa merita* interpretation. As in considering reprobation, Ockham does not use "predestination" to refer to God's eternal *choice*, but to the *giving* of eternal life. Not only is this clear from the almost interchangeable way in which he uses the terms "eternal life" and "predestination", but also because, if

---

[18] OTh IV, p. 606: "Sed de praedestinatio videtur esse magis dubium. Et quantum ad hoc potest dici sine praeiudicio et assertione quod alicuius praedestinationis est aliqua causa et ratio, et alicuius non est talis ratio et causa."

[19] OTh IV, pp. 606-607: "Praedestinationis primorum videtur esse aliqua ratio, quia sicut damnati ideo reprobantur quia praevidentur peccaturi finaliter,—cum 'Deus non prius est ultor quam aliquis sit peccator'—ita est de quibusdam praedestinantur quia praevidentur finaliter perseverare in caritate, et Deum non conferreret eis vitam aeternam nisi prius mererentur vitam aeternam."

[20] OTh IV, pp. 606-607: "Aliqui autem solum ex gratia speciali sunt ordinati ad vitam aeternam, ita quod sibi ipsis non sunt derelecti sicut alii, sed praeveniuntur ne possint ponere obicem ne perdant vitam aeternam. Sicut fuit de Beata Virgine et de quibusdam aliis, qui praeveniebantur gratia divina ne peccarent et perderent vitam aeternam... Causa autem quare istos praedestinat sine omni ratione et alios propter rationem, non est nisi divina voluntas. Sicut causa quare beatus Paulus fuit percussus a Deo et conversus sine meritis quibuscumque praeviis, et alius non sic, non est causa nisi divina voluntas."

Ockham were referring to the primary significate of "predestination", he would be making the absurd claim that God's very being is caused by human actions. Furthermore, his account of how Paul and Mary are predestined supports this interpretation. The decision to predestine some according to merit and some without regard to merit presupposes a logically prior and free decision by God to set up the process of predestination so that merits are usually taken into account. Ockham is implicitly appealing to his distinction between God's power viewed absolutely and God's power viewed in the context of what He has ordained.[21] Had God so chosen He could grant eternal life without regard to merits in every case; after all, for Ockham, God's eternal will is not determined by human actions; God has so ordered the universe, however, that the execution of His will follows a pattern which takes into account the actions of humans.

Ockham's use of the distinction between these two ways of considering God's power is much more sophisticated than that of 13th-century theologians, but in this case such sophistication does not amount to innovation. If we take for example Thomas Aquinas, we see that Ockham's claim that eternal life is granted according to merit is in no way inconsistent with SPE as it was understood at the time. Distinguishing between predestination and its effects, Aquinas had claimed that one effect could cause another. So for instance, although predestination (for Aquinas, the eternal elective will of God) has no created cause, glory, which is an effect of predestination, is caused by merit, which is another effect of predestination. In fact, the causal relationship between merit and glory is stronger on Aquinas's theory than on Ockham's. Aquinas does not mention any examples of individuals being given eternal life without merit, nor does he distinguish between "real" causality and mere propositional priority. Merits, either one's own or the meritorious intercession of someone else, are a *sine quibus non* for eternal life.[22]

Aquinas's strong statements about the role of merits in salvation are mitigated by his claims that only those in a state of grace may perform meritorious acts and that only those chosen by God's free and eternal election persevere in a state of grace. Nor is Aquinas unique in this regard. Except for those 14th- and 15th-century au-

---

[21] See: Courtenay, *Capacity and Volition*, pp. 117-123, for Ockham's appropriation of this distinction. Ockham and the *pactum* theologians are unique in their extensive use of the distinction in their soteriology, but not in their understanding of the distinction in general.

[22] Aquinas, *Summa*, q. 23, a. 8, (Leonine, vol.2).

thors who assumed an extreme anti-Pelagian attitude, most Scholastics protected from Pelagianism rather strong statements about the ability of human free will by placing them within the context of an equally strong doctrine of God's free and externally undetermined election.[23] According to Heiko A. Oberman, Ockham's failure to surround his optimistic positions on human free will with the traditional doctrine of predestination results in Pelagianism.[24] Clearly then, the important principle is not *how* one receives eternal life, but rather involves events that occur earlier in the process of predestination. We should ask then, first, to what extent is merit an effect of grace? Second, why does God grant such grace to one individual and not another, or rather why does God elect some and not others?

Ockham's discussion of grace also contradicts a *post praevisa merita* reading. The relationship between grace and merit according to Ockham depends on the distinction between God's power considered absolutely and the scope of His operations according to His revealed will. According to God's power taken in the first way, human merit can exist in the absence of a habit of grace, but still requires God's gracious acceptance of any given act if it is to be meritorious; according to God's power taken in the second way, however, meritorious acts are performed only by those infused with divine love. Thus,

> that an act be meritorious without any such supernatural habit <of love> informing <the soul> does not include any contradiction, because no act can be meritorious from what is purely natural to it, nor from any created cause, but <only> from the grace of God voluntarily and freely accepting it as meritorious. And therefore, just as God willingly and freely accepts a good motion of the will as meritorious when it is elicited by the possession of love, so from His absolute power, <God> can accept the same motion of the will even if He has not infused love <into the willer>.[25]

---

[23] The most obvious example is Scotus, who has been accused of holding a Pelagian doctrine of justification and a determinist doctrine of predestination. Alister McGrath describes Scotus's soteriology as an "Iron Age settlement containing a highly vulnerable central area strongly defended by outer defensive ditches"; McGrath, "The Anti-Pelagian Structure of 'Nominalist' Doctrines of Justification", p. 108.

[24] Oberman, *Harvest*, pp. 185-217; idem "Trent", pp. 208-209.

[25] OTh III, d. 17, q. 2, pp. 471-472: "...quod non includit contradictionem aliquem actum esse meritorium sine omni tali habitu supernaturali formaliter informante. Quia nullus actus ex puris naturalibus, nec ex quacumque causa creata, potest esse meritorius, sed ex gratia Dei voluntarie et libere acceptante. Et ideo sicut Deus libere acceptat bonum motum voluntatis tamquam meritorium quando elicitur ab habente caritatem, ita de potentia sua absoluta posset acceptare eundem motum voluntatis etiam si non infuderet caritatem."

Ockham does not claim that it is possible for a human being to perform a meritorious act of his own power, and thus earn salvation; he claims the opposite. Just because a work is done in a state of grace does not entail that God must reward it. Rather, the merit of the act lies within God's gracious acceptance of the act, regardless of whether the agent was infused with the love of God at the time of the action.[26] God is obligated to reward meritorious action only insofar as He has freely bound Himself to do so, and only insofar as He graciously considers an action meritorious. Thus, on God's power considered absolutely, while merit does not necessarily presuppose an infused habit of grace, no act is meritorious without God's forensic grace. Moreover, according to how God has ordered the process of salvation, no act can be meritorious unless it is performed by one who possesses a habit of grace. Therefore, human merit presupposes two kinds of grace, since, according to the process of salvation as ordered by God, acts must both be done in a state of infused grace and also be graciously accepted by God as meritorious.

On what basis, then, does God grant these two gifts of grace? Certainly it is not on account of foreseen merits, since merits are an effect of grace on both God's absolute and ordained power. But there are certain passages which suggest that Ockham considered God's offer of grace to be general. When describing how God predestines in such special cases as those of Paul and Mary, Ockham states that God grants a type of grace which they are unable to resist <ne possint ponere obicem>.[27] The implication is that in typical cases one is reprobate not because God did not offer grace, but because the reprobate resisted the offer of grace by maintaining in themselves an obstacle to it. What differentiates individuals like Paul and Mary from typical people is not that the former are given grace and the latter earn it, but that they are offered different kinds of grace. The typical person is offered resistible grace; Mary and Paul are made an offer they cannot refuse.

---

[26] OTh III, p. 472: "Verumtamen illum actum esse meritorium non est in potestate naturae humanae—sive habeat caritatem sive non habeat—sed est in libera Dei acceptatione." McGrath interprets these passages in the same way I do. He argues that merit is the cause of eternal life according to Ockham, but the meritoriousness of an act is imputed to it by God and is not intrinsic to the act itself (McGrath, "Anti-Pelagian").

[27] Note that while both Aureol and Ockham argue for a GE account of predestination, Aureol uses the example of Paul's conversion as the paradigm case for passive non-resistance, but Ockham cites this as the exception which proves the rule. Since Ockham allows some positive human use of free will as a cause of predestination, the case of Paul reflects a suspension of the typical process, whereas for Aureol it is the only example which clearly shows the process.

Other passages, too, suggest a GE account. In attacking Aquinas, Ockham claims that such human activities as becoming disposed to grace and removing impediments to it are not effects of predestination or grace, but precede it, and in a certain sense, are the reason why God gives grace:

> But generic good works done in a state of mortal sin are in some way a cause why God gives grace to someone. Whence, according to the saints and doctors, although works done in a state of mortal sin are of no effect with regard to eternal life, nor are they remunerated in eternal life, nevertheless they are remunerated temporally, and they ought to be done so that God may sooner give to someone the grace by which he does merit eternal life. Therefore, such good works in some way dispose <someone> to grace and, consequently, to an effect of predestination, although not sufficiently or strictly meritoriously.[28]

This claim that preparation is a cause, but not a meritorious cause, of grace does not make sense in either a SPE or a *post praevisa merita* account. According to a GE account, however, grace is offered to all, but there is some non-meritorious reason which differentiates the predestined from the reprobate. For Aureol, it was passive non-resistance to grace; for Ockham, it is an appropriate preparation for its infusion.

Even though Ockham does seem to favor a GE account, he has fully integrated it into his own theological perspective. Aureol would not call preparation a good work, or a positive act in any sense. Ockham, however, incorporates preparation into the *pactum* whereby God can determine Himself to respond to human actions without those actions conditioning the divine will. Combining GE with a positive human role in the *ordo salutis* reduced any particular impact that Aureol's innovation would have on the Oxford soteriological controversy. For all of Ockham's sophistication, his soteriological views were seen by late medieval anti-Pelagian authors, and some modern ones as well, as a reincarnation of an old nemesis best refuted by a reaffirmation of tradition. And this is only the first time that

---

[28] OTh IV, p. 600: "Sed opera bona ex genere facta in peccato mortali sunt aliquo modo causa quare dat alicui gratiam. Unde secundum Sanctos et Doctores, quamvis opera facta in peccato mortali nihil faciant ad vitam, nec remunerabantur in vitae aeterna, tamen remunerantur temporaliter, et sunt facienda ut citius Deus det alicui gratiam qua mereatur vitam aeternam. Igitur aliquo modo, quamvis non sufficienter nec simpliciter meritorie, talia opera bona disponunt ad gratiam, et per consequens ad effectum praedestinationis.

"Nam licet quidquid in homine ordinans ipsum ad salutem— tamquam quo posito est dignus vita aeterna— comprehendatur sub effectu praedestinationis, non tamen omne quocumque modo ordinans, scilicet disponendo vel impedimentum amovendo, comprehenditur sub effectu praedestinationis."

Aureol's influence at Oxford on this topic would become buried by the indigenous issues.

Robert Holcot

As is the case with Ockham, there is also disagreement among modern scholars over Holcot's doctrine of predestination. Alois Meissner claims that Holcot's views on predestination, like those of most Dominicans of the time, followed the doctrine of Aquinas. Meissner especially stresses the fact that Holcot, like Aquinas, holds the position that I have been referring to as SPE.[29] Heiko A. Oberman, on the other hand, claims that Holcot defends a doctrine of predestination based on the foreknowledge of merits (*post praevisa merita*).[30] Neither position takes into account Holcot's theological context, nor the fact that Holcot's views on predestination develop over time.[31] Between his lectures on the *Sentences* as a student and his Bible lectures as a master, Holcot moves from an unenthusiastic acceptance of SPE to his own notion of GE.

In Book II, question 1 of his lectures on the *Sentences*, Holcot discusses predestination in the context of a larger discussion of God's just government of the world. When isolated from the rest of the discussion, Holcot's argument appears to be an endorsement of SPE, combining elements of his own Dominican tradition and the Franciscan semantic analysis. First, any answer to the question, "whether in the predestined there is some cause for his predestination", must specify what "*praedestinatio*" means. Holcot distinguishes between four meanings of the term:

> This term "predestination" is equivocal. <Taken> in one way it means an action; <taken> in another way it means a passion. <Taken> in a third way we can say that eternal glory is predestination, or that grace is predestination. And <taken in this third way>, every gift given to man by God by which man progresses towards beatitude can generally be called predestination. <Taken> in a fourth

---

[29] Alois Meissner, *Gotteserkenntnis und Gotteslehre nach dem englischen Dominikanertheologen Robert Holkot*, (Limburg an der Lahn, 1953), pp. 102-104.

[30] Oberman, *Harvest*, pp. 243-248.

[31] The importation of the 15th-century distinction between predestination *ante praevisa merita* and *post praevisa merita* is especially unhelpful. Not only is the distinction foreign to the 14th century, but it is also unable to take into account the flexibility of the term "*praedestinatio*". Moreover, a rejection of the Dominican position, or of SPE in general, does not entail a rejection of predestination based on the eternal will of God. SPE, GE, and, of course, DPE all reject the claim that foreknowledge of merits conditions the divine will.

way, this term "predestination", like the term "to build", does not stand for a <simple> thing, but it is a term which we use for the sake of eloquence and brevity in place of a complex. Thus the term "to build" denotes someone bringing together and uniting wood and stones and other such things into a particular shape. And in such a way the term 'predestination' is taken in the place of the following complex <construction>: "God wills to give someone eternal life which he does not <yet> possess, but will possess".[32]

For Holcot considers only the third and fourth senses of the term are relevant to the question.[33] He considers each of them separately, and superficially his treatment of them seems to defend SPE. A closer examination, however, reveals that Holcot's own opinion is less than clear. At the time of his lectures on the *Sentences*, there is a tension in Holcot's thought between the traditional understanding of SPE and his own understanding of human capacity and divine justice. This tension is most evident in his treatment of the third sense of "predestination". Like Aquinas, he distinguishes between predestination and its effects, and thus identifies predestination with election, while construing grace and glory as its effects. But unlike them, he expands the set of effects beyond grace, merit, and glory, to include the creation of individuals. Since according to the distinction between predestination and its effect, one effect can cause another, Holcot can argue that the individual person, who is an effect of predestination, can cause other effects such as good works:

> If we speak <about "predestination" taken> in the third way, then the sense <of the question> is: whether there be some cause on the part of the predestined why he will possess grace and glory. And it seems that, <taken> in this way it must be said that some effects of predestination (i.e. being predestined) have <their> cause in the predestined, and some do not. But the aggregate of the effects of predestination does not have a cause in the predestined. This is clear, be-

---

[32] Robert Holcot, *Quaestiones super IV libros Sententiarum*, (Lugduni, 1497), II, q. 1, U: "Prima est iste terminus 'praedestinatio' equivoce dicitur. Uno modo sonat in actionem; alio modo in passionem. Tertio modo possumus dicere quod gloria aeterna est praedestinatio, vel gratia est praedestinatio. Et generaliter omnem donum collatum homini a Deo quo homo bene utitur ad beatitudinem potest vocari praedestinatio. Quarto modo iste terminus 'praedestinatio' per nulla re supponit— sicut iste terminus 'edificare'—sed est terminus quo utimur propter eloquentiam et breviloquium loco unius complexi. Unde iste terminus 'edificare' denotat aliquem apponere et coniungere ligna et lapides et huiusmodi in certam figuram. Et sic iste terminus 'praedestinatio' accipitur loco talis complexi: Deum velle dare alicui vitam aeternam quam ille non habet, sed habebit."

[33] *Ibid.*: "Dici potest quod 'praedestinatio' primo modo loquendo nullam causam <habet>, cum sit Deus. Si loquamur secundo modo, tunc sensus quaestionis est 'nunquid praedestinatus habeat causam sui in se'. Et si loquamur de homine, manifestum est quod sic, quia componitur ex materia et forma quae sunt esse sui. Sed hoc nihil est ad propositum."

cause the good work of a person has a cause in the person, and nevertheless is one effect of predestination. But the creation of the soul, formation of the body, and other such things do not have a cause in the predestined, nor, consequently, does the entire multitude of works which are called "effects" of predestination.[34]

As significant as this change is, however, it would not constitute a deviation from SPE, if Holcot eliminates grace and glory as the sort of effects of predestination which are caused by human beings. According to Aquinas, human beings merit eternal salvation through works that they do in a state of grace. But Aquinas is also careful to point out that grace is given according to the uncaused, divine will to save particular persons. Holcot does not make a similar statement. Nor does Holcot answer the question that he has posed; that is, he does not specify whether meritorious works constitute the sort of effects which lie outside the scope of human causality (as, for instance, do the creation of a person's soul or the formation of his body), or, rather, the sort which have a cause in the individual.

Taking "predestination" in the fourth sense would seem to force Holcot to answer the question he has avoided in analyzing the third. On this final understanding "predestination" refers to election—God's willing to give grace and glory to someone. Both the way Holcot frames the question and his answer point to a defense of SPE:

> If we speak about <"predestination"> in the fourth way, the sense <of the question> is this: whether on the part of the predestined there is some cause of his predestination; that is whether God will have ordained Himself to give eternal life to someone on account of something in the predestined or on account of the fact that He foreknows someone to be predestined in the future; that is whether the following causal <sequence> is true: God predestined and preordained Peter to eternal life because He knew that at the final moment <of his life> Peter will have believed in God and loved God. And this sense is treated as apropos to our purposes by theologians. And it is said that this is not the case, on the contrary <it is held> that the following causal <sequence> is true: namely because God preordained Peter to eternal life, therefore at the final moment <of his life Peter> was

---

[34] *Ibid.*: "Si autem loquamur tertio modo, tunc est sensus: an sit aliqua causa ex parte praedestinati quare ipse habebit gratiam et gloriam. Et sic videtur dicendum quod aliquis effectus praedestinationis (id est praedestinatus) habet causam in praedestinato, et aliquis non. Sed tota multitudo effectuum praedestinationis non habet causam in praedestinato. Hoc patet quia bona operatio homini habet causam in homine, et tamen est unus effectus praedestinationis. Creatio vero animae et forma corporis et huiusmodi non habent causam in ipso homine praedestinato, nec per consequens tota multitudo operationum quae sunt effectus praedestinationis."

going to believe in God and to love <Him>... Nevertheless, the following causal <sequence> is not true: therefore God preordained Peter to eternal life because Peter was going to believe etc., but rather the contrary <is true> according to the saints.[35]

Yet even this passage does not reveal Holcot's opinion, for once again he does not answer the question. Rather he recites how the question is treated by other theologians and summarizes what seems to be the correct interpretation of sacred writings. It is as if Holcot is attempting to distance himself from a position which he is constrained to hold.

Holcot's treatment of reprobation presents a similar situation. According to SPE, reprobation occurs because God does not will grace and glory to everybody. Those to whom God does not will grace fall into sin and are reprobated on account of foreknowledge of that sin. Therefore, predestination and reprobation have different causes, inasmuch as predestination is caused by God's elective will, but reprobation is caused by human sin. Here again, Holcot presents a SPE account, and here again, he puts it in the mouths of others:

> It seems, therefore, that theologians speak one way about predestination and the predestined, and another way about reprobation and the reprobate. For concerning the predestined the causal <sequences> such as the following are true: because Peter is predestined, Peter will be saved. In the reprobate, however, causal <sequences> such as the following ought not be conceded: because God reprobated Judas, therefore Judas sinned, and therefore he was damned. But rather the contrary <ought to be conceded>: because Judas was going to sin, therefore God reprobated him.[36]

Not only does Holcot distance himself from this opinion, but the authority whom he cites to explain how reprobation does not cause

---

[35] *Ibid.*: "Si loquamur quarto modo, sensus est iste: utrum a parte praedestinati sit aliqua causa suae praedestinationis; hoc est, an Deus ordinaverit se alicui daturum vitam aeternam propter aliquid in praedestinato, vel propter hoc quod praescit aliquid futurum in praedestinato; hoc est, an talis causalis sit vera: Deus praedestinavit et praeordinavit Petrum ad vitam aeternam quia scivit Petrum crediturum in Deum et finaliter dilecturum Deum. Et iste sensus tractatur proprie ad propositum apud doctores. Et dicitur quod non, immo econverso est haec causalis vera: quia scilicet Deus praeordinavit Petrum ad vitam aeternam, ideo Petrus fuit crediturus in Deum et finaliter dilecturus...haec tamen causalis non est vera: ideo Deus praeordinavit Petrum ad vitam aeternam quia fuit crediturus et cetera, sed econtrario secundum sanctos."

[36] *Ibid.*: "Videtur ergo doctores aliter loquuntur de praedestinatione et praedestinato et aliter de reprobatione et reprobis. Nam de praedestinato tales causales sunt verae: quia Petrus est praedestinatus, Petrus salvabitur. In reprobis autem non debet tales concedi: quia Deus Judam reprobavit, ideo peccavit, et ideo damnabitur. Sed econtrario: quia Judas erat peccaturus, ideo Deus eum reprobavit."

sin, Anselm in *De casu diaboli*, seems to support an understanding of reprobation more akin to GE than to SPE.[37] Applying Anselm's discussion of the devil's rejection of divine perseverance to Judas's reprobation, Holcot argues that reprobation is caused by Judas's refusal of the divine offer of grace:

> ...<Anselm>, speaking to his disciple, offers the following example saying: "I offer something to you and you accept it. I do not give, therefore, because you accept, but therefore you accept because I give. And the giving is the cause of the accepting. I offer <something> to another and he does not accept it. He does not, therefore, not accept because I do not give, but therefore I do not give because he does not accept."...Accordingly, the true causal <sequence> ought to be formed thus: "Therefore God does not give grace to Judas nor to the devil because he would not accept it."[38]

Although this passage is used to support a distinction between the causality of predestination and reprobation, it does not make a good case for SPE. Assuming, as Holcot does, that there is no pertinent distinction between the fall of an angel and the reprobation of a man, this passage supports the notion that God offers grace to all people. While it may still be true that predestination and reprobation have different kinds of causes, this difference is not due to the fact that the divine salvific will pertains only to certain individuals. According to this account, Judas is an object of the divine salvific will, but rejects the offer of grace. In so applying Anselm's argument to the reprobation of Judas, it appears that Holcot is, even at this point of his career, more comfortable with the notion that God's salvific will pertains to all people, rather than to certain particular ones.

Understanding Holcot as sympathetic to the concept of GE not only makes sense of the ambiguity of his discussion of predestination itself, but also reconciles passages in his lectures on the *Sentences* which seem to contradict SPE.[39] In the discussion immediately preceding the section on predestination, Holcot claims that God will save all who follow His laws. "Thus it is not <God's> intention,

---

[37] *S. Anselmi Opera Omnia*, vol. I, pp. 235-240. I do not claim that Anselm held a doctrine of general election. Anselm never connects his discussion of the devil's rejection of divine perseverance to the mortal realm. Holcot departs from Anselm's text when he treats the cases of Judas and the devil as similar.

[38] Holcot, *In Sent.*, II, q. 1, U: "...loquens ad discipulum suum ponit ei exemplum tale: 'Porrigo inquit tibi aliquid et tu accipis. Non ideo do quia tu accipis, sed ideo accipis quia ego do. Et datio est causa acceptionis. Porrigo alteri, et non accipit. Ille non ideo non accipit quia non do ego, sed ideo non do quia ille non accipit.'... Secundum sic debet causalis formari vera: 'ideo Deus non dedit Judae vel diabolo gratiam quia ille non accipit.'"

[39] Oberman, *Harvest*, pp. 244-245.

strictly speaking, that all be saved, but He wills that everyone who lives according to His established laws will be saved."[40] If one is approaching this text with a simple dichotomy between predestination *post praevisa merita* and *ante praevisa merita* in mind, one would certainly characterize Holcot as endorsing the former. If, however, one is familiar with GE as Aureol conceives of it, one recognizes the formulaic interpretation of *I Timothy* 2:4 used as the basis for GE: "God wills that all men be saved", provided that 'X'.

If Holcot was still unsure of his understanding of the relation between election, grace, and merit as a student, as a Master of Theology he left his doubts behind. In his lectures on the book of *Wisdom* he has moved to an unambiguous endorsement of GE, although, like Ockham, Holcot has a much more exalted view of human capacity than Aureol would admit. While Holcot does not address predestination specifically in his surviving Bible commentaries, several points in his *Wisdom* lectures Holcot so remarks on how man receives grace as to illuminate his commitment to GE at this stage. In lecture 145, where Holcot is again discussing divine government, he asks whether God necessarily gives grace to those who prepare themselves for it and answers in the affirmative. Since he is operating from a notion of GE, however, Holcot in no way means to say that man's disposition affects the divine will. The arguments that he uses emphasize that God offers His grace regardless of the recipients disposition.

> Furthermore, *Revelation* 3:<20 says>: "I stand at the door and knock. If anyone opens it for me, I will enter in to him and eat with him." But he who disposes himself by doing what is in him opens himself, and therefore <God> necessarily enters. This is confirmed, since when the man opens himself, <God> either enters or does not enter. If He does not enter, then He knocks without reason, which is impious to say. If He enters, then He gives grace.
>
> Furthermore, Anselm in chapter 3 of *De casu diaboli* says that there is a cause why God did not give grace and perseverance to the devil: because he did not want to accept it. Therefore, the devil did not not accept grace because God did not give it, but rather, therefore, God did not give it because he would not accept it. <This is> because whoever prepares himself to receive grace, necessarily receives it.[41]

---

[40] Holcot, *In Sent.*, B. II, q.1, T: "Unde non est intentio sua simpliciter et absolute quod omnes salventur, sed vult quod quicumque vixerit secundum leges statutas salvetur."

[41] *Robertus Holkoti super libros Sapientiae*, (Hagenau, 1494), Lect. 145, p. 127ra: "Praeterea Apoc. 3: 'Ego sto ad ostium et pulso. Si quis aperuerit mihi, intrabo ad eum et cenabo cum eo.' Sed iste ergo disponit se faciendo id quod in eo est aperit sibi, ergo intrat necessario. Confirmatur, quia isto aperiente sibi aut intrat aut non

Here, plainly, Holcot has abandoned the idea that predestination and reprobation have different sorts of causes. On his reading of *Revelation* 3:20, the cause for both predestination and reprobation lies in human action, not divine election, since God gives everyone the chance to open the door to His grace. Similarly, Holcot has altered his interpretation of Anselm's account of the fall of the devil so that it not only explains the reprobation of humans, but their predestination as well. Instead of merely showing how the reprobate justly merit their punishment, Holcot uses this passage to illustrate that all humans have the ability and the *opportunity* to accept and receive grace.

While Ockham's use of GE is implicit, Holcot has explicitly adopted a GE account of predestination and grace. But, like Ockham, he has incorporated GE within the context of issues that Oxford theologians had established. So, while for Aureol individuals are predestined on account of their passive non-resistance to the universal offer of grace, Holcot stipulates two conditions for reception of grace: passive non-resistance to it and, as we have seen, active preparation for it. Holcot claims that this positive disposition does not constitute a Pelagian form of merit by distinguishing between full or condign and appropriate or congruent merit.

> And therefore God spontaneously gives first grace to a man insofar as he is naturally disposed to grace and is not presenting an obstacle to grace through an evil use of free choice. But although an appropriate disposition is required before first grace, nevertheless it does not merit grace by full merit, but only by an appropriate merit.[42]

Aureol had rejected the distinction between full and appropriate merit, and his concept of GE has no room for it. According to Aureol God offered His grace to all people by His very nature. If an active response were required in this case, then both salvation and

---

intrat. Si non intrat, ergo frustra pulsat, quod impium est dicere. Si intrat, ergo dat gratia. Praeterea, Anselmus de casu diaboli capitulo 3 dicit, quod illa est causa quare Deus diabolo non dedit gratiam et perseverantia quia ipse noluit accipere. Unde non ideo non accepit diabolus perseverantia quia Deus non dedit, sed ideo Deus non dedit quia ipse non accepit. Quia quicumque se parat ut accipiat, necessario recipit."

[42] *Ibid.*, Lect. 116, p. 101rb: "Et ideo Deus sponte dat homini primam gratiam, homini inquantum se ad gratiam disponenti naturali et non praebenti obicem gratiae per malum usum liberi arbitrii. Licet autem ante primam gratiam requiratur dispositio conveniens, illa tamen non meretur gratiam merito condigno, sed congrui tantum."

In this passage, Holcot does not stress the "activeness" of preparation as he does in the preceding passage. Given that the notion of active preparation can so easily be interpreted as simply meriting grace, we should not be surprised that Holcot seems to pull back from it at times.

damnation would be primarily in the hands of human beings. There would be, in short, no distinction between divine grace and what was naturally within the power of human free choice, and therefore good use of free will would be meritorious. Aureol's stress on passive non-resistance to grace is his most important safeguard against Pelagianism.

For Holcot, on the other hand, God does not offer grace of necessity, but only on account of a pact which He has made with mankind.[43] Since both the offer of grace and the promise that it will be conferred on those who prepare for it are contingent upon the decision of God, Holcot is not presented with the same problem as Aureol. The positive preparation for grace is meritorious only insofar as it is accepted by God as meritorious in accordance with the pact He has made with mankind. While Aureol safeguarded his position by limiting the human capacity to respond to grace, Holcot sought to avoid Pelagianism by explaining the process of salvation as a contract freely entered into by both parties.

Thomas Bradwardine

Because Ockham and Holcot had appropriated GE into a *pactum* account which allows room for positive cause of predestination on the part of the predestined, Bradwardine considered Holcot's views on grace and predestination as part of the anthropologically-oriented Pelagianism which he considered to be rampant in contemporary theology.[44] There is no evidence that Bradwardine ever addressed Aureol's account of GE: none of the positions that Bradwardine cites as Pelagian in the chapters of the *De causa Dei* on grace and predestination resemble Aureol's views. He seems to be totally unaware of Aureol's doctrine. His own doctrine of predestination addresses the need to reaffirm the priority of divine election over human free will in the case of the predestined—a position ideally suited to re-

---

[43] *Ibid.*, Lect. 145, p. 127ra: "...posset tamen Deus mutare legem circa aliam personam, si vellet. Et talis quantumcumque se disponeret non haberet quia dispositio hominis nullam causalitatem habet respectu gratiae de necessitate, sed tamen de congruo quia gratia excedit omnem operationem naturalem. Nec est possibile quod homo mereatur per quodcumque opus naturale morale, puta gratiam de condigno."

[44] Bradwardine composed *De causa Dei* during the late 1330s. He probably began writing it while still a fellow of Merton College at Oxford, but the bulk of it was written during his stay in the household of Richard de Bury. See Oberman, *Bradwardine*, pp. 10-22. We know that Bradwardine had completed *De causa Dei* and that it was circulating on the Continent by the time Rimini lectured on the *Sentences* at Paris in 1343-1344 (Rimini, *Lectura*, vol. 7, p. 365).

futing those who ascribe too much to the role of human free will in
the *ordo salutis*, but one that does not address a critique of particular
election itself.

In Book I, chapters 35-39, of the *De causa Dei*, Bradwardine presents and attacks what he sees as the major varieties of Pelagian doctrines of grace. In each case the positions involve some claim that
grace is given on account of some positive use of human free will.
There is no indication that Bradwardine is concerned with any GE
account of the gift of grace. His attack on Holcot's doctrine is directed at the implications of Holcot's *pactum* account for the role of
human free will. In chapters 37-39, Bradwardine attacks positions
which are associated with Holcot.[45] The position outlined in chapter
37 claims that God gives grace to those who prepare for it,[46] while
the position condemned in 38 is clearly based on the interpretation of
Revelation 3:20 found in Holcot's *Wisdom* lectures.[47] In chapter 39,
four times longer than the previous four chapters together,
Bradwardine denies the distinction between *meritum de congruo* and
meritum de condigno, a distinction, Bradwardine charges, employed by a
vast number of Scholastic theologians.[48] Granting that Holcot is only
one of many attacked in chapter 39, it is still the case that the more
specific attacks in 37 and 38 have nothing to do with GE. In fact,
Bradwardine condemns Holcot for the very notion which distinguishes Holcot from Aureol: Holcot's claim that first grace is a result of a
positive human act. As for Bradwardine's attack on the distinction
between *meritum de condigno* and *meritum de congruo*, Aureol, because of
his conception of GE, is one of the only theologians of the period not
to employ it in this regard. When one turns to Bradwardine's chapters on predestination, one finds a similar focus on theories that

---

[45] The positions recounted in chapters 35 and 36 refer to Pelagius and his ancient followers. Bradwardine, (*De Causa Dei*, I, ch. 35, p. 307): "Contra Pelagium,
quod gratia datur a Deo non praecedentibus meritis comparatur." *Ibid.*: "Contra
Procuratores Pelagii assertentes quod et si merita non sunt causa collationis gratiae
principales, sunt tamen causa sine qua non confertur...Dicunt enim aliqui talium
quod merita non sunt causa principalis gratiae nobis datae, sed causa sine qua non
datur. Sed quis non videat istos et eorum similes haeresim Pelagianam tantum vo-
caliter declinare et ipsam realiter praedicare?"

[46] *Ibid.*, p. 316: "Contra quosdam Pelagianos dicentes hominem posse ex se tantum debite praeparare, quod si faciat, Deus dabit sibi gratiam suam gratis."

[47] *Ibid.*, ch. 38, pp. 319-324: "Contra Pelagianos dicentes quod Deus praevenit
hominem in gratiae collatione pulsando et homo ipsam acceptionem gratiae ape-
riendo et consentiendo, ex se tamen pulsanti et sic ipsam quodammodo promeren-
do."

[48] *Ibid.*, ch. 39, pp. 325-364: "Contra quosdam putantes hominem ex se tantum
posse mereri primam gratiam de congruo, non de condigno... Iste error est famosi-
or caeteris diebus et nimis multi per ipsum in Pelagianum praecitium dilabuntur."

stress the meritorious ability of human free will. The opinion which Bradwardine spends the most effort refuting is one which claims that, although individuals are either predestined or reprobated by God, the level of glory or punishment received depends on good or evil use of human free will.[49] The only Medieval author whom I know held such a view was the Thomas of England cited and attacked by Aureol in his own treatise on predestination. In this instance, Bradwardine is, knowingly or not, *following* Aureol, whom Rimini, of all people, credits with decisively refuting this opinion.[50] Finally, in chapter 47, Bradwardine lists and condemns various opinions which argue that predestination is based on merit.[51]

Consistent with his attack on those who seem to glorify human free will, Bradwardine's own doctrine of predestination is primarily concerned with upholding the priority of the grace of God in the process of predestination. Conversely, he is not concerned with constructing precise accounts of election or reprobation. Although some of his claims may be construed as advocating DPE, Bradwardine's doctrine is more properly situated in the SPE tradition. His definition of predestination, for instance, is based on the majority account endorsed by Aquinas:

> <Predestination> is the eternal prevolition of God or the preordination of the divine will regarding the future. And this can be taken in two ways. In one way <it is taken> generally, namely as the divine preordination with respect to some future thing, and in this way <the term "predestination"> is convertible with "providence". In another way it is taken specifically, namely as the preordination of the divine will regarding a rational creature (either angelic or human), and this is the common way that Scripture, the canons, and the doctors speak <of it>.[52]

Bradwardine's definition of reprobation, however, is less clear:

> But reprobation is taken as the eternal unwillingness [noluitione] of God, whereby He is unwilling to confer grace upon someone, and as

---

[49] *Ibid.*, ch. 46, pp. 427-433.

[50] Rimini, *Lectura*, I, d. 40-41, a. 1, (vol. 3, p. 328, ll. 13-15): "Nam, sicut dicit unus doctor, et in hoc bene, non solum deus praedestinat quemquam ad praemium aeternum, sed etiam ad determinatum praemii gradum..."

[51] *De Causa Dei*, I, ch. 47, pp. 436-441, esp. 436: "Obiiciunt autem Pelagiani contra praemissa de praedestinatione et reprobatione, conantes ipses vel omnino vel saltem ostendere ipsas esse secundum merita personarum."

[52] *Ibid.*, I, ch. 45, p. 421: "Ipsa est aeterna praevolitio Dei, sive praeordonatio voluntatis divinae circa futurum. Et haec dupliciter potest sumi. Uno modo generaliter, scilicet pro praeordinatione divina respectu cuiuscumque futuri, et sic est convertibile cum providentia... Alio modo specialiter, scilicet pro praeordinatione voluntatis divinae circa creaturam rationalem (angelicam vel humanam), et iste communis modus loquendi Scripturae, Canonicae, et Doctorum."

its effects, namely the privation of grace or abandonment (which is also called 'obduration').[53]

"Obduration" can be taken in two ways. In one way as reprobation (namely, active obduration), that is as the divine will being unwilling [nolente], or not willing [non volente], or willing not [volente non] to render <grace and glory>, and in this way no superior or prior cause need be assigned on the part of men.[54]

The problem in interpreting Bradwardine lies in his use of "*nolle*" which can mean either "to be unwilling" or "to will a negative result", precisely the distinction between SPE and DPE. Moreover, his indifference to the distinction between "*non velle*" and "*velle non*" implies that it does not matter how one interprets "*nolle*". From these statements, therefore, it is impossible to determine Bradwardine's understanding of election.

Elsewhere, however, Bradwardine maintains that predestination and reprobation are not equal, coordinate actions of the divine will:

And yet just as the volition of God can be taken in two ways, namely simply and in a certain respect, <predestination> of the good and <predestination> of the evil, double predestination of this sort corresponds to it: simply and in a certain respect, of the good and of the evil... Most frequently, nevertheless, the saints say that predestination refers only to the good. This is because predestination of the evil is not predestination simply and *per se*, but only *per accidens*; and being *per accidens* is akin to non-being.[55]

What Bradwardine has in mind here is something like Scotus's account of SPE, which he endorses with a few qualifications regarding the latter's notion of divine justice.[56] Thus when Bradwardine uses

[53] *Ibid.*, p. 426: "Reprobatio vero accipitur pro aeterna Dei noluitione gratiae alicui non conferendae et pro eius temporali effectu, scilicet gratiae privatione seu desertione, et haec vocatur obduratio."

[54] *Ibid.*, II, ch. 32, p. 617: "Pro his tamen sciendum quod 'obduratio' dupliciter potest sumi. Uno modo pro reprobatione, scilicet obduratione activa, id est, pro voluntate divina nolente seu non volente aut volente non mollire, et sic non habet causam superiorem et priorem ex parte hominum assignandum."

[55] Bradwardine, *De causa Dei*, I, ch. 45, p. 421: "Et adhuc sicut volutio Dei accipitur bino modo, simpliciter scilicet et secundum quid, bonorum videlicet et malorum... sic et ei duplex huiusmodi praedestinatio correspondet, simpliciter et secundum quid, bonorum et malorum...Saepissime tamen dicunt Sancti quod praedestinatio est tantum bonorum, quod ideo est, quia praedestinatio malorum non est praedestinatio simpliciter et per se, sed tantum per accidens, et ens per accidens propinquum est non enti..."

[56] *Ibid.*, p. 441: "Quidam tamen, ut Scotus super 1 Sententiarum distinctione 41, volentes vitare reprobationem esse causaliter ex operibus reprobati et etiam crudelitatem in Deo, dicunt quod Lucifer sive Judas primo offertur voluntati divinae in suis puris naturalibus sine culpa, et sic non vult eum damnare; secundo Deus vult et ex

terms like *"nolle"*, and *"velle non"* to describe reprobation, we should not understand him as endorsing a DPE account in which God has an active will to damn. God wills damnation for the reprobate only in so far as He has not willed their salvation.

Although many of the significant soteriological developments of the "new English theology" involved new conceptions of God and his relationship with humanity, controversy centered on the implications that such doctrines bore for the role of human free will in salvation. Even when we find Oxford authors such as Ockham and Holcot, who seem to have been influenced by the Parisian discussion of divine election, they incorporate that influence into the Oxford paradigm. Issues such as election, predestination, and reprobation were clearly secondary in this paradigm. So much so indeed, that the most ardent and prolix anti-Pelagian author of the Middle Ages treats predestination as a footnote. While the soteriological developments of the Oxford theologians would continue to be the main nemesis of anti-Pelagian authors until the Reformation, the roots of the post-Reformation predestinarian controversies are wholly Parisian.

---

hoc scit se cooperaturum cum eo ad substantiam actus mali, et sic ipsum peccaturum mortaliter commitendo, vel non cooperaturum eo ad substantiam actus boni, et sic ipsum peccaturum mortaliter ommitiendo, et quatenus praevidet eum talis, vult ei damnationem et poenam. Ratio tamen Scoti nequaquam evidenter hoc probat, sicut praecedentia manifestant, est enim similis argumento de iniquitate et praemisso. Veruntamen si ista positio stet cum praemissis hic et 45 huius, et Deum ab omni iniquitate et crudelitate plane excuset, et placet Satrapis, placet mihi." See also, Oberman who, in *Bradwardine*, p. 140, claims that Bradwardine attempted to adhere as closely as possible to Scotus in his doctrine of predestination.

CHAPTER FIVE

GENERAL ELECTION VS. DOUBLE-PARTICULAR ELECTION
Thomas of Strassbourg and Gregory of Rimini

Aureol's influence on Oxford soteriology was quickly incorporated into the anthropological terms of the Oxford debate. At Paris the development of GE created a debate concerning predestination in its own right. Moreover, the debate shifted to theologians in the Augustinian order and became a major component of late Medieval Augustinian anti-Pelagianism. Aureol's influence on Latin predestinarian thought in general occurred outside the Franciscan discussion which produced it. In the mid-1330s, Thomas of Strassbourg, in a rare move, broke from Aquinas and Giles of Rome on the question of the cause of predestination. Strassbourg rejected the common SPE account and adopted Aureol's GE account with some significant modification. Strassbourg's use of GE meant that GE was not only a viable option in Parisian theology when Gregory of Rimini lectured 1343-1344, but it was one held by the most important member of Rimini's own order since Giles of Rome. Moreover, Strassbourg's own modifications of the doctrine help explain why Rimini saw GE as a unique challenge to orthodoxy and initiated a second front in the anti-Pelagian offensive.

Thomas of Strassbourg

Aureol's influence on Parisian Augustinians in the two decades after he read the *Sentences* is well-documented. All three of the known Augustinian authors in this period were familiar with Aureol.[1] In the mid-1320s Gerard of Siena and Michael of Massa debated the merits of Aureol's theology.[2] Gerard attacked Aureol, among others, in his self-appointed role as defender of the thought of Giles of Rome; Michael of Massa charged Gerard with entering a debate beyond his skill.[3] Aureol's influence continued in the 1330s, when Thomas

---

[1] Trapp, "Augustinian Theology", pp. 160ff.

[2] For the dating of these two, see Zumkeller, "Die Augustinerschule", p. 174.

[3] Trapp, "Augustinian Theology", pp. 160-173. Unfortunately, Massa did not address predestination in his commentary on the *Sentences*. See Michael of Massa, *In libros Sententiarum*, Bologna, Universita 2214.

of Strassbourg rejected SPE as it was held by Thomas Aquinas and
Giles of Rome, in favor of Aureol's GE account.[4]

In contrast with most of the theologians studied thus far, Strassbourg's understanding of election is not clearly indicated in the definitional phase of his treatment of predestination and reprobation.
Based on these passages alone, Strassbourg would appear to endorse
SPE. Yet, his claim that reprobation is primarily the foreknowledge
of sin according to which God denies grace and punishes the sinner is
consistent with both the SPE and GE accounts of election.[5] His discussion of the various meanings of "predestination" seems, however,
clearly to support an SPE account. As a technical soteriological term,
"predestination", in Strassbourg's view, refers to God's direction of
humans to eternal beatitude.[6] Moreover, for Strassbourg divine predestination includes both God proposing to save some and also
"sending" them on their way to beatitude through the gift of grace:

> One must pay attention to <the fact> that "to destine" seems to signi-
> fy in two ways. For "to destine" is the same as "to propose"... Second,

---

[4] The only other study of Strassbourg's doctrine of predestination is John L.
Shannon, *Good Works and Predestination in Thomas of Strassbourg*, (Baltimore, 1940).
Shannon's thesis suffers from two flaws. First, his main goal is to harmonize
Strassbourg's doctrine of predestination with that of Aquinas and Giles of Rome.
Strassbourg, however, on this point is quite self-consciously departing from his
teachers. Second, while Shannon notes the resemblance of Strassbourg's doctrine to
Aureol's, he does not argue for any connection. This is because he does not take
into account the development of the doctrine of predestination in the generations
between Aquinas and Strassbourg. This largely accounts for Shannon's admitted
confusion on some points of Strassbourg's doctrine.

[5] Thomas of Strassbourg, *Commentaria in quattuor libros Sententiarum*, (Venice, 1564),
I, d. 40, q. 1, a. 1, p. 110ra-b: "Quantum ad primum articulum, quid sit reprobatio,
est advertendum quod 'reprobatio' tria videtur implicare, scilicet, praecognitionem
culpae, subtractionem gratiae et praeparationem poenae. Deus enim ab aeterno
praecognovit culpam illius quem reprobat, et propter hoc ipsum gratia finaliter pri-
vat et poenam aeternam ei praeparat. Quoad primum, ipsa reprobatio nihil videtur
addere super simplicem praecognitione divinae praescientiae. Quoad secundum,
non addit aliquid positive, sed solum privative. Quoad tertium, addit aliquid positive. Ex his potest ipsa reprobatio sic describi: reprobatio est aeterna praecognitio
mali usus liberi arbitrii, ratione Deus decrevit aliquem hominem in praesenti vita
privare gratia et in futura punire aeterna poena."

[6] *Ibid.*, p. 110rb: "Quantum ad secundum articulum, quid sit praedestinatio, est
advertendum quod praedestinatio dupliciter potest considerari. Uno modo generaliter prout potest competere rationali—ac etiam intellectuali—creaturae respectu
quorumcumque beneficiorum a Deo collatorum. Alio modo specialiter respectu
hominum in aeternam beatitudinem dirigendorum. Primo modo describit beatus
Augustinus praedestinationem in libro De fide ad Petrum sic dicens, 'praedestinatio
est gratuitae donationis praeparatio'. Secundo modo ait idem Augustinus in libro
De praedestinatione sanctorum, 'praedestinatio est destinatio alicuius in finem', vel
sic: 'preadestinatio est est praeparatio gratiae in praesenti et gloriae in futuro'. Sunt
etiam multae aliae descriptiones praedestinationis datae per Apostolos et alios diversos doctores quas ad praesens gratia brevitatis ommitto."

"to destine" is the same as "to send", according to which a letter is said to be "destined", i.e. "sent". And both ways <in which "to destine" signifies> are satisfactory for <my> purpose. For according to the first, God is said to predestine the elect from eternity, because He had from eternity an eternal purpose for being merciful with respect to them. And, taken in the second way, God is properly said to predestine the elect from the fact that He seems to send and direct them by means of grace to that end which is beatitude and glory.[7]

As on any SPE account, according to this description, God seems to choose some and to give grace to those He has chose simply because He has chosen them. There is no mention of human action in any stage of this process. Strassbourg argues, then, that the difference between predestination and reprobation is that in the former divine grace causes a person's salvation, while in the latter God simply notes a person's sin and damns him:

And through this the difference between the foreknowledge of the damned and the predestination of the elect is also clear. For "foreknowledge" indicates the simple awareness that <God> has concerning the damned, and if a divine purpose is in some way implied along with awareness, this is not <a purpose> according to which God proposes to act, but rather according to which God proposes to desist from acting. But "predestinatio" does not indicate a simple awareness, because the term <also> implies or includes a divine purpose—along with its efficacy—of having mercy or glorifying. And therefore, although the evil are not damned on account of God's impelling them into sin or towards sin, nevertheless none of the good is saved, unless God directs, sends, and impels them to glory by means of His grace.[8]

When Strassbourg turns to the question of why some are predestined and some are reprobated, he clearly endorses a GE account.

---

[7] *Ibid.*: "Est advertendum quod 'destinare' duo videtur significare. Nam 'destinare' idem est quod 'proponere', iuxta quod ait Apostolos, 'unusquisque prout destinavit in corde suo etc'. Et 2 Macchabeorum dicitur, 'Eleazarus destinavit non admittere illicita'. Secundo 'destinare' idem est quod 'mittere', iuxta quod dicitur littera 'destinata', id est 'missa'. Ut utroque modo satis est ad propositum. Nam iuxta primum modum Deus dicitur ab aeterno ipsos electos praedestinare, quia ab aeterno respectu eorum habuit propositum miserendi. Et secundo modo Deus dicitur electos proprie praedestinare, eo quod videtur eos mittere et dirigere per hoc medium, quod est gratia, in hunc finem, qui est beatitudo et gloria."

[8] *Ibid.*: "Et per hoc etiam patet differentia inter praescientiam damnatorum et praedestinationem electorum. Nam praescientia dicit simplicem notitiam quam habet de damnandis, et si cum notitia aliquo modo implicat divinum propositum, hoc non est secundum quod Deus proponit agere, sed potius secundum quod Deus proponit ab actu cessare. Sed praedestinatio non dicit simplicem notitiam, quia implicat sive includit divinum propositum cum sui efficacia ad miserendum et glorificandum. Et ideo, licet mali non damnentur ex hoc quod Deus eos impellat in culpam seu ad culpam, tamen nulli boni salvantur, nisi Deus mediante sua gratia eos dirigat et mittat seu impellat ad gloriam."

The reprobate, he tells us, are damned because they have resisted God's universal offer of grace by possessing an obstacle to it in the form of the evil use of free will. Strassbourg's description of reprobation follows Aureol's on every significant point, including the use of *I Timothy* 2:4 and the analogy likening God's offer of grace to the way the sun shines:

> As for adults, the cause of reprobation can be said to be the evil use of free choice enduring in them at the end of <their> life <as> foreknown by God from eternity. So, because God knew from eternity that such a man will wrongfully have used his free choice at the end of <his> life, therefore God decreed from eternity that His grace finally be withdrawn from such a person who, by his own temerity resists the divine inflowing of grace to the end, and that <he be> reprobate from the glory of eternal beatitude on the grounds that he is unfit...
>
> For it ought to be imagined for our purposes that, just as the sun diffuses <its> rays everywhere and, to the extent that it is possible, it illuminates everything by this sort of diffusion, nevertheless, if some things pose an obstacle to the rays diffused in this way, they remain in darkness, so God considered from His goodness makes the sun of spiritual grace rise over the good and the evil, since considered from His goodness He wills that no one perish, but rather "wills that all men be saved and come to recognition of the truth". Nevertheless, since from eternity He foresaw in some an obstacle of this sort resisting the grace diffused in the aforementioned way, thus such are said to be reprobated by God in the aforementioned way.[9]

Hence, unlike the Oxford theologians Ockham and Holcot, Strassbourg does not hesitate to "imagine" how and why God saves

---

[9] *Ibid.*, p. 112rb-va: "Quantum ad adultos, causa reprobationis dici potest malus usus liberi arbitrii usque ad finem vitae in ipsis duraturus, ab aeterno a Deo praescitus. Unde quia Deus scivit ab aeterno talem hominem in fine vitae suae abuti suo libero arbitrio, ideo a tali homine, influxi divinae gratiae sua temeritate finaliter resistente, Deus ab aeterno decrevit suam gratiam finaliter subtrahere et a gloria aeternae beatitudinis tanquam inhabilem reprobare...

"Est enim imaginandum in isto proposito quod sicut sol radios ubique diffundit et quantum in se est huiusmodi diffusione omnia illuminat, si tamen aliqua huiusmodi diffusis radiis obicam ponunt, illa tenebrosa manebunt, sic Deus solem gratiae spiritualis quantum est ex parte suae bonitatis oriri facit super bonos et malos, quia quantum est ex parte bonitatis ipse neminem vult perire, sed magis 'vult omnes homines salvos fieri et agnitionem veritatis venire'. Quia tamen ipse in aliquibus ab aeterno praevidit obicam resistentem huiusmodi gratiae diffusae modo praedicto, ideo tales modo quo dictum est a Deo dicuntur reprobari." See also, *ibid.*, III, d. 12, a. 1, p. 22ra: "Ad quintum dicendum quod Deus gratiam non subtrahit nisi quia homo gratiae obicem ponit. Et ideo quamvis sine gratia non possimus vitare peccata. Tamen Deus non est causa peccati, sed homo ponens obicem gratiae. Nam secundum Dionysius, 'sicut sol iste materialis, quantum de se est non ratiocinans neque praeeligens, radios suae claritatis rebus corporalibus iuxta modum suae capacitatis infundit, sic Deus', etc."

and damns, and so he explicitly employs Aureol's GE account. But
this does not mean that Strassbourg follows Aureol on every point.
Although they both argue for a created cause of predestination from
the premise that predestination and reprobation are parallel but opposite processes, they do not argue for the same cause. For Aureol,
the opposite of resisting grace is not resisting grace; there is no positive act on the part of the predestined. Strassbourg, however, focus-
es more on the nature of the obstacle to grace as sin and the evil use
of free choice. Since the opposite of the evil use of free choice is
good use of free choice, the cause of predestination must be good
use of free choice:

> One should notice, however, that, because opposites have opposite
> causes, and predestination and reprobation are in some way oppo-
> sites, we can, therefore, assign a cause of predestination from the op-
> posites of the causes of reprobation. So that one may match these op-
> posites one by one, I say—always deferring, of course, to a better
> opinion—that the cause of predestination of those adults seems to be
> good use of free choice foreknown from eternity by God to have en-
> dured in them to the end. And God contemplating from eternity the
> good use of free choice, proposed to give grace to such men having
> that sort of use at the end of the present <life>, so that by means of
> grace in the present, they may come to glory in the future.[10]

Even given Strassbourg's operating on a GE understanding of the
offer of grace, this claim, that the good use of free choice is the cause
of predestination, is alarming in the context of the Latin theological
tradition. On the face of it, such a claim seems to be clearly
Pelagian. The universal offer of grace appears to be reduced to the
general influence of God on creation, and salvation is left up to individual rational creatures. While this is exactly how Rimini will interpret this claim, Strassbourg's position, though certainly incautious, is
much more complex.

---

[10] *Ibid.*, I, d. 41, q. 1, a. 2, p. 112va: "Quantum ad secundum articulum, quae sit
causa praedestinationis, est advertendum quod, quia oppositorum oppositiae sunt
causae, praedestinatio autem et reprobatio aliquo modo sunt opposita, ideo causam
praedestinationis assignare possumus ex oppositis causarum reprobationis. Ut igitur
singula singulis per oppositum valeant <co>respondere, dico, salvo tamen semper
meliori iudicio, quod causa praedestinationis ipsorum adultorum videtur esse bonus
usus liberi arbitrii ab aeterno a Deo praecognitus finaliter duraturus. Et bonum
usum finalem Deus ab aeterno contemplans, proposuit talibus hominibus huiusmodi usum habituris sic dare gratiam finaliter in praesenti, ut mediante gratia in praesenti perveniant ad gloriam in futuro." We should notice how Strassbourg qualifies
this statement by the use of the common scholarly caveat, "salvo tamen semper meliori iudicio". It signals here, as in other authors, a realization that there may be
dangers in breaking with tradition and adopting this opinion. Taken along with the
tentative way in which Holcot came to accept GE, we can see how radical Aureol's
doctrine must have seemed at the time.

In his refutation of the common opinion held by Aquinas and Giles of Rome, Strassbourg explains what he means by good use of free will as a cause of predestination. Aware that he is deviating from an opinion held by two theologians whom he holds in high regard;[11] Strassbourg is, consequently, careful to answer the objections that he thinks would be raised by them. For our purposes, two objections concerning the relationship of grace to merit are most important. The first is that all good use of free choice is an effect of predestination; the second is that, if there is some meritorious cause of grace on the part of humans, then it is not grace.[12] Strassbourg's reply to these objections can be confusing, if they are taken out of the context of a scholastic debate. If they are both read not just as refutations of the opinion Strassbourg opposes, but also as arguments for his own position, then his responses seem contradictory.[13]

In reply to the first objection, Strassbourg insists that not all good use of free will is an effect of predestination:

> Good use of free choice can be understood in two ways. In one way <it can be understood> as simply [*de condigno*] meritorious of eternal life, or even appropriately [*de congruo*] <meritorious>, according to the relative disposition or motion towards sanctifying grace (concerning which motion <more> will be said below). In the second way, it can be taken as the good use of free choice belonging to the moral goodness to which man can <incline> from his purely natural ability; and even the moral philosophers wrote concerning this goodness. Therefore, taking the goodness of the use of free choice in the first way, the minor is true. Taking goodness of this sort in the second way, the minor is not true, because one ought not reduce this goodness to a supernatural principle; instead, the good disposition of man—presupposing the common and universal influence of God—suffices to attain such goodness... Therefore, this argument is besides the point.[14]

---

[11] *Ibid.*, p. 112va-b: "Sed hiis praedictis videtur obviare positio magnorum Doctorum loquentium in illa materia, scilicet sancti Thomae et venerabilis Doctoris fratris Aegidii..."

[12] *Ibid.*: "Praeterea, illud quod est effectus praedestinationis non potest esse causa eius; sed bonus usus liberi arbitrii est effectus praedestinationis; ergo non valet illud quod superius posuisti. Maior patet, quia idem non potest esse causa et effectus respectu eiusdem. Minor etiam patet, quia omne bonum quod se tenet ex parte praedestinati videtur esse effectus praedestinationis.

"Praeterea, si praedestinatio haberet causam se tenente ex parte praedestinati, tunc gratia Dei haberet causam ex parte praedestinati. Falsitas consequentis patet, quia si gratia esset ex meritis, iam gratia non esset gratia, sicut ait Apostolus."

[13] Shannon commits this error and tries to harmonize the two passages. This is one of the major flaws in his thesis. See Shannon, pp. 121-135.

[14] Strassbourg, *Commentaria*, I, d. 41, p. 112va-b: "Ad secundam dicendum quod 'bonus usus liberi arbitrii' potest dupliciter intelligi. Uno modo ut est meritorius vitae aeternae de condigno, vel etiam de congruo, secundum propinquam dispositionem vel motionem ad gratiam gratum facientem, de qua motione dicetur infra. Secundo potest accipi 'bonus usus liberi arbitrii' penes bonitatem morum in quam

It would be wrong to interpret this passage as drawing a distinction between those types of free choice that can be a cause of predestination and those that are an effect of predestination. Strassbourg makes it clear that morally good acts are not even meritorious *de congruo*, and thus not soteriologically significant. Strassbourg does not claim that morally good acts are a cause of predestination, only that they are not effects. The last line in the passage gives away his intention: he is not turning the objection around in his favor; he is instead rejecting it as pertinent to the question at hand.

Strassbourg's reply to the next objection indicates his explanation of how good use of free choice is a cause of predestination. The point of departure is the assertion that appropriate merits are the cause of predestination. Yet Strassbourg does not believe that assertion is unorthodox; as he points out, both Aquinas and Giles have held the opinion that the predestined merit glory congruously. But since glory is a kind of grace, it follows that other kinds of grace, such as initial grace, can be merited congruously as well:

> Nevertheless, grace can have a cause which is appropriately meritorious. And although perhaps to some this may seem incorrect, still it necessarily follows from the common doctrine of these doctors <Aquinas and Giles>, because they say that, even though before a man possesses love and sanctifying grace he cannot simply merit eternal life, he can, nevertheless, appropriately <merit it>. <And> following these same doctors, the glory of eternal life is perfected grace. From this it follows that <someone> not possessing grace can appropriately merit perfected grace. Consequently, it can be suitably and correctly said that <someone> who does not have grace can appropriately merit initial grace, that is, the grace of forgiveness...[15]

bonitatem potest homo ex puris naturalibus; de qua etiam bonitate scripserunt philosophi morales. Primo ergo modo accipiendo bonitatem usus liberi arbitrii, tunc minor est vera. Secundo modo accipiendo huiusmodi bonitatem, minor non est vera, quia non oportet illam bonitatem reducere in supernaturale principium, sed sufficit ad eam consequendam bona consuetudo hominis praesupposita communi et univesrali Dei influentia, et de hac bonitate locutus sum superius. Ideo argumentum non est ad propositum."

[15] *Ibid.*: "Ad tertiam dicendum quod gratia Dei non potest habere causam meritoriam de condigno, quia tunc gratia non esset gratia. Tamen gratia potest habere causam de congruo meritoriam. Et quamvis forte alicui illud videatur abusivum, tamen de communi doctrina istorum doctorum necessario sequitur, quia ipsi dicunt quod, licet homo priusquam habeat caritatem et gratiam gratum facientem non possit mereri vitam aeternam de condigno, potest tamen de congruo. Modo secundum eosdem doctores, gloria vitae aeternae est gratia consummata. Ex quibus sequitur quod non habens gratiam potest mereri de congruo gratiam consummatam. Et per consequens convenienter et sine abusione dici potest quod non habens gratiam potest mereri de congruo gratiam initiam, puta gratiam veniae, de qua procedit praedictum argumentum." See also, *Commentaria*, II, dd. 26-27, q. 1, a. 3, p. 179va: "Quantum ad tertium articulum, dico primo quod homo non existens in gratia non

Strassbourg describes the type of good use of free choice that is appropriately meritorious of predestination by referring to the parable of the prodigal son. The relationship of the sinner to God is like that of the prodigal son to his father. The son certainly did not earn his reacceptance into his father's house through any action of his own. He was always welcome to return home; all he had to do was reject his sinful ways and ask his father to take him back.[16] In the same way, Strassbourg continues, God universally and continually offers His grace to all. Thus, like Holcot before him, Strassbourg invokes the image of God knocking on a door: all the sinner need do is open the door and accept divine grace.[17] For Strassbourg, the assent to the offer of grace is the good use of free choice that causes predestination. He explains the relationship between divine grace and human action in this way:

---

potest mereri gratiam de condigno. Quia si homo consitutus in puris naturalibus posset mereri de condigno gratiam gratum facientem, de qua loquimur in praesenti, cum per talem gratiam homo sufficienter consequatur vitam aeternam quae est finis supernaturalis, tunc ex puris naturalibus possemus consequi finem supernaturalem, et per consequens finis supernaturalis non esset supernaturalis, quod est contradictorio. Praeterea, illud cui causaliter omne meritum nostrum inititur hoc mereri non possumus, gratia est huiusmodi, iuxta illud Augustini. Quid est meritum ante gratiam, cum omne bonum meritum nostrum in nobis non faciat, nisi gratia. Praeterea, si ex nostris naturalibus possumus de condigno mereri gratiam, tunc gratia esset debitum absolute. Et per consequens gratia non esset gratia."

[16] *Commentaria*,II, d. 26-27, q. 1, a. 3, p. 179vb: "Secundo dico quod existens sine gratia potest mereri gratiam de congruo, quia congruum esse videtur quod misericors pater prodigum et vagabundum filium, quamvis abierit in regionem longinquam variis se involens generibus peccatorum, reduentem ad gremium paterni domicilii cum pietate suscipiat et errata volenti corrigere, gratiam largiatur. Sed ipse Deus est misericors pater, iuxta illud Apostoli, 'Benedictus Deus et pater Domini nostri Iesu Christi', pater misericordiarum et Deus totius consolatius qui consolatur nos in omni tribulatione nostra. Peccator vero qui quantum ad vitae suae correctionem facit totum quod in se est, assimilatur praedicto filio prodigo dicenti in evangelio, 'Surgam et vadam ad patrem meum et dicam ei, "Pater peccavi in caelum et coram te, iam non sum dignus vocari filius tuus, fac me sicut unum de mercenariis tuis"'. Unde si faceret totum quod in se est, etiam Paganus existeret, Deus nunquam dimitteret, quin veritatem suae fidei sibi panderet et infunderet gratiam Spiritus Sancti, quod bene apparuit de Cornelio ad quem Deus miraculose misit Apostolum Petrum. Modus autem reduendi seu gratiam consequendi, <quamvis> in praedicta parabola satis sit expressus."

[17] *Ibid.*: "Potest tamen dici quod primo per gratiam praevenientem ipse Deus admonet per aliquos impetus spirituales ipsum peccatorem quorum perceptione ipse peccator incipit reatum suum cognoscere et aliqualem habere displicentiam peccatorum. Talibus enim admonitionibus Deus stat ad ostium et pulsat et petiti a nobis nostram conversionem et quia ex nobis ipsis converti non possumus, igitur ad ipsum clamare debemus illud, 'Converte nos Domine ad te et convertemur'. Ad quod respondet Dominus illud, 'Convertimini ad me et ergo convertar ad vos', id est, 'sequimini admonitionem meam et facite quod <in> vobis est et ego convertar ad vos communicando vobis gratiam meam'."

In and of himself, a man cannot sufficiently prepare himself for sanctifying grace, since just as natural forms are not joined to matter except through the prior motion <i.e. act> of a natural agent, in the same way supernatural forms, such as grace, are not joined to the souls of adult human beings without a supernatural agent supernaturally moving the soul itself. Nevertheless, because God with such motions does not take a person by force, but rather entices <him>, nor does He infuse grace, unless <the person> assents to such motions, our entire justification and preparation for grace is, therefore, both from God and from us. But these are from us in one way and from God in another way, because <they> are from God as an efficient cause, but from us consensually; <they are> from God principally, but from us, so to speak, instrumentally.[18]

While this is clearly a GE account of predestination, Strassbourg has made some significant modifications. As Aureol does on his GE account, Strassbourg allows for a cause on the part of the predestined for their predestination without denying the priority of divine grace. God is still the first, efficient cause of predestination in those who are predestined, but He does not cause predestination without the cooperation of the predestined. Furthermore, this cooperation is limited merely to consenting to the infusion of divine grace. But unlike Aureol and like Holcot, Strassbourg considers the human cause of predestination to be positive and in some sense meritorious. Even though Strassbourg was evidently not familiar with the "new English theology" and explicitly endorsed GE as a fully developed doctrine of predestination, he has still imported the notion of congruous merit and positive human action in order to explain the human role in predestination.[19]

---

[18] *Commentaria*, II, d. 28-29, q. 1, a. 2, p. 181ra-b: "Quantum ad secundum articulum, dico breviter quod homo praecise ex se non potest se ad gratiam gratum facientem sufficienter praeparare, quia sicut formae naturales non inducuntur in materiam nisi per motum prius factum ab agente naturali, sic forma supernaturalis, puta gratia, non inducitur in animam adulti hominis sine supernaturali agente supernaturaliter movente ipsam animam. Quia tamen in huiusmodi motionibus Deus hominem non violentat, sed allicit; nec sibi infundit gratiam nisi talibus motionibus assentiat, ideo tota nostra iustificatio et ad gratiam Dei praeparatio est a Deo et a nobis. Aliter tamen et aliter, quia a Deo est efficienter, a nobis autem consentienter; a Deo principaliter, a nobis autem quasi instrumentaliter. Hinc est quod auctoritates sacri canonis huiusmodi praeparationem quandoque attribuunt a nobis, sicut illud Zacchareus, '"Convertimini ad me", ait Dominus exercituum, "et ergo convertar ad vos"'."

[19] There is no good evidence that any of the theological works produced by scholars identified with the "new English theology" were known at Paris until the late 1330s. See Tachau, *Vision*, pp. 315-352; Courtenay, *Schools and Scholars*, pp. 163-167. According to Trapp, "Augustinian Theology", pp. 179-180, Strassbourg does not cite any Oxford-trained theologians.

Strassbourg's independent modification of GE was to prove historically important. While the modifications to GE made in the context of Oxford thought tended to obscure the implications of GE, Strassbourg highlighted them. As a result, although his junior confrere, Gregory of Rimini, would focus his attack on Aureol's understanding of election, he would also use Strassbourg's version as a foil for his own doctrine of reprobation, thereby giving Rimini the occasion to develop the implications of his anti-Pelagian attitude on divine election. Thus, both Aureol's and Strassbourg's versions of GE were instrumental to the development of Rimini's equally radical DPE account, to which it is now possible to turn.

Gregory of Rimini

In the several scholarly generations after Aureol, GE won important adherents on both sides of the Channel, without being itself the subject of a focused attack. This scenario changed when Gregory of Rimini began his Parisian lectures on the *Sentences* in 1343. While continuing the attack begun by Halifax and Bradwardine on the perceived Pelagian tendencies of the anthropological aspects of the Oxford *pactum* soteriology, Rimini also condemned what he considered to be Pelagian doctrines of predestination held by important Parisian theologians such as Henry of Ghent, Thomas of England, and, above all, the GE-doctrines of Peter Aureol and Thomas of Strassbourg. In doing so, Rimini went beyond a defense of the traditional Scholastic understanding of SPE.

There has been, relatively speaking, a great deal written about Rimini's doctrine of predestination. Some historians have even noted that his doctrine was unique among Scholastics; but none have noted that Rimini's understanding of predestination as DPE, along with Aureol's doctrine of GE, constitutes a significant change in the history of Latin theology.[20] With the development of DPE as a response to GE, the Scholastic consensus concerning predestination was irrevocably shattered. From this point on there would be three doctrinally viable doctrines of predestination in Western theology. The Reformation did not cause this pluralism; it merely reinforced a diversity that was already present in theological discussion.

---

[20] Both Schüler and Leff realize that Rimini's understanding of an active divine will to reprobate is uniquely his. Schüler is most concerned with showing how such a view is faithful to Augustine; Leff stresses the uniqueness of this view, but does not find it historically significant. See Schüler, *Prädestination*, pp. 51-69; and Leff, *Rimini*, pp. 198-203. These studies are useful, however, for understanding Rimini's views on predestination in relation to other aspects of his thought.

Moreover, the essentially reactionary nature of Rimini's doctrine has been missed altogether. Yet his entire discussion of the causes of predestination and reprobation is structured as a response to the opinions of Aureol and Strassbourg, with a few side arguments aimed at Henry of Ghent and Thomas of England.[21] Indeed, regardless of whether Rimini's doctrine of predestination is faithful to Paul and Augustine, it is not the case that DPE is merely the result (as some have supposed) of a deeper understanding of Augustine on the part of Rimini. Instead, DPE was developed by a scholar who was both immersed in the Augustinian corpus and deeply involved in the various soteriological conflicts of his time. It was on account of this context of conflict that Rimini turned to the anti-Pelagian Augustine in particular and interpreted "this" Augustine in a more radically theocentric way than had any Latin theologian since Gottschalk. Moreover, Rimini's doctrine of predestination addressed a specific controversy over divine election, not a general late Medieval "Pelagianism". Hence, it is no coincidence that the most significant and controversial aspect of Rimini's doctrine, that there is an eternal, active divine will to damn certain people, also provides his strongest defense against GE.

The Development and Definition of DPE

Rimini evidently did not endorse DPE from the first, but rather seems to have moved from an ambiguous understanding of particular election to DPE while revising his lectures on the *Sentences* at Paris. Early manuscript copies of his lectures contain texts which, while absent in other manuscripts, were once to have been found in the lost autograph of Rimini's text. Experts now concur that these so-called "additions" are instead earlier remarks which were deleted from later versions of the work.[22] Fortunately for our purposes, the inclusion of the "additions" in the critical edition allows us to see the development in Rimini's understanding of predestination.

---

[21] Vignaux, *Predestination*, pp. 165-175, notes Aureol's role as an opponent to Rimini, but does not see how this effects the development of Rimini's own doctrine.

[22] See, *Lectura*, vol. I, xiv-xvii, xciii-xcvii, where the editors argue that the "additions" are deletions. In light of the editors argument, William Courtenay reversed his own conclusions that the "additions" are later revisions. For his earlier position, see Courtenay, "Mirecourt", p. 157; for his later position, see the reprint of the same article in *Covenant and Causality in Medieval Thought: Studies in Philosophy, Theology, and Economic Practice*, [coll. essays], (London, 1984), p. 174a. See also: Katherine Tachau, review of *Gregorii Ariminensis OESA Lectura Super Primum et Secundum Sententiarum*, ed. Damasus Trapp OESA et al., *Speculum* 64 (1988), pp. 929-933.

The first article of Rimini's treatise on predestination is a short definitional exposition of the terms "predestination" and "reprobation". Rimini appears to have completely rewritten this section in the later versions of his lectures, presumably because he recognized that his earlier definitions of "predestination" and "reprobation" had been ambiguous and confused. Thus, at one point he holds a position concerning predestination and the divine will that is more appropriate for an SPE or GE account, namely: "...God cannot predestine what He does not foreknow, although He could foreknow what He does not predestine, for foreknowledge concerns even evil things, but predestination concerns only good things."[23] Yet immediately after this passage Rimini adopts the view that predestination and reprobation are equally attributed to the divine will:

> It is clear, therefore, that the nominal definition of "predestination", properly given, is understood as the eternal purpose of God by which He appointed some beforehand to whom to give grace. And thus, "reprobation" signifies the eternal purpose of God by which He pre-ordained not to give grace to such <a person>, but instead preordained eternal punishment, a just <punishment> suited for their sins.[24]

Even this passage, however, does not clearly endorse any one understanding of predestination. Even though Rimini attributes reprobation to the divine will, it is unclear whether God reprobates on account of human sin or merely on account of His will. The phrase *"preaordinavit autem iustam pro peccatis aeternam poenam"* can be read in more than one way. On the one hand, it can support an SPE-account. According to this reading, Rimini would be arguing that God ordained eternal punishment for some as a suitable punishment for their foreknown sins. On the other hand, the phrase could be read as an endorsement of DPE. On this reading, he would be arguing that even though God's will to punish does not take into account foreknown human sin, His preordination of eternal punishment for some is not unjust, since the sinners deserve the punishment anyway.[25] Sinners get what they deserve, but not *because* they deserve it.

---

[23] Rimini, *Lectura*, I, a. 1, (vol. 3, p. 322): "deus non potest praedestinare, quae non praescit, quamvis possit praescire, quae non praedestinat, nam praescientia est etiam de malis, praedestinatio vero de bonis tantum."

[24] *Ibid.*: "Patet ergo, quid nomine 'praedestinationis' proprie datur intelligi, quia scilicet aeternum dei propositum, quo quibusdam gratiam dare praestituit. Sic etiam per reprobationem significatur aeternam dei propositum, quo praeordinavit talem non dare gratiam, praeordinavit autem iustam pro peccatis aeternam poenam."

[25] At this point, Rimini's understanding of predestination is much like Bradwardine's, straddling the fence between a traditional SPE account and a more

The revised version (of 1343-1344) of this part of the treatise suffers from no such ambiguity. In this version he defines predestination and reprobation as follows:

> Therefore, predestination is the will or purpose itself for giving eternal life, but to give eternal life and to call and to justify are effects of predestination. But reprobation is the will to not <*velle non*> have mercy or, what is the same, the purpose for not giving eternal life; but to not have mercy and to not give eternal life are effects of reprobation...[26]

Insofar as this definition of predestination is concerned, Rimini has not broken any new ground, for such a statement as he offers is consonant with either the Thomist or the Franciscan view of SPE. Furthermore, the major divergence from Aureol's understanding would be the re-identification of predestination with the eternal, elective will of God. Rimini's definition of reprobation, however, puts him as far outside the mainstream as Aureol, but in the opposite direction. Here, after all, Rimini has not only re-identified reprobation with the eternal, elective will of God, but he has claimed that "reprobation" refers to a positive, active divine willing.

Rimini bases this last claim on an interpretation of two key passages in *Romans* (9:11-13 and 9:18) that lead him to a doctrine of double-particular election.[27] He argues that the words "diligere" and "odire" in verse 13 are synonymous with "velle miserere" and "velle indurare" in verse 18.[28] So verses 11 through 13 may be read according to Rimini: "When they had not yet been born or done any-

---

radically anti-Pelagian DPE account. It is tempting to make the argument that at this stage of his career Rimini was, like Bradwardine, unaware of the Parisian understanding of GE. It is likely, however, that Rimini was exposed to Aureol's work when Rimini began his theological training at Paris in the early 1320s. It is also quite possible that Rimini had access to Aureol's writings while teaching at the various northern Italian Augustinian *studia*. The most accessible description of Rimini's career is in Leff, *Rimini*, pp. 3-4; but see also, Venicio Marcolino, "Der Augustinertheologe an der Universitaet Paris", *Werk und Wirkung*, pp. 127-194, which supercedes Leff. My assumption is supported by the prominent role that Aureol plays in Rimini's lectures as one of his central opponents (see *Lectura*, vol. 7, pp. 358-359, for a complete list of citations of Aureol in Rimini's lectures).

[26] Rimini, *Lectura*, vol. 3, p. 323: "Est ergo praedestinatio ipsum velle seu propositum dandi vitam aeternam; dare autem vitam aeternam et vocare et iustificare sunt praedestinationis effectus. Reprobatio vero est velle non misereri seu, quod idem est, propositum non dandi vitam aeternam; non misereri autem seu non dare vitam aeternam est effectus reprobationis..."

[27] Vulgate, Ad Romanos, 9:11-13, 18: "¹¹cum enim nondum nati fuissent aut aliquid egissent bonum aut malum, ut secundum electionem propositum Dei maneret, ¹²non ex operibus sed vocante dictum est ei, quia maior serviet minori, ¹³sicut scriptum est, 'Iacob dilexi, Esau autem odio habui'...¹⁸ergo cuius vult miseretur et quem vult indurat."

[28] Rimini, *Lectura*, I, d. 40-41, a. 1, (vol. 3, p. 323).

thing good or evil... I willed to have mercy on Jacob and I willed to harden Esau." Unlike Aquinas, Alexander of Hales, or Scotus, Rimini concludes that the divine elective will pertains to both the predestined and the reprobate. Rimini reiterates this conclusion by arguing that, since with respect to any particular person, God either gives this person eternal life or not, it follows that with respect to any particular person, this person has been either predestined or reprobated from eternity by the divine will. Rimini bases this argument on two passages from Augustine that he treats as axiomatic. First, whatever God does, He does willingly. Second, whatever God wills, He has always and will always will. Thus, if God damns somebody, He damns that person according to an eternal, active will.[29]

In order to support this new understanding of predestination, Rimini redefines the relationship between the divine willing and divine foreknowledge as they pertain to predestination. While in his earlier version Rimini drew a sharp distinction between predestination and foreknowledge, he now collapses the distinction:

> Predestination, therefore, is the preparation and disposition for giving eternal life. Moreover, a disposition and a purpose are the same, and this is the proper signification of the term "predestination". Nevertheless, because it is not possible for God to predestine unless He is foreknowing, therefore the saints frequently define "predestination" by way of foreknowledge. Indeed, as Augustine says in the book <De bono perseverantiae>, sometimes they use the term "foreknowledge" in place of the term "predestination".[30]

Noting this reinterpretation of divine foreknowledge as it bears upon predestination allows us better to understand the otherwise ambiguous conclusion with which Rimini ends the definitional part of his treatise: "For any particular person whatsoever, God has ei-

---

[29] *Ibid.*, p. 324: "Quod probatur sic: Cuilibet homini deus dabit vel non dabit vitam aeternam; igitur quilibet homo fuit ab aeterno praedestinatus vel reprobatus. Antecedens patet. Consequentia probatur, quia, si alicui dabit, constat quod volens dabi, quia deus non nis volens quicquam facit, ut dicit Augustinus Enchiridio capitulo 103. Si cui autem volet dare, semper illi voluit dare, cum ipse nihil possit velle voluntate accedente et nova, ut patet per eundem 15 De Trinitate capitulo 20. Igitur cuicumque dabit vitam aeternam, ab aeterno voluit illam sibi dare, et per consequens ab aeterno fuit praedestinatus. Et similiter sequitur quod cuicumque non dabit, ab aeterno voluit illi non dare, igitur ab aeterno fuit reprobatus."
[30] *Ibid.*: "Praeparatio ergo et dispositio dandi vitam aeternam est praedestinatio; dispositio autem et propositum idem, et haec est propria significatio huius nominis 'praedestinatio'. Quia tamen non est possibile deum praedestinare nisi praesciendo, ideo sancti frequenter praedestinationem definiunt per praescientiam, immo, ut eodem libro dicit Augustinus, aliquando nomine praescientia pro nomine praedestinationis utuntur."

ther preordained or foreknown either the eternal kingdom or eternal punishment; therefore every person whatsoever is either predestined or reprobated from eternity".[31] It would be both grammatically and theologically acceptable to read this conclusion, in an SPE sense, to mean that the predestined are preordained to the eternal kingdom, while the reprobate are foreknown to face eternal punishment. But according to Rimini, there is no significant difference between fore-knowledge and predestination, nor, therefore, between foreknowl-edge and preordination. Thus, it would be more consistent with Rimini's previous statements to read the coordinates as conjunctive, rather than disjunctive. On such a reading then, with respect to God's predestining, foreknowledge and preordination are the same; indeed, with respect to God's will, predestination and reprobation are equal, differing only in their respective effects on particular human beings. In this later version of his *Sentence*'s lectures, Rimini has clearly departed from Scholastic tradition. His reasons for doing so become clear as soon as he begins his second article. There, in citing the opinions to which he is responding in this treatise, Rimini distinguishes between two types of predestinarian error. First, there are those who argue for a positive cause for predestination on the part of the predestined. Chief among them is Strassbourg.[32] On the other hand, there are those who argue for a negative cause for pre-destination on the part of the predestined—and here Rimini quotes Aureol at length.[33] Then he lays out the five conclusions he will de-fend in this treatise: (1) No one is predestined on account of the fore-knowledge of human free will; (2) no one is predestined on account of the foreknowledge of an absence of an obstacle to grace; (3) God predestines solely on account of mercy; (4) no one is reprobated on account of the foreknowledge of the evil use of free will; and (5) no one is reprobated on account of the foreknowledge of the presence

---

[31] *Ibid.*, p. 323: "Secundo sic: Cuilibet homini deus ab aeterno praeordinavit vel praescivit regnum aeternum vel poenam aeternam; igitur quilibet homo fuit ab aeterno praedestinatus vel reprobatus."

[32] *Ibid.*, a. 2, p. 325: "Secundum autem hunc intellectum aliquorum doctorum volentium reddere causam, quare isti vel illi sunt praedestinati vel reprobati, quidam reddiderunt causam positivam dicentes quod propter bona opera vel usum bonum liberi arbitrii, quam deus praescivit aliquos habituros, praedestinavit eos, et proter malum usum futurum in aliis illos reprobavit." The editors point out in n. 8 that Strassbourg is cited by name in the margin by Rimini.

[33] *Ibid.*, p. 326: "Demum alii dixerunt quod praedestinationis nulla est in praedestinatis causa positiva, privitiva tantum, scilicet absentia finalis obicis per cul-pam originalem vel actualem respectu gratiae dei, reprobationis vero est causa pos-itiva in reprobis, scilicet talis obex peccati gratiae." There follows a lengthy verba-tim quotation from Aureol (p. 326).

of an obstacle to grace.[34] His arguments for these conclusions reveal that they form an integrated attack on GE.

The Case for Particular-Election

Arguing for the first three conclusions, Rimini does not so much make a case against GE, as he makes a case for particular-election. In these passages we can most clearly see how alien a GE understanding of the economy of salvation was to Rimini. The arguments for the first three conclusions and the arguments for the last two should be read separately. The first three *assume* a particular-election understanding of predestination and reprobation. They are intended to reaffirm the traditional understanding of election and reveal the novelty of GE.

Rimini's arguments for the first conclusion (that no one is predestined on account of a foreknown use of free will) is directed primarily against those theologians who argue for a positive cause for predestination on the part of the predestined. Yet, even at this point, Rimini's attitude towards Aureol's understanding of election is apparent: although they begin from the same premise and arrive at the same conclusion, their understandings of how such a conclusion should be reached are fundamentally different. Like Aureol, Rimini argues against a positive cause of predestination on the part of the predestined from the fact that positing such a cause does not take into account all the predestined: "Since some who are predestined were not going to have any good use of free will, therefore no one is predestined on account of such use."[35] Again like Aureol, Rimini's example is the children who die immediately after baptism. Moreover, when he refutes the claim that such children are judged on account of the sins they would have committed, if they had lived, Rimini cites Aureol's argument to the same effect as supporting his own position.[36]

---

[34] *Ibid.*: "...prima est quod nullus est praedestinatus propter bonum usum liberi arbitrii, quem deus praescivit eum habiturum, qualitercumque consideretur bonitas eius. Secunda, quod nullus est praedestinatus, quia praescitus fore finaliter sine obicem habituali et actuali gratiae. Tertia, quod quemcumque deus praedestinavit, gratis tantummodo et misericorditer praedestinavit. Quarta, quod nullus est reprobatus propter malum usum liberi arbitrii, quem illum deus praevidit habiturum. Quinta, quod nullus est reprobatus, quia praevisus fore finaliter cum obice gratiae."

[35] *Ibid.*, p. 326: "Prima conclusio deducitur primo sic: Aliqui praedestinati fuerunt non habituri ullum bonum usum liberi arbitrii; igitur nullus praedestinatus propter talem usum."

[36] *Ibid.*, pp. 329-330.

Yet having established that the prospect of children dying immediately after baptism sufficiently deals with the argument for positive
causes on the part of the predestined for their predestination, Rimini
then parts company with Aureol. The latter had adduced the example of such children to show that, instead of a positive cause, theologians should attribute a negative or, more exactly, a "privative"
cause to the predestined. For Rimini, however, such a cause is not
an option. If there is no positive cause on the part of the predestined, then, Rimini assumes, there is no cause whatsoever on the
part of the predestined. Instead, the cause of predestination lies solely in the divine will.

For both Aureol and Rimini—and for Latin theologians generally—the good use of free will is an effect of grace. Aureol had departed from Scholastic tradition by saying that grace is offered to all
human beings. Rimini, by contrast, defends the priority of grace
through the claim that grace is not only a gift of God but also a gift
offered only to those particular people whom God has predestined.
Rimini supports his understanding of particular election by appealing to a passage from Augustine's *De praedestinatione sanctorum* where
Augustine paraphrases *Romans* 8:30 to support a particular election
account:

> For those whom <God> predestined He also called (namely by that
> call which is in accordance with His purpose), not therefore others.
> But those whom He predestined, He also called, but not others; but
> those whom He so called, He also justified, but not others...[37]

This commitment to particular election explains how Rimini can
follow the same line of reasoning as Aureol and come to such a different conclusion. In Rimini's arguments for his second conclusion
(that no one is predestined on account of the foreknown absence of
an obstacle to grace), which is directed specifically against Aureol,
Rimini returns to Aureol's example of children dying immediately
after baptism. This time, however, he attacks the assumptions by
which Aureol had constructed a GE-account of predestination. Rimini recalled that, according to Aureol, someone is either baptized
or not due to the natural course of temporal events. So, for instance,
if a person is born of unbelieving parents or dies soon after death,
there is no baptism—not, however, thanks to divine reprobation,
but rather due to God's not choosing to interfere with the course of
nature in this case. Conversely, if someone is baptized, then this,

---

[37] Augustine, *De praedestinatione sanctorum*, in *Patrilogia cursus completus. Series latina*,
ed. J-P Migne, (Paris, 1844-1864), vol. 44, p. 986. Hereafter: PL; Rimini, *Lectura*, I,
d. 40-41, a. 2, (vol. 3, p. 329).

too, is due to such circumstances as believing parents, and not pre-destination. For Rimini, such a claim is tantamount to Pelagianism. To prove that this is so, he describes two hypothetical situations which could follow from such a doctrine. First, even if baptism itself follows from a circumstance such as believing parents, the desire of the parents to have their child baptized must be an effect of divine grace, since it would be a good use of free will. If not, then it would be possible for an unbeliever who is knowledgeable about Christian customs to seek baptism and have his sins remitted solely out of his own free will.[38] Second, if the child who dies immediately after baptism were baptized according to the course of nature, then grace and eternal life would not be gifts of God as Scripture says, but effects of a purely natural event.[39]

These scenarios, however, do not address Aureol's intent. In these examples, Rimini assumes a particular-election account on which human action is either (a) a result of purely human use of free will or (b) a special gift of grace given only to those particular people chosen by God. But if one considers Rimini's example from Aureol's GE perspective, then Pelagianism is not the *necessary* conclusion. The non-believer in the first of Rimini's cases exemplifies exactly what Aureol had in mind when he described passive non-resistance to grace. Familiar with Christians and their customs, and not rejecting them, the non-Christian wishes to participate in the life of the Church. Nor does his desire to be baptized or his actual baptism earn him grace that had not yet been offered; rather these are the means by which he accepts the grace already offered. Furthermore, an analysis of the second example according to Aureol's theory

---

[38] Rimini, *Lectura*, I, d. 40-41, a. 2, (vol. 3, pp. 334-335): "Praeterea, quidquid sit de hoc, utrum scilicet ex solo naturali cursu et non ex speciali providentia dei aliquis praedestinatus nascatur de parentibus fidelibus, tamen quod eius parentes velint et faciant ipsum baptizari, non ex cursu naturali aut etiam ex libero arbitrio solum hoc provenit, sed ex speciali gratia dei, qui in eis 'operatur' illud bonum 'velle et perficere pro' sua, dei scilicet, 'bona voluntate', ut dicit Apostolus. Et confirmatur, quia, si parentes sine speciali dei motione vellent et facerunt filium baptizari, eadem ratione posset unus Iudaeus vel gentilis inter christianos conversatus et de consuetudine baptizari christianorum ex experientia informatus ex virtutue liberi arbitrii velle baptizari et baptismum petere et suscipere, deo hanc voluntatem in eo non specialiter operante, et per consequens ex puris naturalibus posset quis de statu perditionis ad stutum salutis et gratiae pervenire; quod forte non exit pelagianae heresis metas..."

[39] *Ibid.*, p. 335: "Praeterea, sequitur secundum hanc responsionem quod ex solo cursu naturali stante communi ordinatione divina quis sit determinate praedestinatus et ordinatus ad vitam aeternam illamque consequatur; quod utique non dubium est adversari catholica fidei, tunc enim non secundum electionem gratiae 'reliquae salvae fierent', nec electi essent 'vasa misericordiae, quae deus praeparavit in gloriam', et innumera dicta scripturae alia falsa essent."

would construe "predestination", "grace", and "eternal life" not as the effects of the course of nature *alone*, but also of God's universal will to save everyone.

Rimini's choice of examples does not reflect a misunderstanding of GE on his part. What it does reflect is the differing understandings of God that lie at the root of the disagreement over election. For Aureol, God by His nature loves His creatures and wills grace and salvation to all of them. Yet, He leaves His creatures free to resist His love and grace. Aureol's God does not choose among His creatures arbitrarily, but rather with respect to their attitudes towards His love. Rimini correctly sees this view of the divine nature and its relationship with creatures as the basis for Aureol's objection to particular election. Accordingly, Rimini singles out and refutes Aureol's notion of a God who offers grace universally.[40]

Rimini admits that God is a universal agent, but also asserts that He is a free agent. As a free agent God is not bound by His nature to act in any way. And, inasmuch as God is the creator of the universe, He can be likened to an artificer who does one thing to one part of the matter he is shaping and another thing to another part of it, as he sees fit.[41] Moreover, not only can God act in whatever way He pleases, but whatever God wills to do, He does. Therefore, if God wills that a particular person be saved, that person will be saved regardless of whether that person resists or not.[42] Rimini's use of the conversion of Paul to explain this illustrates the differences between him and Aureol. For Rimini, the conversion of Paul is an instance of God's irresistibly infusing grace into a hitherto hardened sinner, whereas Aureol had interpreted it as exemplifying the appropriate human response to a resistible offer. Nor does Rimini take Paul's case to be the exception to the rule as Ockham does. Sanctifying grace, according to Rimini, is always irresistible and offered only to a few.

Given this understanding of God and the divine offer of grace, Rimini can state in his third conclusion:

---

[40] *Lectura*, I, d. 40-41, a. 2, (vol. 3, p. 343).

[41] *Ibid.*, p. 345: "Ad secundum dico quod, si illa prima propositio sumatur pro una universali, falsa est, et habet instantiam de agente libero. Artifex namque non agit in quamlibet partem obiectae materiae, sed in aliquam sic et in aliquam non, ut sibi placet. Deus autem liberrimus est in agendo."

[42] *Ibid.*: "Nec valet ad obsistendum dicere quod, quibus non dat huiusmodi dona, in eis invenit impedimentum, quia nullum impedimentum est possibile esse, ubi vult agere, sicut patet in conversione Pauli, cui maiorem gratiam contulit quam multis iam fidelibus et iustis, in quibus nullum erat impedimentum, et aliis etiam minus indispositis quam ipse non tribuit."

Whoever is predestined has been predestined by the mercy and graciousness of the divine will alone…and neither is anyone predestined on account of good works or the good use of free choice, nor on account of a lack of sin or whatever else renders man unworthy of eternal life, which God foresaw as future; but rather these things follow from his predestination.[43]

The Case for Double-Particular Election

As strong as this statement is, however, it does not end the discussion. Although Rimini has made a strong case *for* particular election, he has not really made a strong case *against* GE. Most importantly, he has not addressed Aureol's critique of SPE on its own terms; this, then, is the task to which Rimini turns in arguing for his last two conclusions. But to make a case against GE, he must eliminate the weakness of SPE. Aureol had argued that SPE was untenable because it was inconsistent: if there is a cause on the part of the reprobate for reprobation, then it follows that there must be some kind of cause on the part of the predestined for predestination. Far from rejecting Aureol's reasoning, Rimini tacitly accepts it. Hence, Rimini's defense of particular election is not an argument for the reasonableness of the causally asymmetrical SPE account. Instead, Rimini argues for an account of particular election which does not suffer from any such inconsistency: double-particular election (DPE).

Rimini undertakes a methodical exegesis of Paul's classic statement concerning divine predestination in *Romans* 9 in order to defend his fourth conclusion (that no one is reprobated on account of the foreknowledge of the evil use of free choice). For Rimini, the history of Jacob and Esau clearly indicates that both predestination and reprobation are equally and solely attributable to the divine will:

> Just as the following words <*Romans* 9:13> declare: "As it is written: 'Jacob I have loved, but Esau I have hated'", the Apostle <Paul> says that, just like the love for or predestination of Jacob, the hatred for or reprobation of Esau "is not from his works, but from God calling <him> according to <His> election", etc. Therefore, just as it cannot be said that Jacob is predestined from past, present, or future works (as has been proven above), in the same way it is not truly said

---

[43] *Ibid.*: "Tertia conclusio, videlicet quod quilibet praedestinatus fuit praedestinatus ex sola misericordia et gratuita voluntate divina, probatur primo quidem ex praecedentibus, per quae monstratum est quod nec propter bona opera aut bonum usum liberi arbitrii nec propter carentiam culpae aut cuiuscumque reddentis hominem indignum vitae aeternae, quae deus praevideret futura, quisquam est praedestinatus, sed potius eius praedestinationem talia consequuntur."

according to the intention of the Apostle, or of Augustine, that Esau is reprobated from future works. For concerning both <the Apostle> said that <it is> "not from works" etc.

And this <interpretation> is supported, because the Apostle, wishing to prove that <reprobation> is not from works, says these words <Romans 9:11>: "For when they had not yet been born or done anything good or evil". Nor did he speak only of Jacob, "when he had not yet been born or done anything good", in order to reveal that he is not even predestined from future <works>, but, having spoken in the plural, <the Apostle> also mentions the doing of evil, in order similarly to declare that Esau was not reprobated from future evil works.[44]

To support this reading, Rimini turns to what is for him the key passage in chapter 9, verse 18: "Therefore, <God> has mercy on whom He wills, and hardens whom He wills".[45] Rimini has already used this passage in the question's first article to show that the predestination of Jacob and the reprobation of Esau were parallel, by proposing that *"miserere"* and *"indurare"* could be substituted for *"diligere"* and *"odire"* in verse 13. Here once again, he resorts to verse 18 to interpret another verse in chapter 9 in support of DPE. In 9:16, Paul says that salvation is "therefore not from willing or running, but from the mercy of God".[46] Citing Augustine's *Ad Simplicianum* in support, Rimini claims that, in light of verse 18, verse 16 implies not only that salvation is due only to the mercy of God, but also that damnation is due solely to God's obduration.[47] Therefore,

---

[44] *Ibid.*, p. 338: "...sicut declarant verba sequentia: 'Sicut, inquit, scriptum est: "Iacob dilexi, Esau autem odio habui"'; hoc autem odium seu reprobationem aeque sicut et Iacob dilectionem vel praedestinationem dicit Apostolus 'non ex operibus eorum esse, sed ex deo vocante ut secundum electionem etc'. Unde, sicut non potest dici quod ex operibus praeteritis, praesentibus vel futuris sit Iacob praedestinatus, ut supra probatum est, sic secundum intentionem Apostoli et Augustini non vere dicitur quod Esau sit ex futuris operibus reprobatus; de utroque namque ait quod 'non ex operibus etc'.
"Confirmatur, quia Apostolus volens probare quod non ex operibus ponit illa verba: 'Cum nondum nati essent {fuissent: Vulgate} aut egissent aliquid boni aut mali', nec solum dixit de Iacob 'cum nondum natus esset aut aliquid boni egisset', ut ostenderet eum non ex operibus suis etiam futuris praedestinatum, sed pluraliter locutus est et actionem mali commemoravit, ut similiter declararet Esau non fuisse ex futuris malis operibus reprobatum."
[45] *Ibid.*
[46] Vulgate, Ad Romanos, 9:16: "...igitur non volentis neque currentis sed miserentis dei."
[47] Rimini, *Lectura*, I, d. 40-41, a. 2, (vol. 3, pp. 338-339): "Secundo, idem probatur ex sequenti verbo Apostoli 'non est, inquit, volentis neque currentis, sed dei est miserentis', et statim concludit 'ergo cuius vult miseretur, et quem vult indurat', id est, 'non miseretur', ut exponit Augustinus, per quorum verborum consequentiam secundum Augustinum colligitur quod, sicut Apostolus dixerat 'non est volentis neque currentis, sed Dei miserentis', sic etiam dici debeat secundum intentionem Apostoli 'non est volentis neque currentis, sed obdurantis' id est non miserentis dei, 'ut obduratio', secundum quod dicit Augustinus, 'sit nolle misereri, non ut aliquid

Just as it is not because a person wills or runs (i.e. works) well that God has mercy on that person, nor is it even that God wills from eternity to have mercy on a person because that person will have had good will and works, so therefore, it is not because a person was going to have had an evil will and evil works that God wills from eternity to have mercy upon him.[48]

Rimini is aware that such a reading of Paul seems to impute injustice to God and to deny human free will, but this, he finds, buttresses his claim. He points out that Paul himself had anticipated the charge that, if reprobation and obduration occur solely on account of the divine will, then humans are not responsible for their sins.[49] Rimini takes this to mean that Paul really has endorsed DPE, since if he did not, why bother dealing with the objection at all?[50] And surely, if he had meant that Esau was reprobated on account of foreknowledge of his sins, Paul would have said so in replying to his own objection. Instead, Paul responds in 9:20-21 that it is not for humans to question the divine will; after all, Paul remarks, the relationship between God and humans is like that of a potter to his clay.[51]

After building his own Scriptural argument, Rimini must then deal with the Biblical passages that Aureol had deployed, particularly *I Timothy* 2:4. First, Rimini argues, this passage cannot be interpreted literally, whether one is arguing for or against a cause of reprobation:

---

ab illo irrogetur, quo sit homo deterior, sed tantum, quo sit melior, non erogetur'." See Augustine, *Ad simplicianum*, PL, vol. 40, I, c. 2, n. 15, p. 120.

[48] *Ibid.*: "Ergo, sicut non quia quis bene vult aut currit, id est operatur, ideo deus eius miseretur, nec etiam deus ab aeterno voluit eius misereri, quia ille habiturus erat bonam voluntatem et opera, sic non quia aliquis erat habiturus malam voluntatem et opera mala, ideo deus ab aeterno voluit eius non misereri."

[49] *Ibid.*: "cum dixisset 'cuius vult miseretur, et quem vult indurat', statim obicit: 'Dicis itaque mihi, ut quid deus queritur', id est 'conqueritur' de his, qui nec bene volunt nec bene operantur? 'Nam voluntati eius quis resistit?' Quasi diciat, cum nullus quicquam possit contra voluntatem dei, si deus quos vult indurat, non possunt illi bene agere, et per consequens nec de eis ipse iuste conqueritur."

[50] *Ibid.*: "Secunda vero obiectio solum locum videtur habere propter reprobationem malorum, sicut et tantum de malis deus conqueritur, quae tamen non haberet locum, si propter mala opera reprobarentur."

[51] *Ibid.*, pp. 339-40: "Praeterea, idem patet ex responsione Apostoli, qui non dixit quod propter mala opera deus reprobat—quod si ita esset, utique dixisset et plane satisfecisset contradicenti—, sed hominem ad considerationem propriae infirmitatis, qua non potest capere alta iudicia dei, revocavit dicens: 'O tu homo quis es, ut respondeas deo?' Et postea adhibuit exemplum de figulo, in cuius potestate et 'ex eadem massa facere vasa in honorem et vasa in contumeliam', ut ex hoc ostenderet deum eos, quibus non vult gratis misereri, sine cuius misericordia nemo potest bona operari, absque iniustitia permittere ex vitiata massa generis humani in interitum ire."

I say to another <objection> derived from the authority of the Apostle <*I Timothy* 2:4> that <it> does not proceed any more against me than against those positing a cause of reprobation <on the part of the reprobate>. For, supposing that <God> reprobates from a cause <on the part of the reprobate>, nonetheless, He does reprobate, and consequently there are some whom He does not will to save. Second, I say that, if the reasoning <behind this objection> were valid, then it would prove that every person is predestined and that none is reprobated, which is erroneous.[52]

Next, Rimini cites Augustine's interpretations of these verses as authoritative. According to Augustine's reading, the Apostle's words could mean either that with respect to the saved, God willed their salvation, or that God wills to save kinds of men.[53]

Finally, Rimini must deal with the objection that, according to DPE, God causes sin. He rejects the inference that, just because sin is not the cause of reprobation, reprobation must be the cause of sin. DPE does not replace the divine foreknowledge of sin in the SPE account with an active divine will that humans sin; rather, DPE replaces the lack of a divine will to give grace with an *active will* to deny grace:

> For to afflict or to punish is not to reprobate. Therefore, God neither reprobates someone so that He may punish <that person>, nor does He punish because He reprobated, but <He punishes> because the one whom He punishes has sinned or has been condemned by sin, of which sin, moreover, divine reprobation is not the cause. For God does not reprobate someone by imparting wickedness, but by not imparting grace; nor <does He reprobate> by impelling someone into sinning, but by not leading that person to good works through His grace.[54]

---

[52] *Ibid.*, p. 348: "Ad aliam ex auctoritate Apostoli incedentem dico primo quod non plus procedit contra me quam contra ponentes causam reprobationis. Nam supposito quod ex causa reprobet, reprobat tamen, et per consequens aliquos non vult salvos fieri. Secundo dico quod, si ratio valeret, probaret omnem hominem esse praedestinatum et neminem reprobatum; quod est erroneum."

[53] *Ibid.* See also, Augustine, *De praedestinatione sanctorum*, IIX, c. 6, n. 18, (PL, vol. 44, p. 971); and *idem*, *Enchiridion*, XXVII, c. 103, (PL, vol. 40, p. 280). While it was common for Medieval Scholastics to cite Augustine's interpretation of *I Timothy* in support of particular election, these interpretations were rejected at the Second Council of Orange in the 6th century. Since, however, the decrees of that council were lost until the 16th century, Medieval Scholastics were unaware that Augustine's doctrines of election, predestination and reprobation did not have the same authority as his doctrine of grace. See Pelikan, *Christian Tradition*, vol. 1, pp. 318-331.

[54] *Ibid.*: "Nam affligere et punire non est reprobare, nec propterea reprobat deus quemquam ut puniat, nec punit quia reprobavit, sed quia ille, quem punit, peccavit aut peccato reus fuit, cuius peccati etiam non fuit causa divina reprobatio. Non enim deus aliquem reprobat impartiendo malitiam, sed eum ad bene agendum per suam gratiam non trahendo."

The distinction that Rimini draws here between the will to reprobate and the will to punish underscores the development in Rimini's
thought over the course of his teaching. On his earlier definition of
reprobation the will to deny grace and the will to punish are each an
aspect of the will to reprobate. If, at that point, Rimini was already
endorsing a DPE account, then he had not yet worked out the rela-
tionships among reprobation, sin, and punishment. On his later definition, however, there is no mention of punishment; reprobation is
merely the will to not have mercy or to not give eternal life.[55]

Once Rimini has established that reprobation is not caused by
human sin, he is able to respond to Aureol's doctrine of reprobation,
for in identifying reprobation with an active divine will, Rimini has
eliminated the basis for Aureol's critique of SPE. Indeed, the argument for the fifth conclusion (that no one is reprobated on account
of the foreseen absence of an obstacle to grace), which is addressed
to Aureol, merely refers to previous arguments.[56] Since Aureol had
defined an obstacle to grace as the presence of sin, Rimini does not
need any new arguments to refute Aureol's doctrine of reprobation.

In order to reject GE and what Rimini considered its Pelagian
tendencies, he also rejected the Scholastic consensus position of
SPE. While doing so may have made for a more logically consistent
account of particular election, it was not a victory without costs. As
we shall see, some of the most ardent anti-Pelagian authors of the
later Middle Ages could not accept Rimini's identification of reprobation with the divine will. Far from resolving a dilemma, Rimini's
doctrine of DPE instead created a "trilemma" which all later Latin
theologians who addressed the problem of predestination would
have to confront.

---

[55] Rimini's distinction between the will to reprobate and the will to punish in article 2 of distinctions 40-41 also strengthens the case that the "additions" in this
question are earlier versions. If the "additio" 151 were a later revision, then Rimini
would have revised article 1 so that it would contradict an argument central to article 2. If we can assume that Rimini would be careful enough to be consistent on
such an important point, then we should consider the *textus ordinarius* of article 1 to
be the revised version.
[56] *Ibid.*, p. 342.

CHAPTER SIX

PREDESTINARIAN PLURALISM IN THE LATER MIDDLE AGES

By 1344, the Scholastic consensus concerning predestination had been replaced by multi-sided debate centering on the nature and extent of divine election. Far from settling the issue, Rimini had instead complicated it. While this debate did not occupy center-stage in the later Middle Ages, it was prominent; and once introduced into the polarized atmosphere of the Reformation, it became a leading point of conflict. Thus a brief survey of the development of this issue up to the Reformation would be a useful way to close this study, even if it is not yet possible to give an exhaustive account of the development of the debate over predestination between 1350 and 1500. Focusing on several major figures will, nevertheless, suffice to demonstrate that the debate not only lived on, but continued to be shaped by a developing theological context. Furthermore, such a focus will permit a reassessment of the current scholarly depiction of late Medieval soteriology.

The most obvious place to look for predestinarian controversy is in the writings of those authors who have been described by modern scholars as "anti-Pelagian". One does find controversy, but it is not the sort that is expected. All of the anti-Pelagian authors who are treated here, insofar as they mention GE, condemn it; they are not, however, unified as to what is the best alternative. Surprisingly, anti-Pelagian authors *within* the Augustinian Order reject Rimini's understanding of DPE in favor of a "reinforced" version of SPE. The basic dilemma they perceive is to maintain a sufficiently strong version of SPE, while not falling into the determinism implied by DPE. Also surprisingly, DPE is adopted *outside* the Augustinian Order by such important late Medieval theologians as Pierre d'Ailly and Marsilius of Inghen.

Anti-Pelagians were not the only authors interested in GE. At least one defender of the Thomist version of SPE took GE very seriously. Aquinas's most influential late Medieval apologist, John Capreolus, saw Aureol's version of GE as the only significant threat to Aquinas's understanding of predestination. But far from resolving the conflict, Capreolus would confirm the fact that between the two positions there is only mutual misunderstanding. Although condemned from many sides, GE survived as a viable theological option on the eve of the Reformation. In fact, it was endorsed by Gabriel Biel, arguably the most influential academic theologian of the later Middle Ages. Biel, a theologian who took the thought of William Ockham as his reference point, defended the more anthropocentric *pactum* version of GE developed by Ockham and Holcot.[1] Unlike Ockham, however, Biel explicitly endorsed GE, rather than just assuming it tacitly.

DPE and Late Medieval Anti-Pelagianism

According to common scholarly opinion, Gregory of Rimini was the founder of a late Medieval anti-Pelagian trend, currently known as the *schola Augustiniana moderna*, within the Augustinian Order.[2] Recently, however, the soteriological unity of this group has been called into question, particularly concerning the doctrine of justification.[3] This same critical attitude ought to be focused on the doctrine of predestination as well. It is true that anti-Pelagian Augustinian Hermits commonly used predestination as one of their weapons against perceived heresy, but it is not the case that Augustinian anti-Pelagians followed Rimini's tactic of endorsing DPE.[4] On the contrary, a cursory analysis of the doctrines of John Klenkok, Hugolino of Orvieto, and John Hiltalingen of Basel—three of the most important anti-Pelagian authors in the Augustinian order during the second half of the 14th century—shows that insofar as predestination is concerned there were anti-Pelagian theologians as worried about avoiding the deterministic implications of DPE as they were with condemning perceived Pelagianism. Caught between Scylla and Charybdis, they adopted a "strong" version of SPE. According to the latter, God does not have an active will to damn, but the will to predestine some also affects those not predestined, since their status as "not predestined", and thus their eventual reprobation, is settled by the divine will to predestine some and not others.[5] Unlike earlier ver-

---

[1] See chapter 4.

[2] See above, Introduction.

[3] See McGrath, "'Augustinianism'?", pp. 247-267.

[4] Hereafter, unless otherwise specified, the term "Augustinian" will refer to theologians belonging to the Order of Augustinian Hermits.

[5] This strong view of SPE presupposes a pessimistic anthropology according to which man, after the Fall, is so inclined to sin that those who are not predestined necessarily merit damnation. For the Augustinian anti-Pelagian understanding of sin and human free will, see Schüler, *Prädestination*; Burger, "Der Augustinerschuler"; Adolar Zumkeller, "Der Augustinertheologe Johannes Hiltalingen von Basel (+1392) über Urstand, Erbsünde, Gnade und Verdienst", *Analecta Augustiniana*, 43 (1980) pp.

sions of SPE, reprobation on this theory is not caused by sins, but rather, someone is reprobated when God does not predestine that person.

The English Augustinian John Klenkok provides the earliest example of this tendency to opt for a strengthened SPE. His lectures on the *Sentences*, delivered at Oxford in 1354-1355, contain doctrines of grace and justification that are explicitly directed against a modern "Pelagianism".[6] But in his doctrine of predestination, Klenkok is equally concerned with avoiding the determinism of DPE: "Reprobation, however, does not refer to an act of the <divine> will, but only to a negation of predestination."[7] Yet this does not mean that humans are responsible for their own particular reprobation. If sin were after all the cause of reprobation, then, according to Klenkok, Paul and Mary Magdalene would have been reprobate.[8] Augustinian anti-Pelagians such as Klenkok emphasized that sin was a constant factor in human life, and thus could not be a reason why some were reprobate and not others.

Klenkok formulated his "strong" SPE in response to the doctrine of Bradwardine whom he considered to have held DPE.[9] Given the fact that Klenkok knew Rimini's works well and that he was presumably sharp enough to realize that Rimini's version of DPE was much stronger than Bradwardine's, Klenkok should also be seen as rejecting Rimini's understanding of predestination. That Klenkok failed to mention Rimini by name should not pose a problem, since Rimini was the minister-general of the Augustinian Order at the time Klenkok lectured on the *Sentences*. His tacit rejection of Rimini is all the more significant, because Klenkok was responsible for transmitting Rimini's anti-Pelagianism to the English Augustinians.[10]

57-162; *idem*, "Hugolin von Orvieto (+1373) über Urstand und Erbsünde", *Augustiniana*, 3 (1953), pp. 165-193; 4 (1954) 25-46.

[6] Adolar Zumkeller, "Johannes Klenkok O.S.A. (+1374) im Kampf gegen den 'Pelagianismus' seiner Zeit: Seine Lehre über Gnade, Rechtfertigung und Verdienst", *Recherches Augustiniennes*, 13 (1978), pp. 231-333; Courtenay, *Schools and Scholars*, p. 315.

[7] John Klenkok, *Expositio litteralis super libros Sententiarum*, 1, d. 40, in Zumkeller, "Klenkok", p. 260, n. 112: "Reprobatio autem non dicit actum voluntatis, sed solum negationem praedestinationis."

[8] *Ibid.*, n. 116: "Hic quidam errantes dixerunt, quod Deus reprobet propter futura peccata, quae homo facturus esset, si viveret, esto quod ea non faciat. Hoc reprobat Augustinus, quoniam sic Paulus et Maria Magdalena reprobati fuissent, antequam nati essent."

[9] *Ibid.*, n. 118: "Unde male dicit Bradwardine, quod positive volendo Deus reprobat et indurat et obdurat."

[10] Trapp, "Augustinian Theology", pp. 223-239; *idem*, "Notes on John Klenkok O.S.A. (+1373)", *Augustinianum* 4 (1964), pp. 358-404.

Still, Klenkok's rejection of Rimini on predestination is readily explicable when we think of him as not merely a conduit of continental theology to Oxford, but also as himself immersed in Oxonian theology. The English soteriological controversy revolved around anthropology, and not election. Moreover, English theologians had been sensitized to the dangers of determinist tendencies by Bradwardine. Thus, in the English context, an endorsement of DPE carried more dangers than benefits.

But even at Paris, where election was a central issue, Augustinian anti-Pelagianism departed from Rimini over predestination. Hugolino of Orvieto was one of the few Augustinian theologians of the 14th century to approximate Rimini's influence.[11] In terms of his soteriology, he has been pictured as carrying on the anti-Pelagian program of Rimini.[12] This program, however, does not for Orvieto include DPE. Instead, he explicitly rejects DPE as an acceptable understanding of predestination, even at the expense of his anti-Pelagian program.

Thus, at the beginning of his discussion of predestination, Orvieto denies that "reprobation" refers to a positive, active divine will:

> But "reprobation" does not denote divine will in a positive sense…, it is therefore <to be taken> negatively as the lack of divine purpose for finally having mercy or for finally preparing for eternal glory. Or <it can be taken> as, so to speak, a spontaneous forsaking, so that <God> does not finally have mercy <on the reprobate>, not so that <the reprobate> be evil, but so that <he> be as he was going to be on his own <ability> with regard to merit. Therefore, to reprobate is to not propose finally to have mercy and freely to forsake those born from the mass of sin.[13]

---

[11] Unlike the writings of most 14th-century authors, a significant portion of Orvieto's major works are available in modern critical editions. For his lectures of the *Sentences*, see *Hugolini de Urbis Veteri OESA Commentarius in Quattor Libros Sententiarum*, ed. Willigis Eckerman OSA, (Wuerzburg, 1984). The first part of his commentary on Aristotle's *Physics* is contained in Willigis Eckerman OSA, *Der Physikkommentar Hugolins von Orvieto OESA*, (Berlin, 1972), pp. 13-99. There is also a relatively large body of secondary work pertaining to Orvieto, for which, see Egon Gindele, ed., *Bibliographie zur Geschichte und Theologie des Augustiner-Eremitenordens bis zum Beginn der Reformation*, (Berlin, 1977), pp. 217-220.

[12] Adolar Zumkeller, "Hugolin von Orvieto (+1373) über Prädestination, Rechtfertigung unde Verdienst", *Augustiniana*, 4 (1954) pp. 109-156; 5 (1955) pp. 5-51; *idem*, "Hugolin über Urstand und Erbsünde".

[13] *Hugolini Commentarius*, I, d. 41, q. 1, a. 1, (vol. 2, p. 382): "'Reprobatio' vero non denotat positive velle divinum, ut est respectu aliqualiter esse semper in tempore, est igitur negative divinum non propositum finaliter miserendi seu ad gloriam aeternam praeparandi finaliter seu est quasi spontanea relictio, ut non finaliter misereatur, non ut sit malus, sed ut sit, qualis ex se futurus sit quoad meritum. Igitur non proponere misereri finaliter nascituri de massa peccati est sponte relinquere, reprobare."

Orvieto has clearly returned to an SPE understanding of predestination, specifically towards a model which resembles the Scotist version. Whereas Rimini had spoken of a divine purpose for denying mercy (*proponere non*), Orvieto carefully explains that reprobation is a lack of purpose (*non proponere*).

But merely moving negatives around does not solve the problem for Orvieto, since he is genuinely concerned with the Pelagian ramifications of GE. Like Rimini's, Orvieto's doctrine of predestination is framed, at least in part, around a response to Aureol's version of GE.[14] He goes so far as to restate Rimini's five conclusions against GE.[15] The problem that this poses for Orvieto is that conclusion four, which is an endorsement of DPE, is the crux of Rimini's attack on GE. For Rimini, the only way to avoid GE was to defend the causal parallelism of predestination and reprobation. Both must refer to an active, positive divine will. Thus, Orvieto must restate conclusion four so that it still refutes GE without endorsing DPE. He attempts to do this by distinguishing between two senses of "reprobation". Taken strictly, "reprobation" refers to the lack of divine purpose for giving grace and glory. He describes this, as he does above, as a forsaking of the reprobate who are mired in the mass of sin. In a broader sense, "reprobation" can refer to a purpose for not giving grace, insofar as it is a purpose for punishing the reprobate.[16] Having drawn this distinction, Orvieto can now restate conclusion four:

> No one is reprobated or forsaken in the eternal present, <if "reprobated" is> taken in the first, strict sense of being merely not predestined, because <he> is foreseen to merit <reprobation> in time. This is proved: There are no works done by a pilgrim <in this life> which either are or can be so evil, but that <1> it is possible for the person to be preserved from them by God; <2> God could show mercy for them; and <3> that God in His eternal <present> could, finally and temporally, will to have mercy. If, therefore, <God> does not will and did not will in His eternal <present> to preserve <the person> in time from an obstacle <to grace> or from sin, and does not will to have mercy (and this is to reprobate and forsake), it follows that, strictly speaking, <God> does not have mercy <on the person> be-

---

[14] It is not clear that Orvieto had direct contact with Aureol's doctrine. Orvieto actually frames his doctrine around Rimini's five conclusions which were themselves a response to Aureol. It seems that Orvieto knew Aureol through Rimini, since he does not engage Aureol in his own right, nor does he quote him directly.

[15] *Hugolini Commentarius*, I, d. 41, q. 1, a. 2, (vol. 2, pp. 385-391).

[16] *Ibid.*, a. 1, pp. 383-384: "Distinctio cadit hic de 'reprobatione', quia reprobatio potest capi praecise, ut est non propositum dandi finaliter gratiam et gloriam, sed reliquendi. Secundo: Prout est propositum non dandi, sed puniendi saltem aliquos ad certum gradum suppliciorum."

cause the person will have done evil, but because <He> did not will <to have mercy on that person>.[17]

By restating the conclusion in this way, Orvieto hoped to avoid the determinism of DPE. But he does so at the expense of refuting GE. Aureol had never claimed that an obstacle to grace conditioned the divine elective will. By restating the tenets of SPE, Orvieto misses the whole issue of Aureol's doctrine of election based on *I Timothy* 2:4: God wills that all men be saved. Therefore, Orvieto's doctrine of reprobation is open to the same critique as Scotus's: if God does not will that the reprobate be saved, then He does not will that *all* men be saved. On his doctrine of predestination, at least, Orvieto was more concerned with avoiding determinism than he was with combating Pelagianism.

The difference between traditional SPE and the anti-Pelagian "strong" SPE is most carefully worked out by John Hiltalingen of Basel. In his lectures on the *Sentences*, given at Paris in 1365-1366, Hiltalingen claims that the traditional understanding of SPE is not strong enough, since according to it reprobation is only a possibility for those who are not predestined. In this case, Hiltalingen is trying to arbitrate between his influential confreres Rimini and Orvieto. Thus, Hiltalingen announces a "first corollary":

> Just as "reprobation" is not expressed well through <such phrases as> "a purpose for not having mercy" or "an unwillingness for having mercy", in the same way it is insufficient to describe <reprobation> through <such phrases as> only "a lack of purpose" or "not to will to have mercy". The first <of these locutions> is against the manner of speaking of master Gregory <of Rimini>; the second is against that of master Hugolino <of Orvieto>. The corollary is proved, because that there be a purpose of which God is unwilling entails a positive relation, but with respect to reprobation God does not have a positive relation. Therefore, the first part is true. The second part is proved, because a lack of purpose alone does not <sufficiently> distinguish being reprobate <i.e. one's reprobation being settled> from a mere possibility. Therefore <reprobation> is insufficiently described through these phrases.[18]

---

[17] *Ibid.*, a. 2, p. 387: "Quarta conclusio: Nulla est in aeterno praesenti reprobatus seu relictus quasi mere non praedestinatus in sensus primo propterea praecise, quia praevisus est temporaliter demereri. Probatur: Nulla viatoris opera sunt vel possunt esse tam mala, quin possibile fuerit deo ab eis viatorem praeservare et quin pro ipsis misericordiam praestare possit deus et quin in suo aeterno possit deus velle temporaliter ac finaliter misereri. Si igitur non vult et non voluit in aeterno suo praeservare in tempore ab obice seu a culpa, nec vult misereri, et hoc est reprobare seu relinquere, sequitur, quod non propterea praecise non miseretur, quia iste operaturus est male, sed quia non vult."

[18] John Hiltalingen of Basel, *Super Quattuor Libros Sententiarum*, I, q. 32, in Adolar Zumkeller, "Hiltalingen", p. 93, n. 99: "Primum corollarium: Sicut reprobatio non

According to Hiltalingen there are only two possible alternatives for
human souls and the divine elective will settles the issue through
predestination.[19] Hiltalingen has closed the logical space between
being merely not predestined and being reprobate.[20] Moreover,
while he does not endorse DPE, he has retained the argument that
the causally significant moment in reprobation is not human sin, but
rather divine election. For Hiltalingen, this solves the problem of an-
swering the critique of GE without completely abandoning the traditional Scholastic understanding of election.

Even though Rimini's doctrine of predestination was rejected within his order, he was not without significant supporters in the later
Middle Ages. Both Marsilius of Inghen and Pierre d'Ailly (whose
doctrine of predestination was one of the most widely read in the
later Middle Ages) explicitly endorse and cite nearly verbatim
Rimini's version of DPE.[21] The only significant departure that they

---

bene per propositum non miserendi vel per nolle misereri exprimitur, sic insufficienter describitur per solum non propositum vel non velle misereri. Primum est
contra modum loquendi magistri Gregorii, secundum contra modum loquendi magistri Hugolini. Probatur corollarium, quia tam propositum quam nolle habent se
positive, sed Deus respectu reprobationis non habent se positive. Igitur prima pars
vera. Secunda pars probatur, quia per solum non propositum non distinguitur reprobatus a mere possibile. Igitur insufficienter describitur sic per eos."

[19] *Ibid.*, p. 89, n. 90: "Praedestinationis a reprobatione principalis distinctiva ratio
est divinae voluntatis aeterna ad alterum electiva determinatio."

[20] I would like to thank Scott MacDonald and his students in the Aquinas sem-
inar (University of Iowa, Summer 1992) for pointing out to me the logical space left
open in the Thomist account of SPE.

[21] Pierre d'Ailly, *Quaestiones super libros Sententiarum cum quibusdam in fine adjunctus*,
(Strassbourg, 1490; reprint: Frankfurt, 1968), I, q. 12, a. 2, F-K; Marsilius of Inghen,
Quaestiones super quattuor libros Sententiarum, (Strassbourg, 1501; repr. Frankfurt, 1966),
I, q. 41, a. 2. Both d'Ailly and Inghen came into contact with Rimini's teaching during their theological studies at Paris in the late 1360s. While Inghen did not actually
comment on the *Sentences* until he resumed his studies at Heidelberg in the 1390s,
given the almost verbatim citation of Rimini concerning merit and predestination, it
seems likely that Inghen's views on this topic were fully formed while still at Paris in
the 1360s. For a more detailed account of Inghen's career, see M.J.F.M. Hoenen,
Marsilius of Inghen: Divine Knowledge in Late Medieval Thought, (Leiden, 1993), pp. 7-25.
D'Ailly lectured on the *Sentences* at Paris during the 1370s; see Norman Kretzmann,
Anthony Kenny, and Jan Pinborg, eds., *Cambridge History of Later Medieval Philosophy*,
(Cambridge, UK, 1982), p. 876. On the popularity of d'Ailly's treatise of predestina-
tion, see Maurice Patronnier de Gandillac, "De l'usage est de la valeur des argu-
ments probables dans les questions du cardinal Pierre d'Ailly sur le 'Livre des
Sentences'", *Archives d'histoire doctrinale et litteraire du moyen age*, 8 (1933) pp. 43-91, esp.
p. 44. D'Ailly's doctrine of predestination has been treated by George Lindbeck,
"Nominalism and the Problem of Meaning as Illustrated by Pierre d'Ailly on
Predestination and Justification", *Harvard Theological Review*, 52 (1959), pp. 43-60, esp.
pp. 44-54. Lindbeck's study is not very useful since he considers Ockham, Rimini,
and d'Ailly to be "Nominalists" who shared the same doctrine of predestination. In
fact, d'Ailly is the first to see the challenge which Ockham's version of GE poses to
DPE.

both make from Rimini is to draw general conclusions stressing the causal structure of DPE beyond what Rimini had argued for in his five original conclusions. Both Inghen and d'Ailly add a sixth conclusion, one that highlights the uncaused nature of divine predestination and reprobation. For Inghen and d'Ailly it is a matter of recasting Rimini's negative argument, that God does not predestine or reprobate on account of any created cause, into a positive conclusion, that God predestines and reprobates merely on account of His will.[22]

Perhaps the most significant deviation from Rimini is d'Ailly's. In addition to reciting Rimini's attack on Aureol's account of GE, he also applies Rimini's arguments to Ockham's version of GE.[23] According to d'Ailly, Ockham has missed the point in distinguishing between strict causality and propositional priority. Claiming that sin in some sense causes damnation is not the same as saying that sin in some sense causes reprobation. But if this is the case, then Ockham has not demonstrated the causal inconsistency of particular election. Thus, d'Ailly argues on Rimini's behalf:

> And although <Rimini> would concede this causal <sequence>: "because he will finally sin, therefore he will be damned", just as Ockham concedes, nevertheless he would deny this: "because he will finally sin, therefore he will be reprobated", which the other <Ockham> concedes. Hence, according to Gregory the two <damnation and reprobation> ought to be considered distinctly in this case. As to the first, "God does not propose to have mercy on him"—the basis of reprobation properly consists in that proposition. And there is no other cause beyond His good pleasure why He proposes in this way...The second is what ought to be considered here, namely to him on whom God proposes not to have mercy, He also prepares for due punishment for sinning. And therefore, although it is not on account of sin that God is unwilling to have mercy, i.e. does not give eternal life, nevertheless He wills to give punishment on account of sin. And thus <Rimini> concedes this causal <sequence>: "because he will sin, God wills to give him punishment". And <Rimini> does not <concede> this <causal sequence>: "because he will sin, God will reprobate him or will not to give him glory", etc.[24]

---

[22] Inghen, *Quaestiones*, I, q. 41, a. 2: "Sexta conclusio quod Dominus ab aeterno hos quos reprobat sua voluntate reprobat, non propter futura peccata quae sunt ipsi facturi, nec etiam propter finalem obicem gratiae quae in eis est inventurus. Haec sequitur duabus conclusionibus praecedentibus. Ex his sequitur conclusio septima...quod nullus praedestinatus est praedestinatus ob aliquam causam quae de futuro debebat in existere. Similiter, nec aliquis reprobatus ob aliquam causam reprobatus est quae in eo in futuro debebat fore."

D'Ailly, *Quaestiones*, I, q. 12, a. 2, H: "Sexta potest addi quod quaecumque Deus reprobavit sine quacumque causa in ipso reprobato eum reprobavit."

[23] D'Ailly, *ibid.*, K.

[24] *Ibid.*: "Et quamvis concederet istam causalem: quia iste peccabit finaliter, ideo damnabitur, sicut Ockham, tamen negaret illam: quia iste peccabit finaliter, ideo

In Inghen's and d'Ailly's treatments we find a strange sort of endorsement of DPE. They present a stronger version of DPE than Rimini himself does, but in both cases they claim to be explicating Rimini's views and not to be putting forth their own. While the Augustinian anti-Pelagians attempted to modify Rimini's views so that these would be more doctrinally acceptable, Inghen and d'Ailly fully endorse DPE without taking on the responsibility that such an endorsement entails. Coupled with Rimini's own popularity on other issues, the influence that Inghen and d'Ailly had on late Medieval and early modern theology allowed DPE to stay alive, but nothing more. It would take the upheaval of the Reformation to give DPE room to grow.

John Capreolus: The Thomist Response to GE

While the attack on GE was carried out mainly by those who were involved in the late Medieval anti-Pelagian cause, GE itself was directed against the traditional Scholastic understanding of SPE. Due to the lack of extant sources, we have not been able to gauge the response of those who held the majority opinion in Aureol's time, that is to say, of those who defended the Thomist version of SPE. Fortunately, the apparent silence of Thomists does not extend beyond the early 15th century when the "Prince of Thomists", John Capreolus (d.1444) wrote his *Defensiones theologiae divi Thomae Aquinatis*.[25] On the issue of predestination, Capreolus saw Aureol as having posed the only significant challenge to the Thomist understanding.[26] But unlike the more soteri-

---

reprobatur, quam alius concedit. Unde secundum Gregorium duo sunt: 'non proposuit misereri huic', et in hoc proprie consistit ratio reprobationis. Et cur sic proposuit non est aliqua causa propter suum beneplacitum, sed simpliciter considerandum est cum Apostolo, 'cuius vult miseretur, et quem vult indurat', id est non miseretur. Aliud est quod est hic considerandum, scilicet, quod tali cuius proposuit Deus non misereri, praeparavit etiam pro peccatis poenam debitam. Et ideo quamvis non propter culpam nolit Deus misereri, id est non dare vitam aeternam, tamen propter culpam vult dare poenam. Et sic concedit istam causalem, 'quia iste peccabit Deus vult ei dare poena', et non istam, 'quia iste peccabit Deus eum reprobat vel vult non dare gloriam', etc."

[25] *Johannis Capreoli Tolosani defensiones theologiae divi Thomae Aquinatis*, 7 vols., ed. C. Paban and T. Pegues, (1900-1908; repr. Main, 1967). Martin Grabmann is the only modern historian to treat Capreolus in any depth. See Martin Grabmann, "Johannes Capreolus, der 'Princeps Thomistarum' und seine Stellung in der Geschichte der Thomistenschule", *Divus Thomas*, 22 (1944), pp. 85-109, 145-170; *idem, Mittalterliches Geistesleben: Abhandlungen zur Geschichte der Scholastik und Mystik*, (Munich, 1936), vol. 2, pp. 475ff. According to Grabmann, Capreolus's chief contribution to Thomism was to establish the mature positions taken in the *Summa*, rather than the earlier lectures on the *Sentences*, as the "official" teaching of Aquinas.

[26] Capreolus, vol. 2, pp. 472-504.

ologically centered attack of the anti-Pelagians, Capreolus's attitude towards GE reveals that Aureol and the Thomists were not even using the same language.

Capreolus's first refutation of Aureol is an excellent illustration of this impasse. Recall that Aureol had attacked Aquinas for saying that predestination had the characteristic of an order or ordering (*ratio ordinis*) in the divine essence. Given Aureol's interpretation of *ratio* as characteristic, Aureol understood Aquinas as arguing that predestination was an order in the divine essence. Moreover, if Aureol is correct, then Capreolus's defense is a distinction without a difference; indeed, he seems to make the Thomist position even more problematic than Aureol had thought it. Thus, Capreolus says:

> To the first <argument of Aureol against Aquinas> it is said that we do not say predestination is some order, but that predestination is the ratio of an order. And when it is asked whether this ratio is objectively in the <divine> intellect etc., I say that the ratio of this order is the divine intellect and divine essence itself; and it is objectively in the <divine> intellect in the same way that the thing known is in the knower.[27]

If Aquinas and Capreolus are using *"ratio"* in the way Aureol claims they are, then Aureol is correct in assuming that they have impugned divine simplicity. But this is not the case. Capreolus clearly sees a difference between *ratio ordinis* and *ordo*. A better reading of both Aquinas and Capreolus would be to translate *"ratio"* as "basis" or, even, "reason for". According to this reading *"ratio ordinis"* would refer to a basis for an order or basis for ordering. Such a reading would make the above statement of Capreolus consistent with the Thomist view, that the divine intellect is the basis for predestination, since predestination is an aspect of providence. Such a reading also reduces the conflict between Aureol and the Thomists from a disagreement over what predestination is, to one over which divine attribute is the basis for it.

We have already considered how Aureol's and Aquinas's differing use of the terms *"predestinatio"* and *"reprobatio"* was fundamental to their disagreement over the causes of predestination and reprobation.[28] For Aquinas, "predestination" and "reprobation" principally referred to the divine *essence*, while for Aureol they referred to the di-

---

[27] *Ibid.*, p. 477b: "Ad primum quidem, dicitur quod non dicimus quod ordo aliquis sit praedestinatio, sed ratio ordinis est praedestinatio. Et cum quaeritur de hoc, an sit obiective in intellectu etc., dico quod ratio illius ordinis est ipse divinus intellectus, et divinus essentia; et est obiective in intellectu ut cognitum in cognoscente."

[28] See above, chapter 3.

vine *actions* of rewarding and punishing. Thus, Aquinas could insist that reprobation has no cause other than divine justice and the divine will, but for Aureol reprobation must have as its cause human sin.

Capreolus addresses two of Aureol's arguments for this position. First, by identifying reprobation with punishment, Aureol claims that reprobation is evil, and thus only intended by God *per accidens*. As such, it cannot reveal divine justice, which is good and intended by God *per se*.[29] Second, since reprobation is punishment, God would be unjust to inflict it upon humans merely on account of His will and without regard to human sin.[30] Capreolus gives the same response to both of these arguments: "reprobation" does not primarily refer to punishment, but rather to the divine foreknowledge of sin and to the divine purpose to punish humans on account of it.[31]

Capreolus did not see GE as a threat to orthodoxy, but rather he saw Aureol as a theologian who just did not understand the sublime truths of SPE. But if Aureol did not comprehend the arguments and terminology of Aquinas, it was equally the case that Capreolus, at least, did not understand the arguments or terminology of Aureol. The conflict between GE and the Thomist version of SPE in the later Middle Ages was less a debate than an agreement to disagree.

Gabriel Biel: GE on the Eve of the Reformation

So far we have surveyed only the late Medieval reaction to GE. Because the documentary evidence of theology in the late 14th and 15th centuries remains so little charted, it is not yet possible to trace GE from the time of Holcot to the 16th century. This problem, however, is mitigated by the fact that we find GE alive and well in the late 15th century. Gabriel Biel (d.1497), perhaps the most influential theologian of his time, held GE as part of his defense of Ockham's doctrine of predestination.[32] But Biel does not merely restate Ockham's doctrine; instead, he explicates the implicit GE com-

[29] Capreolus, pp. 501b-502a.
[30] *Ibid.*
[31] Capreolus, p. 503a: "Non enim reprobatio est mala, aut per accidens intenta, immo per se. Praesciens enim Deus quorundam peccata, quae ab ipso nullo modo sunt intenta, proposuit eos non liberare in praesenti, immo deserere, et in futuro punire, quod est reprobatio."
p. 504b: "...dicitur quod falsum supponit, scilicet quod nos dicamus Deum infligere alicui poenam sine illius demerito. Non enim reprobare est poenam dare, sed est proponere debitam poenam reddere..."
[32] The standard treatment of Biel is Oberman's *Harvest*, in which Oberman is especially interested in Biel's soteriological views. Biel's doctrine of predestination, like Ockham's, has been the subject of dispute among historians of theology; Ockham

ponent of Ockham's doctrine. Since Biel's doctrine of predestination and its dependence on Ockham have been discussed often and at length, it may suffice to point out briefly how Biel's doctrine of predestination not only preserved and passed on GE to the Reformation period, but how in drawing upon the language of both Ockham and Holcot, it is the most striking example of the *pactum* version of GE in the Middle Ages.[33]

Biel begins his discussion of the causes of predestination and reprobation by drawing the same distinctions as had Ockham, often quoting verbatim.[34] Thus, "predestination" refers primarily to God and secondarily to the gift of eternal life; "reprobation" refers primarily to God and secondarily to the inflicting of eternal punishment. The term "cause" can be taken either strictly, as naming a thing through which the existence of another thing follows as an effect, or loosely, in the sense of "propositional priority". For Biel, like Ockham, God, as the primary significate of "predestination" and "reprobation", has no cause on either sense of that term. Nor do the secondary significates of "predestination" and "reprobation" have a cause on the strict sense of that term. Hence, for Biel, as for Ockham, causes can be ascribed only to the secondary significates of "predestination" and "reprobation", and then only if "cause" is taken loosely. From this starting point, Biel next derives three conclusions, which he quotes directly from Ockham's text: (1) sin is the cause of reprobation; (2) in most cases meritorious works are the cause of predestination; and (3) in some instances, such as Paul and Mary, God predestines for no reason.[35]

The second conclusion holds the key to interpreting Biel. Taken out of context, it seems to be an example of predestination *post praevisa merita*. But as Biel recognized Ockham's intent, in this case "predestination" refers to the granting of eternal life and "cause" refers to a propositional priority. By substituting these terms, Biel reached a proposition which no Scholastic would deny: "those who persevere

---

and Biel are usually treated together in this regard. Thus, my argument that Biel defends GE will have the same implications for the arguments of these historians as my claim that Ockham defended GE. See above, chapter 4.

[33] We do know that Jean Gerson, who was active in the late 14th and early 15th centuries, moved from a *pactum* version of GE in his early works to a SPE in his highly influential *Consolatio theologiae*. See Mark S. Burrows, "Jean Gerson after Constance: 'Via Media et Regia' as a Revision of the Ockhamist Covenant", *Church History*, 59 (1990), pp. 467-481.

[34] *Gabrielis Biel Collectorium circa quattor libros Sententiarum*, ed. Wilfridus Werbeck and Udo Hofmann, (Tübingen, 1973), vol. 1, I, d. 41, a. 1, pp. 728-729. See above, chapter 4.

[35] Biel, pp. 729-730.

in meritorious works are predestined". This formulation, of course, raises the question of what Biel means by "meritorious works". Like Ockham and Holcot, Biel distinguishes between human deeds that are intrinsically worthy (*condignus*) of divine reward and those that are merely appropriate (*congruus*) in terms of the covenant that God has established between Himself and human beings.[36] According to the *pactum* scheme, God has set in order (or ordained) His acceptance of congruous actions as if they were meritorious of eternal life, even though they are not intrinsically meritorious. Biel draws a further distinction by refraining from calling the reason for the infusion of grace an "appropriate *merit*" (*meritum de congruo*), but terming it rather a merely "appropriate *disposition*" (*dispositio de congruo*) for the divine infusion of grace according to the covenant. For Biel, therefore, the human cause of grace and glory is not meritorious in any sense.

With these distinctions in mind, we can look at two passages of Biel's which refer explicitly to GE. At one point, he discusses the role of the human will in the process of predestination: "It is within the power of man to use his <free> choice either well or poorly, either to maintain an obstacle to God's grace or to remove it. For by his will, he can cease from sinning and will to not sin."[37] Taking the first sentence alone, this would seem like an endorsement of GE. Yet even if Biel understands the will to not sin as the creation of a disposition rather than a meritorious action, it seems that the human will initiates the process of predestination. But only a few lines later, Biel explains that God initiates the process through His general offer of grace:

> God assists all those not maintaining an obstacle <to grace>, bestowing grace on them, nor does He withdraw <the grace> necessary for salvation from any adult who has the use of reason and is doing what is within him <to do>.[38]

---

[36] *Ibid.*, p. 731: "...dicitur quod in multis etiam praecedit gratiam bonus usus liberi arbitrii tamquam dispositio de congruo, quae est etiam ratio infusionis gratiae, capiendo 'rationem' modo dicto in conclusione secunda. Nec tamen propter hoc gratia non est gratia, quia non datur propter bonum usum liberi arbitrii tamquam meritum condignum, sed dispositio de congruo, qua non existente, non infunderetur."

[37] *Ibid.*, p. 732: "In potestate hominis est bene et male uti suo arbitrio et sic ponere obicem gratiae Dei vel positum removere. Potest enim cessare a voluntate peccandi et potest velle non peccasse."

[38] *Ibid.*, p. 733: "Deus ad est omnibus obicem non ponentibus, offerens gratiam, nec alicui adulto rationis usum habenti et quod in se est facienti subtrahit necessaria ad salutem."

In addition to citing *I Timothy* ("God wills that all men be saved"),
Biel also cites *Revelation* 3 ("I <Christ> stand at the door and knock.
If anyone opens the door, I will come in..."), which Holcot had used
to explain the cooperation between the divine offer of grace and the
active human response.[39]

Biel's understanding of an appropriate disposition is much like
Holcot's understanding of a congruous merit: it is a minimal, yet
sufficient, response to the universal offer of divine grace.[40] The
avoidance of sin does not merit grace; it only allows previously offered grace to be infused. Like Ockham and Holcot, Biel has incorporated GE into the soteriological covenant between God and humans. While Aureol would surely have objected to the active role of
humans in the process, his understanding of predestination in terms
of a general election and a universal offer of grace could hardly have
asked for a more influential defender on the eve of the Reformation.

---

[39] *Ibid.*, p. 733.
[40] See above, chapter 5.

CONCLUSION

Since Augustine and the Pelagian controversy, Western soteriology has been dominated by the dichotomy between grace and merit. Yet precise statements concerning the respective roles of human and divine action in the *ordo salutis* come only after the dam had burst in the 16th and 17th centuries. Until then Latin theologians had been bound only by the Patristic understanding of Pelagianism (that the human will is capable of fulfilling the commandments necessary for salvation) and the ancient understanding of *fatum* or determinism. In short, God must be responsible for salvation, but humans must be culpable for their own damnation. Working within this framework Medieval Scholastics had arrived at a consensus concerning predestination by the 13th century: single-particular election (SPE). According to SPE, God actively wills to save particular individuals and therefore these individuals receive grace. Those for whom God does not will salvation do not receive grace, and thus remain in sin and justly merit damnation. The term "predestination" refers to the divine will to save particular individuals; "reprobation" refers to the foreknowledge of sins in those towards whom God does not have such a will.

In the 14th century this consensus view was challenged by two alternatives. In 1317 Peter Aureol, claiming that SPE is deterministic, argued for general election (GE). According to GE, God offers grace to all, and an individual's salvation or damnation follows according to that person's response to the offer. In 1344 Gregory of Rimini, judging GE to be Pelagian, reacted by advocating double-particular election (DPE), whereby God not only wills to save some individuals, but actively wills to damn others. New methodological approaches peculiar to late Medieval Franciscan theology, particularly its use of logic and semantics, provided the occasion for the re-emergence of predestinarian pluralism in Latin theology. Scotus's formal distinction and Aureol's connotative distinction between the divine attributes allowed them to argue for a, then novel, voluntaristic account of predestination. The semantic analysis of terms such as "predestination" and "reprobation" which these two inherited from Alexander of Hales and Bonaventure became the raw material for controversy. Fully exploiting the logical and semantic assumptions of the Franciscan approach to the problem of predestination, Peter Aureol broke with his Franciscan brothers and Scholastic theology in general.

Within a few generations of Aureol, the Scholastic consensus had been shattered. Aureol's GE account quickly won important adherents on both sides of the Channel and in each of the three major mendicant orders: William Ockham O.F.M. and Robert Holcot O.P. at Oxford, and Thomas of Strassbourg O.E.S.A. at Paris. In the person of Gabriel Biel, GE would be introduced into the theological debates of the Reformation. Opposition to GE, in the form of DPE and strong SPE accounts, merely abetted the fragmentation process.

WORKS CITED

Adams, Marilyn McCord, "Ockham on Identity and Distinction", *Franciscan Studies*, 36 (1976), 25-44.

——, *William Ockham*, 2 vols., (Notre Dame, 1987).

Alexander of Hales, *Glossa in quattor libros Sententiarum*, (Bonaventure, 1951-1957).

Anselm of Canterbury, *Monologion, Anselmi Opera Omnia*, vol. 1, ed. Franciscus Salesius Schmitt, (Edinburg, 1946).

Augustine of Hippo, *De Trinitate, Corpus Christianorum. Series Latina*, (Turnhout, Belgium, 1953-).

Bonansea, B.M., *Man and His Approach to God in John Duns Scotus*, (N.Y., 1983).

Bonaventure, *Opera omnia*, (Quaracchi, 1883).

Burger, Christoph Peter, "Der Augustinschüler gegen die Modernen Pelagianer: Das 'auxilium speciale dei' in der Gnadenlehre Gregors von Rimini", *Gregor von Rimini: Werk und Wirkung bis zur Reformation*, ed. Heiko A. Oberman, (Berlin, 1981), pp. 195-240.

Burrows, Mark S., "Jean Gerson after Constance: 'Via Media et Regia' as a Revision of the Ockhamist Covenant", *Church History*, 59 (1990), pp. 467-481.

Copleston, Frederick, *A History of Philosophy, Volume II: Augustine to Scotus*, (Garden City, NY, 1944).

Courtenay, William J., *Adam Wodeham: His Life and Writings*, (Leiden, 1979).

——, *Capacity and Volition: A History of the Distinction of Absolute and Ordained Power*, (Bergamo, 1990).

——, *Covenant and Causality in Medieval Thought: Studies in Philosophy, Theology, and Economic Practice*, [coll. essays], (London, 1984).

——, "John of Mirecourt and Gregory of Rimini on Whether God Can Undo the Past", *Recherches de Theologie ancienne et medieval*, 39 (1972), pp. 224-253 & 40 (1973), pp. 147-174.

——, "Nominalism and Late Medieval Religion", *The Pursuit of Holiness*, ed. C. Trinkaus and Heiko A. Oberman (Leiden, 1974), pp. 26-59.

——, "Ockham, Chatton, and the London Studium: Observations on Recent Changes in Ockham's Biography", *Die GegenwartOckhams*, ed. W. Vossenkuhl and R. Schönberger, (Weinheim, 1990), pp. 327-337.

——, *Schools and Scholars in Fourteenth-Century England*, (Princeton, 1987).

Courtenay, William J. and Tachau, Katherine H., "Ockham, Ockhamists and the English-German Nation at Paris, 1339-1341", *History of Universities*, 2 (1982), pp. 53-96.

Decker, Bruno, *Die Gotteslehre des Jakob von Metz: Untersuchungen zur Dominikanertheologie zu Beginn des 14. Jahrhunderts, Beiträge zur Geschichte der Philosophie des Mittelalters*, 42/1 (Münster, 1967).

Donnelly, John Patrick, *Calvinism and Scholasticism in Vermigli's Doctrine of Man and Grace*, (Leiden, 1976).

Doucet, Victorin, "The History of the Problem of the Authenticity of the Summa", *Franciscan Studies*, 7 (1947), pp. 26-41, 274-311.

Dreiling, Raymundus OFM, *Der Konzeptualismus in der Universalienlehre des Franziskanerzbischof Petrus Aureoli, Beiträge zur Geschichte der Philosophie des Mittelalters*, 11/6 (Münster, 1913).

Dumont, Stephen, "The Univocity of the Concept of Being in the Fourteenth Century: John Duns Scotus and William of Alnwick", *Medieval Studies*, 49 (1987).

Durand of Saint-Pourcain, *In libros Sententiarum. Redactio tertia*, (Venice, 1571).

Etzkorn, G., "Walter Chatton and the Controversy on the Absolute Necessity of Grace", *Franciscan Studies*, 37 (1977), pp. 32-75.

Francis Mayronnes, *In libros Sententiarum*, (Venice, 1520; repr. Frankfurt, 1966).

Gabrielis Biel, *Collectorium circa quattor libros Sententiarum*, eds. Werbeck, Wilfridus and Hofmann, Udo, (Tubingen, 1973).

de Gandillac Patronnier, Maurice, "De l'usage est de la valeur des arguments probables dans les questions du cardinal Pierre d'Ailly sur le 'Livre des Sentences'", *Archives d'histoire doctrinale et litteraire du moyen age*, 8 (1933) pp. 43-91.

Gelber, Hester Goodenough, *It Could Have Been Otherwise: Modal Theory and Theology Among the Dominicans at Oxford, 1310-1340*, forthcoming.

——, "Logic and the Trinity", (Ph.D. Dissertation, University of Wisconsin, 1974).

Giles of Rome, *In libros Sententiarum*, (Frankfurt, 1969).

Gindele, Egon, ed., *Bibliographie zur Geschicte und Theologie des Augustiner-Eremitenordens bis zum Beginn der Reformation*, (Berlin, 1977).

Grabmann, Martin, "Johannes Capreolus der 'Princeps Thomistrarum' und seine Stellung in der Geschicte der Thomistenschule", *Divus Thomas*, 22 (1944) pp. 85-109, 145-170.

——, *Mittalterliches Geistleben: Abhandlungen zur Geschicte der Scholastik und Mystik*, (Munich, 1936).

Grane, Leif, "Gregor von Rimini und Luthers Leipziger Disputation", *Studia Theologia*, 22 (1968), pp. 29-49.

Gregorius Ariminensis OESA, *Lectura super primum et secundum Sententiarum*, 7 vols., eds. Damasus Trapp and Venicio Marcolino, (Berlin, 1979).

Henninger, Mark, *Relations*, (Oxford, 1989).

Henry of Ghent, *Quodlibeta*, (Paris, 1518; repr. Frankfurt, 1961).

——, *Summa Quaestionum Ordinarium*, (Paris, 1520; repr. Bonaventure, NY, 1953).

Hervaeus Natalis O.P., *In libros Sententiarum*, (Paris, 1647).

Hilary of Poitiers, *De Trinitate, Patrilogia Latina*, (Paris, 1878-1890).

Hocedez, E., *Richard de Middleton: sa vie, ses oevres, sa doctrine*, (Paris, 1925).

Hoenen, M.J.F.M., *Marsilius of Inghen: Divine Knowledge in Late Medieval Thought,* (Leiden, 1993).
Hugolino of Orvieto, *Hugolini de Urbis Veteri OESA Commentarius in Quattor Libros Sententiarum,* ed. Willigis Eckerman OSA, (Wuerzburg, 1984).
——, *Der Physikkommentar Hugolins von Orvieto OESA,* ed. Willigis Eckerman, (Berlin, 1972).

James III, Frank E., "A Late Medieval Parallel in Reformation Thought: Gemina Praedestinatio in Gregory of Rimini and Peter Martyr Vermigli", *Via Augustini: Augustine in the Later Middle Ages, Renaissance, and Reformation,* ed. Heiko A. Oberman and Frank E. James III, (Leiden, 1991), pp. 157-188.
Johannes Capreolus, *Johannis Capreoli Tolosani defensiones theologiae divi Thomae Aquinatis,* 7 vols., ed. C. Paban and T. Pegues, (1900-1908; repr. Main, 1967).
John Duns Scotus, *Opera omnia,* ed. Charles Balic, (Vatican City, 1950-).
——, *Opera omnia,* ed. Luke Wadding, (1639; repr. 1891-1895).
John of Damascus, *De fide orthodoxa,* ed. Eligius Buyteart, (Bonaventure, NY, 1955).

Knuutila, Simo, "Change and Contradiction: A Fourteenth-Century Controversy", *Synthese,* 40, (1979), pp. 189-207.
Kretzmann, Norman, "Continuity, Contrariety, Contradiction, and Change", *Infinity and Continuity in Ancient and Medieval Thought,* ed. *idem,* (Cornell, 1982), pp. 270-296.
Kretzmann, Norman, Kenny, Anthony, and Pinborg, Jan, eds., *The Cambridge History of Later Medieval Philosophy,* (Cambridge, UK, 1982).

Langston, Douglas C., *God's Willing Knowledge: The Influence of Scotus's Analysis of Omniscience,* (London, 1986).
Leff, Gordon, *Bradwardine and the Pelagians: A Study of his De Causa Dei and Its Opponents,* (Cambridge, UK, 1957).
——, *Gregory of Rimini: Tradition and Innovation in Fourteenth-Century Thought,* (New York, 1961).
Lindbeck, George, "Nominalism and the Problem of Meaning as Illustrated by Pierre d'Ailly on Predestination and Justification", *Harvard Theological Review,* 52 (1959).
Lindner, B., *Die Erkenntnislehre des Thomas von Strassbourg, Beiträge zur Geschichte der Philosophie des Mittelalters,* 27/4-5, (Münster, 1930).

MacDonald, Scott, ed., *Being and Goodness: The Concept of the Good in Metaphysics and Theology,* (Ithaca, 1991).
Maier, Anneliese, "Literarhistorische Notizen uber Petrus Aureoli, Durandus und den 'Cancellarius'", *Gregorianum,* 29 (1948), pp. 213-251.
Marsilius of Inghen, *Quaestiones super quattuor libros Sententiarum,* (Strassbourg, 1501; repr. Frankfurt, 1966).
Mayer, Cornelius P. and Eckermann, Willigis, eds., *Scientia Augustiniana,* (Wuerzburg, 1975).

McGrath, Alister E., "The Anti-Pelagian Structure of 'Nominalist' Doctrines of Justification", *Ephemerides Theologicae Lovanensis*, 57 (1981), pp. 107-119.

——, "'Augustinianism'? A Critical Assessment of the So-Called 'Medieval Augustinian Tradition' on Justification", *Augustiniana*, 31 (1981), pp. 247-267.

——, *Intellectual Origins of the Reformation*, (Oxford, 1987).

——, *Iustitia Dei*, 2 vols., (Cambridge, UK, 1986).

McSorley, Harry, *Luther: Right or Wrong?*, (Minneapolis, 1969).

Meissner, Alois, *Gotteserkenntnis und Gotteslehre nach dem englischen Dominikanertheologen Robert Holkot*, (Limburg an der Lahn, 1953).

Michael of Massa, *In libros Sententiarum*, Bologna, Universita 2214.

Muller, Richard, *God, Creation and Providence in the Thought of Jacob Arminius*, (Grand Rapids, 1990).

Murdoch, John E., "*Mathesis in philosophiam scholasticam introducta*: The Rise and Development of the Application of Mathematics in Fourteenth-Century Philosophy and Theology", in *Arts liberaux et philosophie au moyen age*, (Montreal, 1969), pp. 215-254.

Oberman, Heiko A., *Archbishop Thomas Bradwardine: A Fourteenth-Century Augustinian, A Study of His Theology in Its Historical Context*, (Utrecht, 1958).

——, "Duns Scotus, Nominalism and the Council of Trent", *The Dawn of the Reformation: Essays in Late Medieval and Reformation Thought*, ed., *idem*, (Edinburg, 1986), pp. 204-233.

——, "'Facientibus Quod in se est Deus non denegat gratiam': Robertus Holcot O.F.M. and the beginnings of Luther's Theology", *Dawn*, pp. 85-103.

——, *The Harvest of Medieval Theology: Gabriel Biel and Late Medieval Nominalism*, (Cambridge, MA, 1963; repr. 1983).

——, "Headwaters of the Reformation: Initia Lutheri—Initia Reformationis", *Dawn*, ed., *idem*.

——, "'Tuus sum, salvum me fac'. Augustinreveil zwischen Renaissance und Reformation", *Scientia Augustiniana*, ed. Cornelius P. Mayer and Willigis Eckermann, (Wuerzburg, 1975), pp. 349-395.

Oberman, Heiko A., ed., *The Dawn of the Reformation: Essays in Late Medieval and Reformation Thought*, (Edinburg, 1986).

——, *Gregor von Rimini: Werk und Wirkung bis zur Reformation*, (Berlin, 1981).

Oberman, Heiko A. and James III, Frank E., eds., *Via Augustini: Augustine in the Later Middle Ages, Renaissance, and Reformation*, (Leiden, 1991).

Pannenberg, Wolfhart, *Die Prädestinationslehre des Duns Skotus*, (Göttingen, 1953).

Pelikan, Jaraslov, *The Christian Tradition: A History of the Development of Doctrine*, 5 vols., (Chicago, 1971- 1987).

Peter Aureol, *Commentariorum in librum primum Sententiarum*, (Rome, 1596).

——, *Scriptum super primum Sententiarum*, 2 vols., ed. Eligius Buyteart, (St. Bonaventure, NY, 1952).

——, *Scriptum super primum Sententiarum*, Paris, Bibliotheque Nationale, MS lat. 15363.

——, *Scriptum super primum Sententiarum*, Vatican City, Biblioteca Apostolica, MS Borghese 329.

——, *Scriptum super primum Sententiarum*, Vatican City, Biblioteca Apostolica MS, Vat. lat. 940.

——, *Scriptum super primum Sententiarum*, Vatican City, Biblioteca Apostolica, MS Vat. lat. 941.

Peter Lombard, *Sententiae in IV libris distinctae*, 3 vols., (Rome, 1971).

Petrus de Aquila, *In libros Sententiarum*, München Staatsbibl., C.L.M. 8879.

Pierre d'Ailly, *Quaestiones super libros Sententiarum cum quibusdam in fine adjunctus*, (Strassbourg, 1490; repr. Frankfurt, 1968).

Richard of Middleton, *Supra quattuor libros Sententiarum*, 4 vols., (Bresciae, 1591).

Robert Holcot, *Quaestiones super IV libros Sententiarum*, (Lugduni, 1497).

——, *Quodlibeta*, in *Seeing the Future Clearly: Questions on Future Contingents By Robert Holcot*, eds. Streveler, Paul, Tachau, Katherine H., Courtenay, William J., and Gelber, Hester Goodenough, (Toronto, 1995).

Roth, Bartolomaeus, *Franz von Mayronis, O.F.M.: Sein Leben, seine Werke, seine Lehre von Formalunterschied in Gott*, Franziskanerische Forschungen, v. 3, (Werl, 1936).

——, *Super libros Sapientiae*, (Hagenau, 1494).

Schmaus, Michael, *Der "Liber propugnatorius" des Thomas Anglicus und die Lehrunterschiede zwischen Thomas von Aquin und Duns Scotus*, part 2; *Die Trintarischen Lehrdifferenzen*, (Munster, 1930).

Schüler, Martin, *Prädestination, Sünde und Freiheit bei Gregor von Rimini*, (Stuttgart, 1934).

Schulze, Manfred, "'Via Gregorii' in Forschung und Quellen", *Werk und Wirkung*, ed. Heiko A. Oberman, pp. 1-126.

Seeberg, Reinhold, *Lehrbuch der Dogmegeschichte*, (Leipzig, 1953).

Shannon, John L., *Good Works and Predestination in Thomas of Strassbourg*, (Baltimore, 1940).

Smalley, Beryl, *English Friars and Antiquity in the Early Fourteenth Century*, (Oxford, 1960).

Spade, Paul, "Quasi-Aristotelianism", in *Infinity and Continuity*, ed. Norman Kretzmann, pp. 297-307.

Stump, Eleonore and Kretzmann, Norman, "Being and Goodness", *Being and Goodness*, ed. Scott MacDonald, pp. 98-128.

Sylla, Edith, "Medieval Quantification of Qualities", *Archive for History of the Exact Sciences*, 8 (1971), pp. 9-39.

Tachau, Katherine H., *Vision and Certitude in the Age of Ockham: Optics, Epistemology and the Foundations of Semantics, 1250-1345*, (Leiden, 1988).

Thomas Aquinas, *Opera omnia*, ed. Robertus Busa, (Stuttgart-Badd, 1980).

——, *Opera omnia. Iussu impensaque Leonis XIII, P.M., edita*, (Vatican City, 1882).

Thomas Bradwardine, *De Causa Dei contra Pelagium*, (London, 1618).

Trapp, Damasus, "Augustinian Theology of the 14th Century: Notes on Editions, Marginalia, Opinions and Book-Lore", *Augustiniana*, 6 (1956), pp. 146-241.

——, "Notes on John Klenkok O.S.A. (+1373)", *Augustinianum*, 4 (1964), pp. 358-404.

Trinkaus, Charles, and Oberman, Heiko A., eds., *The Pursuit of Holiness*, (Leiden, 1974).

Urban, Wolfgang, "Die 'Via moderna' an der Universitaet Erfurt am Vorabend der Reformation", *Werk und Wirkung*, ed. Heiko A. Oberman, pp. 311-330.

Vignaux, Paul, *Justification et Predestination au XIVe siecle. Duns Scot, Pierre d'Aureole, Guillaume d'Occam, Gregoire de Rimini*, (Paris, 1934).

William Ockham, *Opera philosophica et theologica ad fidem codicum manuscriptorum edita*, (St. Bonaventure, NY, 1976-1985).

——, *Opera Theologica. Scriptum in librum Sententiarum. Ordinatio*, vols. 1-4, eds. Gideon Gal, Stephen Brown, G. Etzkorn, and F. Kelly.

——, *Opera Philosophica. De praedestinatio et de praescientia Dei respectu futurorum contingentibus*, vol. 1, ed. Philotheus Boehner.

——, *Predestination, God's Foreknowledge and Future Contingents*, trans. Marilyn McCord Adams and Norman Kretzmann, (New York, 1969).

Wippel, John F., *The Metaphysical Thought of Godfrey of Fontaines: A Study in Late Thirteenth-Century Philosophy*, (Washington, D.C., 1981).

Zumkeller, Adolar OSA, "Der Augustinertheologe Johannes Hiltalingen von Basel (+1392) über Urstand, Erbsünde, Gnade und Verdienst", *Analecta Augustiniana*, 43 (1980), pp. 57-162.

——, "Hugolin von Orvieto (+1373) über Urstand und Erbsünde", *Augustiniana*, 3 (1953) pp. 165-193; 4 (1954), pp. 25-46.

——, "Johannes Klenkok O.S.A. (+1374) im Kampf gegen den 'Pelagianismus' seiner Zeit: Seine Lehre über Gnade, Rechtfertigung und Verdienst", *Recherches Augustiniennes*, 13 (1978), pp. 231-333.

——, "Konrad Treger's Disputation Theses of 1521", *Via Augustini*, eds. Oberman and James, pp. 130-156.

INDICES

INDEX OF SUBJECTS

Page numbers following "n." refer to instances in which the item occurs in a footnote.

INDEX OF NAMES AND PLACES

Page numbers following "n." refer to instances in which the item occurs in a footnote.

Studies in the History
of Christian Thought

EDITED BY HEIKO A. OBERMAN

1. McNEILL, J. J. *The Blondelian Synthesis.* 1966. Out of print
2. GOERTZ, H.-J. *Innere und äussere Ordnung in der Theologie Thomas Müntzers.* 1967
3. BAUMAN, Cl. *Gewaltlosigkeit im Täufertum.* 1968
4. ROLDANUS, J. *Le Christ et l'Homme dans la Théologie d'Athanase d'Alexandrie.* 2nd ed. 1977
5. MILNER, Jr., B. Ch. *Calvin's Doctrine of the Church.* 1970. Out of print
6. TIERNEY, B. *Origins of Papal Infallibility, 1150-1350.* 2nd ed. 1988
7. OLDFIELD, J. J. *Tolerance in the Writings of Félicité Lamennais 1809-1831.* 1973
8. OBERMAN, H. A. (ed.). *Luther and the Dawn of the Modern Era.* 1974. Out of print
9. HOLECZEK, H. *Humanistische Bibelphilologie bei Erasmus, Thomas More und William Tyndale.* 1975
10. FARR, W. *John Wyclif as Legal Reformer.* 1974
11. PURCELL, M. *Papal Crusading Policy 1244-1291.* 1975
12. BALL, B. W. *A Great Expectation.* Eschatological Thought in English Protestantism. 1975
13. STIEBER, J. W. *Pope Eugenius IV, the Council of Basel, and the Empire.* 1978. Out of print
14. PARTEE, Ch. *Calvin and Classical Philosophy.* 1977
15. MISNER, P. *Papacy and Development.* Newman and the Primacy of the Pope. 1976
16. TAVARD, G. H. *The Seventeenth-Century Tradition.* A Study in Recusant Thought. 1978
17. QUINN, A. *The Confidence of British Philosophers.* An Essay in Historical Narrative. 1977
18. BECK, J. *Le Concil de Basle (1434).* 1979
19. CHURCH, F. F. and GEORGE, T. (ed.). *Continuity and Discontinuity in Church History.* 1979
20. GRAY, P. T. R. *The Defense of Chalcedon in the East (451-553).* 1979
21. NIJENHUIS, W. *Adrianus Saravia (c. 1532-1613).* Dutch Calvinist. 1980
22. PARKER, T. H. L. (ed.). *Iohannis Calvini Commentarius in Epistolam Pauli ad Romanos.* 1981
23. ELLIS, I. *Seven Against Christ.* A Study of 'Essays and Reviews'. 1980
24. BRANN, N. L. *The Abbot Trithemius (1462-1516).* 1981
25. LOCHER, G. W. *Zwingli's Thought.* New Perspectives. 1981
26. GOGAN, B. *The Common Corps of Christendom.* Ecclesiological Themes in Thomas More. 1982
27. STOCK, U. *Die Bedeutung der Sakramente in Luthers Sermonen von 1519.* 1982
28. YARDENI, M. (ed.). *Modernité et nonconformisme en France à travers les âges.* 1983
29. PLATT, J. *Reformed Thought and Scholasticism.* 1982
30. WATTS, P. M. *Nicolaus Cusanus.* A Fifteenth-Century Vision of Man. 1982
31. SPRUNGER, K. L. *Dutch Puritanism.* 1982
32. MEIJERING, E. P. *Melanchthon and Patristic Thought.* 1983
33. STROUP, J. *The Struggle for Identity in the Clerical Estate.* 1984
34. 35. COLISH, M. L. *The Stoic Tradition from Antiquity to the Early Middle Ages.* 1.2. 2nd ed. 1990
36. GUY, B. *Domestic Correspondence of Dominique-Marie Varlet, Bishop of Babylon, 1678-1742.* 1986
37. 38. CLARK, F. *The Pseudo-Gregorian Dialogues.* I. II. 1987
39. PARENTE, Jr. J. A. *Religious Drama and the Humanist Tradition.* 1987
40. POSTHUMUS MEYJES, G. H. M. *Hugo Grotius, Meletius.* 1988
41. FELD, H. *Der Ikonoklasmus des Westens.* 1990
42. REEVE, A. and SCREECH, M. A. (eds.). *Erasmus' Annotations on the New Testament.* Acts —Romans — I and II Corinthians. 1990
43. KIRBY, W. J. T. *Richard Hooker's Doctrine of the Royal Supremacy.* 1990
44. GERSTNER, J. N. *The Thousand Generation Covenant.* Reformed Covenant Theology. 1990
45. CHRISTIANSON, G. and IZBICKI, T. M. (eds.). *Nicholas of Cusa.* 1991

46. GARSTEIN, O. *Rome and the Counter-Reformation in Scandinavia*. 1553-1622. 1992
47. GARSTEIN, O. *Rome and the Counter-Reformation in Scandinavia*. 1622-1656. 1992
48. PERRONE COMPAGNI, V. (ed.). *Cornelius Agrippa, De occulta philosophia Libri tres*. 1992
49. MARTIN, D. D. *Fifteenth-Century Carthusian Reform*. The World of Nicholas Kempf. 1992
50. HOENEN, M. J. F. M. *Marsilius of Inghen*. Divine Knowledge in Late Medieval Thought. 1993
51. O'MALLEY, J. W., IZBICKI, T. M. and CHRISTIANSON, G. (eds.). *Humanity and Divinity in Renaissance and Reformation*. Essays in Honor of Charles Trinkaus. 1993
52. REEVE, A. (ed.) and SCREECH, M. A. (introd.). *Erasmus' Annotations on the New Testament*. Galatians to the Apocalypse. 1993
53. STUMP, Ph. H. *The Reforms of the Council of Constance (1414-1418)*. 1994
54. GIAKALIS, A. *Images of the Divine*. The Theology of Icons at the Seventh Ecumenical Council. With a Foreword by Henry Chadwick. 1994
55. NELLEN, H. J. M. and RABBIE, E. (eds.). *Hugo Grotius – Theologian*. Essays in Honour of G. H. M. Posthumus Meyjes. 1994
56. TRIGG, J. D. *Baptism in the Theology of Martin Luther*. 1994
57. JANSE, W. *Albert Hardenberg als Theologe*. Profil eines Bucer-Schülers. 1994
59. SCHOOR, R.J.M. VAN DE. *The Irenical Theology of Théophile Brachet de La Milletière (1588-1665)*. 1995
60. STREHLE, S. *The Catholic Roots of the Protestant Gospel*. Encounter between the Middle Ages and the Reformation. 1995
61. BROWN, M.L. *Donne and the Politics of Conscience in Early Modern England*. 1995
62. SCREECH, M.A. (ed.). *Richard Mocket, Warden of All Souls College, Oxford, Doctrina et Politia Ecclesiae Anglicanae*. An Anglican Summa. Facsimile with Variants of the Text of 1617. Edited with an Introduction. 1995
63. SNOEK, G.J.C. *Medieval Piety from Relics to the Eucharist*. A Process of Mutual Interaction. 1995
64. PIXTON, P.B. *The German Episcopacy and the Implementation of the Decrees of the Fourth Lateran Council, 1216-1245*. Watchmen on the Tower. 1995
65. DOLNIKOWSKI, E.W. *Thomas Bradwardine: A View of Time and a Vision of Eternity in Fourteenth-Century Thought*. 1995
66. RABBIE, E. (ed.). *Hugo Grotius, Ordinum Hollandiae ac Westfrisiae Pietas (1613)*. Critical Edition with Translation and Commentary. 1995
67. HIRSH, J.C. *The Boundaries of Faith*. The Development and Transmission of Medieval Spirituality. 1996
68. BURNETT, S.G. *From Christian Hebraism to Jewish Studies*. Johannes Buxtorf (1564-1629) and Hebrew Learning in the Seventeenth Century. 1996
69. BOLAND O.P., V. *Ideas in God according to Saint Thomas Aquinas*. Sources and Synthesis. 1996
70. LANGE, M.E. *Telling Tears in the English Renaissance*. 1996
71. CHRISTIANSON, G. and T.M. IZBICKI (eds.). *Nicholas of Cusa on Christ and the Church*. Essays in Memory of Chandler McCuskey Brooks for the American Cusanus Society. 1996
72. MALI, A. *Mystic in the New World*. Marie de l'Incarnation (1599-1672). 1996
73. VISSER, D. *Apocalypse as Utopian Expectation (800-1500)*. The Apocalypse Commentary of Berengaudus of Ferrières and the Relationship between Exegesis, Liturgy and Iconography. 1996
74. O'ROURKE BOYLE, M. *Divine Domesticity*. Augustine of Thagaste to Teresa of Avila. 1997
75. PFIZENMAIER, T.C. *The Trinitarian Theology of Dr. Samuel Clarke (1675-1729)*. Context, Sources, and Controversy. 1997
76. BERKVENS-STEVELINCK, C., J. ISRAEL and G.H.M. POSTHUMUS MEYJES (eds.). *The Emergence of Tolerance in the Dutch Republic*. 1997
77. HAYKIN, M.A.G. (ed.). *The Life and Thought of John Gill (1697-1771)*. A Tercentennial Appreciation. 1997
78. KAISER, C.B. *Creational Theology and the History of Physical Science*. The Creationist Tradition from Basil to Bohr. 1997
79. LEES, J.T. *Anselm of Havelberg*. Deeds into Words in the Twelfth Century. 1997
80. WINTER, J.M. VAN. *Sources Concerning the Hospitallers of St John in the Netherlands, 14th-18th Centuries*. 1998

81. TIERNEY, B. *Foundations of the Conciliar Theory*. The Contribution of the Medieval Canonists from Gratian to the Great Schism. Enlarged New Edition. 1998

82. MIERNOWSKI, J. *Le Dieu Néant*. Théologies négatives à l'aube des temps modernes. 1998

83. HALVERSON, J.L. *Peter Aureol on Predestination*. A Challenge to Late Medieval Thought. 1998. ISBN 90 04 10945 5

Prospectus available on request

BRILL — P.O.B. 9000 — 2300 PA LEIDEN — THE NETHERLANDS